Life "In Christ"

Life "In Christ"

Pastoral Theology and Common Worship

PETER M. B. ROBINSON
& GEORGE R. SUMNER

foreword by EPHRAIM RADNER

CASCADE *Books* • Eugene, Oregon

LIFE "IN CHRIST"
Pastoral Theology and Common Worship

Cascade Books
An Imprint of Wipf and Stock Publishers
199 W. 8th Ave., Suite 3
Eugene, OR 97401

www.wipfandstock.com

PAPERBACK ISBN: 979-8-3852-4929-9
HARDCOVER ISBN: 979-8-3852-4930-5
EBOOK ISBN: 979-8-3852-4931-2

Cataloguing-in-Publication data:

Names: Robinson, Peter M. B. [author]. | Sumner, George R. [author]. | Radner, Ephraim [foreword writer].

Title: Life "in Christ" : pastoral theology and common worship / Peter M. B. Robinson and George R. Sumner.

Description: Eugene, OR: Cascade Books, 2026 | Includes bibliographical references and index.

Identifiers: ISBN 979-8-3852-4929-9 (paperback) | ISBN 979-8-3852-4930-5 (hardcover) | ISBN 979-8-3852-4931-2 (ebook)

Subjects: LCSH: Public worship. | Pastoral care. | Pastoral theology. | Pastoral theology—Anglican Communion. | Liturgies. | Pastoral prayers.

Classification: BV4011 R635 2026 (paperback) | BV4011 (ebook)

VERSION NUMBER 03/02/26

Contents

Foreword

At the start of this remarkable work on something they call "pastoral theology," Robinson and Sumner note how so many other disciplines necessarily come into play under this heading. Pastoral theology takes in "liturgical theology, homiletics, pastoral care, counseling, church leadership, missiology, cultural and intercultural understanding, youth ministry, children's ministry," along with "biblical studies, systematic theology, and church history." Yet this panoply of knowledge-forms and skills is actually rooted in and accountable, they write, to a quite specific reality: "Our participation in the body of Christ, the faith of the church, and Christ himself. It is precisely here that pastoral theology must finds its place."[1] Precisely here, "in Christ" and his church.

Unlike many academic works, for which opening methodological commentary has become a dreary and tiresomely drawn out "throat clearing" (in Jeffrey Stout's phrase), the opening of *Life "In Christ": Pastoral Theology and Common Worship* is a necessary read. For pastoral theology, over the past century at least, has mostly left Christ and his church behind, searching for its own content in the thickets and byways of culturally constricted accounts of social, political, and psychological theories and frameworks. Theology could float away in the dogmatic ether, practitioners suggested, but pastoral theology was to be ordered as the antidote to practical irrelevance, rooting reflection on Christian faithfulness in social need and interaction. For decades throughout the twentieth century and beyond, educators insisted that Christian ministers, in their seminary and ongoing formation, needed to diminish the role of classical theological understanding and instead embrace more comprehensively the means (and the theories behind these means) of changing people according to the strategies of social theory and purpose.

1. Page 5.

This is what "pastoral theology" was prepared to do. Practical, praxis, functional, embodied, applied, concrete, action-oriented, reparative, experiential, integrative, transformative, liberative: As qualifiers of the purpose of pastoral theology, these categories promised a new effectiveness to ministerial education and its professional outcomes. Now Christian pastors could make a difference, therapeutically, politically, economically, communally.

Except that the jumble of effective strategies on offer were intricately confusing, often at odds with each other, and inevitably evanescent in their cultural traction. Therapeutic models change, political imperatives morph, the levers of the economy shift or simply break, the character of communities and communal identities dissolve and reshape themselves. It is not as if the disciplines of social science (let alone of classical theology) are *not* relevant to the task of the Christian's life of faithfulness; only that they are so historically ancillary to its center as to require a kind of disciplinary reticence from the start. For in the unsettled dusts of those ongoing changes of culture and historical experience that mark the shape of human life, the "transforming of persons" that the gospel, in the hands of the pastoral theologians, was meant to achieve disappeared in the swirling mists. Who can discern the real forms that move behind the haze of reconfigured societies and their self-explications?

In this context, the "method" of pastoral theology is hardly a simple introductory exercise of academic self-certification. It bespeaks the true challenge of the gospel itself: Who is God and what does God do for us and speak to us? Robinson and Sumner's outline of "pastoral theology" turns us back to these gospel questions. In the late nineteenth century Catholics developed a discipline called "fundamental theology" that attempted to define the credibility of divine revelation and the church's authority to transmit it. In Robinson and Sumner's description, pastoral theology properly exists (in my own paraphrase) as a kind of "ecclesial fundamental theology," one that could be condensed into the opening words of John's Gospel: God speaks his Word, who is from the beginning, and the Word *is* life itself, and gives life. That Word both creates all things—human beings, you and I together—and sets them on a path of purposeful life. As lived in the world, however, that created life turns to all the wrong places, and loses its way. The Word becomes flesh, dwelling among us, and explicating—speaking—God himself. The Word takes his place in the world of changes and limited, broken, and false explications, and exhibits the truth in shining and transformative splendor. This is what "the gospel" says, and its details are given in the "Gospels" themselves, in all their intricate scriptural constellations: *Here!* we are told, *in this living Word and all he does,* is the changed life of Christian faith. This is the foundation of anything we can and should say about Christ, the church, the Christian life, that is, about pastoral theology.

Thus, when it comes to the "methodology" of pastoral theology, Robinson and Sumner stress three aspects. First, a return in our focus and reflection to God's active work, not to the human tasks that social theory imagines as exhaustive of explications of existence. They are not alone in this insistence (they rightly cite Andrew Purves), but it is strikingly novel nonetheless. God's central act *is* Jesus Christ, born of the Virgin Mary by the power of the Holy Spirit. Hence pastoral theology's first and fundamental focus is not on human interaction, but on the action of God, Father, Son, and Spirit. Second, the work of God is *pro nobis*, for us, as confessed in the Creed. By the incarnation, the Son of God assumes the lineage of Adam; by the cross he draws all people to himself; and by the gift of the Spirit in baptism, he joins to himself those who in faith humbly receive him. Robinson and Sumner make therefore this second fundamental assertion: Pastoral theology must primarily consider God's Word and our response to him in terms of the body of Christ that we call "the church." If God acts, God forms the church as his Son's body. Finally, they argue, that body is the measure of human transformation—given in all the forms of Scripture's depiction of the Son traversing the world—and this leads to a particular place, the "path" that is the purpose of God's creating in the first place: that we might be "to the praise of [God's] glory" (Eph 1:12), a divine "temple" of worship and adoration (Eph 2:22; Rev 22:1, 3).

To speak of pastoral theology in these terms seems so obvious. Yet it is completely alien to most contemporary assumptions and approaches to pastoral theology. And however obvious intellectually, the form of Robinson and Sumner's handbook in pastoral theology turns out to be a counterintuitive shock even to those readied for casting aside old approaches. Crossing the threshold of the great church crisis in Germany of 1933, Bonhoeffer spoke of the Christian life embodied in the church, not as an expression of "opinions" and theories about the how social life fits together—"what do people say" about it all. Rather, he insisted, the church that is given in Jesus the Christ, the Son of God, "is concerned only with singing, praying, preaching, doing, and reaching out with the confession, always and only."[2] As the true shape of pastoral theology, this simple and exclusive "concern" is thus presented by Robinson and Sumner in a startling form: the service of Holy Communion, according to the Anglican *Book of Common Prayer* (*BCP*).

Here we get to the nub of Robinson and Sumner's profound recasting of formation. It was Aidan Kavanagh, as they point out, who characterized worship as "primary theology," compared to the "secondary" forms of theology like systematics and other studies. In worship, we "speak *to* God, not *about* God," and of course, worship itself is initiated by a prior divine address. What is theology, after all, other than "the word of God," spoken, given, received, and offered back? God acts, the church is formed by grace as Christ's body, and the word is now spoken among "us," God, man, the God-Man. The sound of praise.

So Robinson and Sumner's manual in pastoral theology is structured around Holy Communion, and each chapter takes up in turn an aspect of this liturgy: gathering, listening to Scripture, confession and absolution, offering, and so on. Those who are not Anglican may find this denominationally provincial. But the volume is not written just or even primarily for Anglicans, nor does it depend on Anglican commitments. One of the abiding virtues of the reformed English worship of the sixteenth century, a virtue articulated in the *BCP*, is that the threefold elements of Christian faith noted above—God acting, in Christ, for his body the church so that the Word might be humanly spoken in praise—determine in a straightforward way the shape of worship itself. Most of the pieces that make up the Lord's Supper or Communion service of the *BCP*—what today we call the "Eucharist"—are shared across Christian traditions. The *BCP's* version is simply a clear and resonant version of it, redolent with crafted citations of and allusions to Scripture, the "words of the Word," that are the driving force of human creaturely life and purpose. Dogma there is in the *BCP*, but this really *is* "primary theology" in its articulation, not a stitching of doctrinal polemics.

The revelation in Robinson and Sumner's outline is how all the aspects of pastoral theology's recent concerns—diverse social, political, therapeutic theories and practices—fall into place within this Christ- and church-centered outline, this Word-speaking orientation toward praise. So, for instance, the opening chapter on "gathering" takes up questions of social epistemology; the discussion of the hearing and proclamation

2. Robertson, *Dietrich Bonhoeffer's Christmas Sermons*, 78.

of Scripture in chapter 4 provides overviews of various theologies of the Bible and of preaching; the chapter on Confession and Absolution provides a telling tour of "secular" therapeutic programs; and the chapter on "offering"—one of the richest in the volume—covers a range of social challenges, including marriage, under the rubric of vocational self-giving.

We can describe the whole approach (as the authors themselves do) in terms of the ancient adage *lex orandi lex credendi*—the law or order of prayer shapes the order of believing. But more than that, prayer itself, in Robinson and Sumner's understanding, is but the expression of the *lex Christi*. "Just as the Lord's prayer is not first and foremost about different techniques for prayer but is grounded in the Son's relationship with the Father, so too pastoral theology is not first and foremost about different ministry techniques, but is about our participation in the Son's relationship with the Father."[3]

Robinson and Sumner do not actually engage the term "pastoral" much at all. But it is worth picking up the term here, because in fact its deep meaning lurks behind all that they write. In scriptural terms, which invent the image from the first, God is the real "shepherd" or "pastor" (Ezek 34:15–16). All human pastors and thus all human pastoral care proves deformed and gives rise to a history of sin (Jer 23:1–2). The figure in whom God's pastoral care is given in the midst of this history is that of his own self and Son, Jesus the Messiah. "I am the good shepherd," he announces (John 10:11). Jesus is "the great shepherd of the sheep" (Heb 13:20), the pastor whose pastoral care embodies the divine act of the creator bringing his creation to its end. To trace pastoral care accurately and faithfully is thus to describe the path of Jesus the Christ, from nativity to death, resurrection to ascension, in service, prayer and supping, and how our own births, marriages, and burials—with all the people involved—then enunciate praise for *this* One Person. There is much that must go into such a tracing. This volume, in its own way, is a record of the multitudinous efforts of the past at doing so. But, in its core, it is a luminous witness to the essence of faithful Christian thanksgiving, the true posture of the church.

Ephraim Radner
Professor Emeritus of Historical Theology,
Wycliffe College, University of Toronto

3. Pages 109–10.

Acknowledgments

A PROJECT LIKE THIS REFLECTS many conversations taking place in both the academy and the church, conversations that hold particular resonance as we assert that pastoral theology, as a discipline, inhabits the space between the two. Deep gratitude is owed to colleagues and friends across both realms, especially the faculty and students at Wycliffe College. Special thanks go to those who endeavor to live faithfully in both the church and the academy or better yet, those who seek to live fully in both worlds at once.

Particular recognition is due to those who read and engaged with drafts or portions of this book along the way: Kira Moolman, Paul Metzger, Victor Austin, Ephraim Radner, Tiffany Robinson, and Stephanie Hodgkins Sumner.

Sincere thanks to Maud Sandbo, whose copyediting was exemplary. We are also grateful to Wycliffe College and the Diocese of Dallas for providing sabbatical time that made this work possible.

1

Locating Pastoral Theology

In the late twentieth century pastoral theologians such as Charles Gerkin sought to realign pastoral care by restoring a theological dimension. Gerkin was critiquing the history of pastoral care in the twentieth century as it grew out of the work of Anton Boisen and Clinical Pastoral Education with its primarily psychotherapeutic approach. For Gerkin, pastoral care begins with God and, as such, pastoral theology needs to be theological. Yet, in the interdisciplinary dialogue he proposed, theology was not clearly defined. Pastoral theologians like Nancy Graham, Heather Walton, Frances Ward, and Don Browning sought to reestablish the legitimacy of pastoral theology by drawing on a shift in epistemology, advanced by people like Alasdair MacIntyre. Recognizing that human beings are practical knowers and that we come to know through narrative and practice as much as by isolated or independent cognition, they have argued for the study of practice in communities as the basis for pastoral theology. While the emphasis on practice is helpful, there was not a corresponding robust ecclesiology grounded in God's economy. As result, the focus is primarily on our endeavors to make sense of both human existence and the divine. Barth's concern to always begin with God and Charles Taylor's emphasis on our tendency to operate solely within the immanent frame lead us to argue for an understanding of God's continuing (and real) presence with us. As such, pastoral theology as a discipline must be guided by Scripture and tradition in the context of the life of local worshiping communities. This directs us toward pastoral theology as ecclesial theology—not theology that is solely observations or analysis of the church but theology (and praxis) that arises in the midst of the church, Christ's body.

In my (Peter) first term teaching pastoral theology full time, a student in his final year expressed his appreciation for a pastoral theology that was theological. I was not surprised to hear this since some of the students who loved systematic theology perceive pastoral theology as simplistic and somewhat naïve. Of course, in ministry the majority of practitioners hold the opposing view, that there is too much emphasis on systematic theology in seminary and not enough emphasis on the practice of ministry. This perspective is reflected in Facebook groups that center on a discussion of "what I didn't learn in seminary." Many years ago pastoral theologian Ray Anderson wryly commented that most pastors in seminary had been inoculated with enough theology to last a lifetime. That certainly resonated with my experience among fellow pastors where there was often an antipathy toward theology, if not an outright rejection of systematic theology, and a desire to find practical tools to effect pastoral ministry. The discipline of pastoral theology often bears the brunt of criticism for an apparent failure of seminaries to address the question of theological integration or to teach students how to translate theology in the context of the practice of ministry. Recent attempts to shift the way we do pastoral theology have sought to address these concerns and reframe our understanding of epistemology by establishing a new basis for doing pastoral theology that begins with praxis while making room for or incorporating a theological framework. Too often this approach prioritizes practice while assuming a narrow understanding of theology that is primarily theoretical or dogmatic and dislocated from the praxis of the worshiping community.

Pastoral or practical theology has an identity crisis, one it has experienced since it became a distinct academic discipline in the eighteenth century.[1]

> The field of practical theology has been throughout its history the most beleaguered and despised of the theological disciplines. . . . To admit in academic theological circles that one is a theologian has been, in recent years, to court embarrassment. To admit that one is a practical theologian invites even deeper skepticism. To admit in a major university that one is a practical theologian has been to invite humiliation.[2]

1. Dingemans, "Practical Theology in the Academy," 82.
2. Browning, *Fundamental Practical Theology*, 3.

Browning bears witness to what most people think of pastoral theology: that it is a suspect or illegitimate partner in theological education. Those who practice pastoral theology are not immune to questions about their own legitimacy alongside discussion of what exactly pastoral theology is supposed to do or accomplish. I often find myself wanting to either apologize or explain what I mean by pastoral theology to students or other faculty.

This lack of clarity in relation to the place of pastoral theology is evident in the struggle to find an appropriate name for the discipline—is it pastoral, practical, or applied theology? All three terms have been used to define the discipline, usually in a manner that reflects individual commitments. Those advocating for *practical theology* emphasize the focus on practice or action; those advocating for *applied theology* perceive the discipline as serving to transition or integrate biblical studies or systematic theology with the church or the individual Christian life; *pastoral theology*, in turn, tends to reflect a focus on ministries of caring and service or more particularly pastoral care. Samuel Park, for example, argues that pastoral theology orients toward pastoral care: "Pastoral theology is theology of pastoral care."[3] The wide variety of definitions of the word *pastoral* indicate, however, that it is a deceptively complex word. This term originated in the practice of caring for sheep or livestock in a pastoral or rural setting (Latin—*pastoralis*) and connotes simplicity, charm, and serenity; these are hardly definitions to inspire confidence in an academic discipline.

In this book we have chosen the term *pastoral theology* precisely because it lays a central emphasis on the church, not only as the focus of the energies of pastoral theology, but as the basis or locus out of which pastoral theology arises. Pastoral theology, which incorporates pastoral care (here we disagree with Park and others who collapse pastoral theology into the practice of pastoral care and particularly the individual to individual care that is often prioritized), arises out of the church being the church. This is not simply the claim that theological reasoning should arise in the context of faith communities but that the active life of the church is itself theologically rich insofar as it reflects and bears witness to the God revealed to us in Jesus Christ in and through the encounter with God in that worship. Aidan Kavanagh is helpful at this point when he speaks of the liturgy as primary theology because we are talking with

3. Park, "History and Method," 65.

God rather than about God.[4] This is theology which only finds its definition, place, and practice in the context of the church as it lives, and has lived, into the relationship with God made possible in Christ: historical, global, local, and particular.

Stretched between the church and the academy and answering to both, pastoral theology as a discipline experiences the tension between the ivory tower of the academy and the concrete particularity of a local community.[5] In the local church a focus on immediate needs and practical skills encourages an emphasis on teaching students what to do rather than how they should relate practice to theology. Indeed, leaders in the church often dismiss theological colleges as hopelessly abstract and bemoan their lack of attention to the practical elements of ministry. And theological educators often retreat into their own areas of specialization to the neglect of the local church. Recent trends toward more local formation have resulted in pastoral theology being one of the first departments to be called into question, under the assumption that theology might best be taught or learned in the field rather than the classroom. Even among denominations which continue to strongly emphasize theology or doctrine, pastoral theology comes under particular criticism for failing to help students integrate theology and praxis. Rather than trying to resolve or eradicate this tension, it is better to acknowledge that the tension exists for a number of good reasons. As already suggested, the first and most important element to this tension is the context of the discipline as both an academic discipline and an expression of the worshiping life of the church. While all theological disciplines are accountable to the church in one way or another, pastoral theology, because it is pastoral, must consistently remember that it originates with and is deeply tied to the life of the church.

That brings us to the second element in the tension that is inherent in pastoral theology, that between the generalist and the specialist. Within the academy, pastoral theology claims to be a distinct discipline or department in the seminary or theological college, but in practice it is

4. Aidan Kavanagh, OSB, described the liturgy as "primary theology," referring to the language we use to talk with God. "Secondary theology" is the language we use to talk about God, or "the body of statements or propositions based upon or derived from reflection upon our interchange with God." Mitchell, *Praying Shapes Believing*, 2. Kavanagh interprets the relationship between the two such that the majority of the influence is from primary theology (*lex orandi*) to secondary theology (*lex credendi*). See Kavanagh, *On Liturgical Theology*.

5. Groome, "Theology on Our Feet," 55–78.

a gathering place for a wide variety of disciplines or specializations, including liturgical theology, homiletics, pastoral care, counseling, church leadership, missiology, cultural and intercultural understanding, youth ministry, children's ministry, etc. In most seminaries—at least those which still have departments—pastoral theology is the largest in terms of the number of faculty and courses. Its very breadth may mean it lacks depth as it seeks to maintain academic credibility as a distinct discipline. There has also been a temptation or tendency for pastoral theology to operate independently to establish its own credentials as a discipline instead of working together with biblical studies and systematic theology. It is no wonder that the shape and influence of the discipline of pastoral theology is difficult to clearly discern. Even as it serves as a gathering place for an array of different disciplines, pastoral theology must remain accountable to the classic theological disciplines of biblical studies, systematic theology, and church history.

Here is the crux of the matter: Rather than being stretched too thin by these different demands and disciplines, the mandate of pastoral theology includes holding other theological disciplines accountable to the church.[6] The problem is not the variety of disciplines in theological studies and their disparate commitments, but the failure to insist that the different disciplines are accountable to each other, and more specifically, that the accountability to one another is grounded in and arises out of our participation in the body of Christ, the faith of the church, and Christ himself. It is precisely here that pastoral theology must find its place as it seeks to bridge the divide between the church and the academy by calling both groups to remember our location in relation to the God who has identified himself with Christ and his body.

AMONG THE PASTORAL THEOLOGIANS

Over the past fifty years many theologians have sought to directly address the tension between practice and theology, including pastoral theologians such as Nancy Graham, Heather Walton, Frances Ward, Dorothy Bass, and Bonnie J. Miller-McLemore. One voice which has had

6. Browning claims that "Christian theology should be seen as practical through and through and at its very heart. Historical, systematic, and practical theology (in the more specific sense of the term) should be seen as subspecialties of the larger and more encompassing discipline called fundamental practical theology." Browning, *Fundamental Practical Theology*, 7–8.

significant influence on this understanding of pastoral theology has been that of Don S. Browning. Browning argues for a recovery of the central place and role of pastoral theology that aligns with the renewed interest in praxis-based philosophy and theology.[7] (Praxis is the careful reflection on practice which is a central element in any approach to pastoral theology.) At the same time he critiques the twentieth-century theological tendency to move from theory to practice, an approach he identifies with theologians such as Karl Barth.[8] He suggests instead that theological scholarship should move from practice to theory and back to practice. Browning argues that for Barth there

> was no role for human understanding, action, or practice in the construal of God's self-disclosure. In this view, theology is practical only by applying God's revelation as directly and purely as possible to the concrete situations of life.[9]

Contrary to Browning's view, what is at issue is not Barth's insistence on beginning with God's self-disclosure in Christ, but rather the way in which Barth understood that self-disclosure. Revelation, for Barth, was always an event rather than a static deposit of information or a set of doctrinal claims or *theoria*. Thus the contrast that Browning suggests

7. "With the rebirth of the practical philosophies, practical theology itself has been reborn. Five years ago, few would admit being practical theologians. Today there is a rush among more dignified and well-established systematic and historical theologians to ask, After all, aren't we all practical?" Browning, *Fundamental Practical Theology*, 3. For Browning all theological scholarship should move from practice to theory to practice. He describes theology as four submovements representing subspecialties of the larger and more encompassing discipline called fundamental practical theology:

- *descriptive theology*;
- *historical theology*—"traditional disciplines of biblical studies, church history and the history of Christian thought" (49);
- *systematic theology*—addressing "general issues and shared themes running through our practices" (52–53); and
- *strategic practical theology*—asking "what should be our praxis in this concrete situation?" (55).

8. Barth "believed that the interpreting community should empty itself of its usual attempts to verify things morally, experientially, or cognitively. The believing community should conform itself totally to the Word of God revealed in Scripture." Browning, *Fundamental Practical Theology*, 7. Browning critiques Barth's model as one that moves solely from theory to practice and suggests that this model dominated most theological education in Europe and North America in the middle decades of the twentieth century.

9. Browning, *Fundamental Practical Theology*, 5.

between theory and practice doesn't actually seem to accord with Barth. In fact, since Barth speaks of revelation as an event, our attention is always directed toward the concrete, practical ways in which God makes himself present to us in encounter.[10] Indeed, Barth would argue that to begin with human experience or phenomena apart from God's identification with humanity in Jesus Christ is itself abstract because it does not deal with the concrete reality of human existence as given to us in Christ. While God is clearly able to make himself present in all kinds of ways, we look first and foremost to the ways in which God has and does make himself present in Jesus Christ and in his body, the worshiping community. The question posed to us by Barth's insistence on beginning with revelation might be more clearly understood as applying to the parameters which must guide our reflection, rather than the order in which reflection happens: we begin with the God who engages with us in the context of human practice. Thus we could say that Browning's insistence on beginning with practice aligns with our claim that pastoral theology arises out of the church, although we would prefer to specify that theological scholarship never moves in a singular pattern or direction but must always be located in the church which holds together theory and practice, or orthodoxy and orthopraxis.[11] Pastoral theology, and indeed theology as a whole, is always an ecclesially based and ecclesially accountable enterprise.[12] (This,

10. Root, in turn, critiques Browning for having little room for divine action; that is, making no "qualitative distinction between time and eternity." He notes that in his critique of Barth, Browning fails to notice that Barth doesn't build his project "on a theory-to-practice perspective, but rather on an articulation of divine practice, of divine action in God's self-revelation." Root, *Christopraxis*, 58.

11. Dingemans notes that in the twentieth century many practical theologians argued that it must begin in ecclesiology: "As a matter of fact, at this moment the majority of academic practical theologians seem to consider 'the functioning of the church in the perspective of the coming Kingdom of God in the world' as the actual field of practical theology" ("Practical Theology in the Academy," 85). Dingemans also notes that recently some practical theologians lay the emphasis "on the liberating work of the gospel in society and in the life of individual believers." Dingemans, "Practical Theology in the Academy," 87.

12. "[The fathers] rarely speak of the Church and of liturgy in explicit terms because for them they are not an 'object' of theology but its ontological foundation, the epiphany, the reality, the self-evidence of that to which then in their writings they 'bear testimony.'" Schmemann, "Debate on the Liturgy," 221. Groome argues that Browning would have been better to describe the "dynamic of theology" using "'life, to tradition, to life.' . . . The latter would signal more clearly that all theology is to begin with consciousness of the lives and issues of people and communities, move critically to appropriate the Scriptures, sacraments, symbols, the creed, code, cult and so on, of the tradition and community . . . and from the beginning intend the outcome to return to

of course, raises a question about the degree to which we are able to put confidence in the church. We will explore this question in greater depth in chapter 4.)

Graham, Walton, and Ward offer a careful exploration of different methods (approaches) to constructing pastoral theologies.[13] Their practical guide to different methodological approaches is very helpful, but their development of the practice-theory-practice approach, which they identify as originating with liberation theology, continues to work with the assumption that we must choose whether to emphasize orthodoxy or orthopraxy rather than affirming the essential and necessary coherence between the two. As an aside, we suggest that as important as the preference for the poor (as advanced by liberation theologians) is to the biblical witness, it cannot function as an overarching hermeneutic without itself distorting theological approaches and constructs. And perhaps here we see reinforced the notion that our presuppositions (which are inevitably theological in one way or another insofar as they say something about God and God's action in the world) will always shape our interpretation. As we will argue a little later, this is where the church's credal affirmation of the God revealed to us in Jesus Christ must serve as the overarching hermeneutic in both biblical interpretation and pastoral theology.

THE BABYLONIAN CAPTIVITY OF PASTORAL THEOLOGY

Andrew Purves argues for a different approach than practice-theory-practice. In *Reconstructing Pastoral Theology* (2004) he claims that for much of the twentieth century pastoral theology began with a primary concern for praxis while dismissing theology proper as too abstract. For Purves, the specialization of disciplines in theological colleges has meant that pastoral theology, which focuses on practical issues and concerns, has drawn on the social sciences rather than a theological framework. Here Purves is echoing many twentieth-century pastoral theologians including Charles Gerkin, Edward Wimberly, or historian Gillian Evans, who refers to the Babylonian captivity of pastoral theology at the hands of

life again—for the life of the world." Groome, review of *Fundamental Practical Theology*, 163.

13. Graham et al., *Theological Reflection*.

the psychological discipline.[14] Purves cites the words of Seward Hiltner, a key figure in the shaping of the modern pastoral theology movement in twentieth-century North America: "the study of concrete experiences like those of pastoral care should lead to a branch of theological study known as 'pastoral theology.'"[15] Note that Hiltner proposes that pastoral theology should develop out of a study of concrete experiences. Dingemans echoes Hiltner's perception that pastoral theology should grow out of concrete experiences when he notes that

> an important shift has taken place in practical theology, from the application of biblical data and statements of faith to the primary task of investigation of Christian practice itself. All over the world, practical theology is understood now as a science of action (*Handlungswissenschaft*) or as a social science.[16]

While concrete experience is central to pastoral theology, how are those concrete experiences to be understood or interpreted? An appropriate appreciation for the social sciences and what we should learn from them is essential, but the abandonment of a theological foundation to pastoral theology unroots it from its center in God's self-disclosure culminating in the person and work of Christ. Purves argues, following Hiltner, that "the discipline has moved in a distinctly clinical, psychotherapeutic, or, more generally, social-scientific direction rather than a theological or doctrinal direction."[17] Pastoral theology has turned to and grounded itself in the social sciences rather than theology.[18] As early as 1976 Gerkin offers something of the same critique: "Some members of the secular helping professions have in the past perceived the Christian minister's commitment to the Christian tradition as a handicapping bias."[19] David Kelsey describes the roots of this resituating of pastoral theology in *Between Athens and Berlin*, in which he observes pastoral theology aligning itself with professional programs such as law and medicine in order to continue to justify its place in the academy. The difficulty is that this shift toward the social sciences and away from theology

14. Evans, *History of Pastoral Care.*

15. Hiltner, "What We Get and Give in Pastoral Care," 14.

16. Dingemans, "Practical Theology in the Academy," 87.

17. Purves, *Reconstructing Pastoral Theology*, xiv.

18. "In the United States at least, from the 1920's, pastoral care came to be cast in a psychological and therapeutic, rather than a theological and liturgical, framework." Purves, *Reconstructing Pastoral Theology*, 5.

19. Gerkin, "Pastoral Ministry Between the Times," 178.

proper is not only a shift away from the church, but it is also a shift away from God's economy. In *Christopraxis: A Practical Theology of the Cross*, after reviewing recent approaches to practical theology which prioritize praxis, Andrew Root suggests a different process: While affirming an emphasis on praxis he insists that God's action in the world is the starting place for understanding practice.[20]

Behind the debate over praxis lies the question of how theology and the social sciences ought to relate to one another. One of the most compelling answers to this question is found in Deborah Hunsinger's *Theology and Pastoral Counseling*.[21] Using the metaphor of being bilingual, she proposes that theology and psychology ought to be understood as standing in a relationship somewhat analogous to the two natures of Christ in the formula of the Council of Chalcedon of 451: in two natures, "unconfusedly, unchangeably, indivisibly, inseparably." From this analogy she derives three rules for the relations between theology and a cognate science: Their claims should be inseparable, differentiated, and ordered.[22] To put the matter negatively, the two kinds of claims cannot be understood as unrelated to one another (since the sufferer is one, and in one and the same world); nor can they be conflated (since understanding before God and in immanent terms are different). As to the third rule, she says that theology, by virtue of its claim about the God who is first and last, needs to have the first and last word, and therefore psychological understanding must be taken up and transposed into the theological, and not vice versa. It is crucial not to suppose that the two kinds of insights are on the same plane. Her understanding gives psychology its own integrity and space, which correspond to the dignity of the human being. But at the end of the day, according to Hunsinger, pastoral theology must be a kind of *theology*, and so must take care to relate the two kinds of discourse in what she calls an asymmetrical relationship. Hers is a concise and precise statement from a therapist and Christian pastoral theologian of the kind of relationship we are seeking to strengthen through this book.

20. Gerkin argues this as well: "Pastoral care, indeed all human care, is finally dependent upon the care of God and our human pastoral care is given sustenance and strength by its participation in that healing, redeeming care that only God can give." Gerkin, "On the Art of Caring," 407.

21. Root identifies Hunsinger and Purves with his fourth model of practical theology—a Barthian or neo-Barthian approach. Root, *Christopraxis*, 75–76.

22. Hunsinger, *Theology and Pastoral Counseling*, 214.

Rather than sidelining or negating the work of psychologists and other mental health professionals, we would affirm their calling at the same time as we clarify the church's role in offering pastoral care. Edward Wimberly is particularly helpful at this point when he offers an important corrective to the narrowing of pastoral theology to a form of pastoral care focused on clergy helping individuals in need: individuals (clergy) ministering to individuals (parishioners).

> The sustaining dimension of black pastoral care has been the function of the total church acting as the caring community. It was not just the pastor who looked after the spiritual and emotional needs of the church members, the whole caring community provided the sustenance for persons and families in crisis situations.[23]

Wimberly argues that the sustaining dimension of black pastoral care (and we might add pastoral theology) has been the function of the whole church. It was not just the pastor who looked after the spiritual and emotional needs of the church members but the whole caring community. Not only does this affirm a broader understanding of pastoral care that includes the whole life and ministry of the church—sustaining, guiding, healing, and reconciling—but it liberates the clergy from overreach in endeavoring to take on roles for which mental health care providers are better equipped.[24]

In one sense, what is at stake in this debate is humility. We need to apprehend the limited nature of human knowledge before God. The danger for the pastoral theologian is to bypass the epistemological foundations of the discipline by turning too quickly to the social sciences without framing our calling in its proper theological context of who God is and what God is doing. Sarah Coakley, referring to the influence of Anton Boisen on the development of Clinical Pastoral Education, suggests that "'pastoral theology' became a matter of the acquisition of certain professional *skills*, with theological accompaniments which were at best derivative from systematic theology, and at worst anti-intellectual replacements of systematic theology with seemingly virtuous goals such as 'global justice' which were strangely untheorised."[25] Such professionalized

23. Moschella and Butler, *Edward Wimberly Reader*, 13.

24. Wimberly draws on the work of Clebsch and Jackle to suggest these four key functions of pastoral care (and by implication, pastoral theology). Moschella and Butler, *Edward Wimberly Reader*, 13.

25. Coakley, "Can Pastoral Theology Be Saved?," para. 13. Coakley traces this shift

knowledge does not make room for the pastoral theologian. The root issue, again, is not a question of the legitimacy of the role of social sciences in informing theological enquiry, but the need to rely upon an approach to epistemology that focuses on the sovereign God's engagement with us in the process of knowing. All human knowing is personal—not only in terms of ourselves as relational creatures, but also with regard to God's own personal engagement with us—an engagement which culminates finally and fully in the person of Jesus Christ and continues in and through the gift of the Holy Spirit.

A PROPOSAL: PASTORAL THEOLOGY AND THE SOCIAL IMAGINARY

Human knowing always incorporates both praxis and theory. It is both cognitive and precognitive. Theory is always rooted in praxis or, to use the helpful category proposed by Charles Taylor, the social imaginary. Human understanding and perception are always grounded in the ways in which we are situated in the world. This is true for Christian knowing just as it is for any form of knowing. The social imaginary includes thoughts, feelings, ideas, and assumptions which are taken for granted. It is, in sum, the framework within which Christian life together, and hence pastoral theology, takes place. The posts and beams of the church's social imaginary are the doctrines and practices of the faith. We can contrast this with the social imaginary of modernity, and especially the very different assumptions about the individual, self-determination, the marketplace of choices, the nature of the emotions, etc., which are essential to modern and postmodern self-understanding.

At this point, we should ask if there is such a thing as a Christian social imaginary. It would be simplistic to suggest that there is a Christian social imaginary that exists independent of the culture in which it is situated. That would be to overlook the basic premises of what Taylor means by the social imaginary in the first place: The practices and patterns of our day-to-day world inevitably shape the way we perceive, understand, and order our lives. It might also appear foolish to suggest that there is

---

back to Schleiermacher and suggests that it "sowed certain unfortunate seeds for the rather different idea of an affectively-oriented, and even anti-rational, rendition of theology which would have its proper place in the professional formation of the clergy for the church's *practical* business of pastoral service." Coakley, "Can Pastoral Theology Be Saved?," para. 6.

only one Christian social imaginary, as there are vast cultural differences among Reformation city churches, illicit Hellenistic congregations, Celtic orders, nineteenth-century missionary societies, contemporary Pentecostal megachurches, etc. At the same time, one can point to features of both doctrine (the Trinity) and practice (baptism, for example) which they all share, and behind these, the Scriptures. In spite of innumerable deformations, one can think of what they share as a "grammar."[26] Given this broad commonality, one can imagine an expression of the Christian social imaginary itself appropriated to modernity, which Taylor struggles to articulate at the end of *A Secular Age*.

So we can deploy the term *Christian social imaginary* in various ways in contradistinction to a modern one, as it retains the distinctiveness of the Christian worldview. This serves as a kind of shorthand for those beliefs, forms, practices, attitudes, and assumptions which are common to the tradition and find instantiation in modern expressions of the faith. Every local worshiping community exists in the tension between a Christian social imaginary (eschatologically ordered) and a variety of secular social imaginaries which are grounded in local cultural expressions. What has become clearer in the post-Christendom era, in spite of vast areas of congruence, are areas of incompatibility between the two.[27]

In our secular age, the primary emphasis on the authority of personal experience combined with a social imaginary which is bounded by or operates only within the limits of the immanent frame allows no space for a transcendent Other who engages with us personally. As Purves suggests, the a priori framework within which we approach questions of praxis is determined by an immanentizing of God: "While attempts have been made to think theologically about pastoral work and about the relationship between theology and psychology, these have been made largely on the basis of an a priori, immanent, and panentheistic view of God that assumes God and humankind are in some kind of relationship of mutuality—a pleasant thought, but one that quite neglects the sovereignty and holiness of the Lord God."[28] This echoes Bonhoeffer's "God of

26. George Lindbeck intended his cultural-linguistic theory to answer just this question.

27. In *Good News in Exile* the authors explore how mainline Protestant churches in the twentieth century lost their distinctiveness while unconsciously adopting many of the elements of a secular social imaginary that were at odds with a Christian social imaginary. See Copenhaver et al., *Good News in Exile.*

28. Purves, *Reconstructing Pastoral Theology*, 5. This echoes Root's concern when he suggests, "Since Don Browning's work . . . practical theology has become a discipline

the gaps," where the only space for the divine to operate or encounter us is in a panentheistic sense, in which we locate God within the context of our own experience (see John Hick or John Shelby Spong).[29]

As Purves has suggested, the consistent challenge for the church in a shift toward practice is how we might still maintain the focus on God's action in the world. Bass, Cahalan, Miller-McLemore, Nieman, and Scharen, in line with many other pastoral theologians in the late twentieth and early twenty-first centuries, argue for beginning with practice. They offer a collaborative approach where they met together to work on their project while also visiting different church contexts, thus reflecting the outworking of the church (gathered community). This primary emphasis on the church as the locus for doing pastoral theology is encouraging, but they do not develop an understanding of the church in its credal formation which is central to this project.[30] At issue is not just attention to the practices of the church but allowing for the way in which the church in its practices is the locus out of which pastoral theology arises. Purves rightly insists that "our exploration of the mystery of human life and experience, the purpose and meaning of faith, and the proper understanding of the call to discipleship are set in the context of the identity, purpose, and acts of God."[31] Working to emphasize the theological in practical theology, Dingemans similarly addresses the work of Christ and the Spirit and how they have been understood in recent developments of practical theology.[32] It is this primary theological frame of reference that allows us to effectively engage with and interpret both the social sciences and practical experience. Again, Hunsinger helps us:

---

fluent in talking about concrete human action (practice), but hesitant in speaking of God's action and nature from the locale of the concrete." Root, *Christopraxis*, 13.

29. Bonhoeffer to Eberhard Bethge, May 29, 30, 1944, in *Letters and Papers from Prison*, 405–7. In a parallel manner we see the burgeoning of new approaches to biblical hermeneutics which put a primary emphasis on the experiential context of the interpreter. Of course, biblical interpretation must take into account particular and local settings, but it founders when it begins with the assumption that the pastor or scholar's role is to interpret the text from another context on behalf of a God who is absent. Theological interpretation of Scripture begins with the assumption that our first calling is to be attentive to the God who makes himself present in and through the text in a manner that is attentive to each and every particular and local situation.

30. Bass et al., *Christian Practical Wisdom*.

31. Purves, *Reconstructing Pastoral Theology*, 31.

32. Dingemans, "Practical Theology in the Academy," 93–94.

> By developing a "Chalcedonian imagination," pastoral theologians can mine various secular disciplines and offer them to theological, spiritual, and pastoral workers as "parables of the truth." These living parables seek to offer human wisdom within an overarching context of prayer as an obedient response to God's promise and command.[33]

Pastoral theology begins with our understanding of God, and is concerned with the initiative of God, with confidence that God is the subject and not simply the object of theological investigation.[34] To begin with God does not mean that God becomes the object of our investigations, but rather that pastoral theology grows out of knowing God in the sense of being in a reconciled relationship with God and God's people in their life together, as God has made and continues to make himself present to us.

> To insist that God, or, more accurately, the ministry of the Father through the Son and in the Holy Spirit, is the subject matter of pastoral theology means then that there is no faithful content to speaking forth and living out the gospel pastorally apart from knowledge of and sharing in the mission of the God who acts savingly in, through, and as Jesus Christ and in the Spirit precisely as a man for all people.[35]

Pastoral theology as a partner with theology proper is the discipline of speaking about the God who has created us, redeemed us, and revealed himself to us (finally and fully in Jesus Christ) even as we as the church allow our lives to be aligned with his desires for us through his encounter with us as a worshiping community. Indeed, Hunsinger points out, "No other discipline that strives to give an account of human life and its purposes is guided by this singular narrative of God with us—neither philosophy nor psychology, neither sociology nor history, nor indeed any of the sciences or humanities."[36] As such, pastoral theology must have robust ties to the disciplines of biblical studies, ethics, and theology proper even as it engages with and learns from other secular fields of

33. Hunsinger, "Pastoral Theology," 4–5.

34. "God is *present* to human beings, not as an idea, principle, or symbol, but as a living person, Jesus Christ, who is both fully God and fully human. Jesus is not only present to us but is also the one through whom we are made present to God. In and through Jesus Christ, we belong to God." Hunsinger, "Pastoral Theology," 5.

35. Purves, *Reconstructing Pastoral Theology*, xxi.

36. Hunsinger, "Pastoral Theology," 6.

study. While the discipline of pastoral theology often has been primarily concerned with practical issues (and especially the social sciences), it is more fitting to recognize that pastoral theology is fundamentally ecclesial theology, both in its primary focus and in how it is shaped and formed as a discipline, and that brings us to the central claim of this book that pastoral theology is first and foremost ecclesial theology.

PASTORAL THEOLOGY AS ECCLESIAL THEOLOGY

Pastoral theology (indeed, all Christian theology) rightly begins with and grows out of the life of the worshiping community: the church as the body of Christ with Christ as its head. We might note here the countertendency in modernity. This tendency not only moved toward the specialization of theological disciplines but also, in the quest for objective or scientific knowing, sought to isolate the study of theology or the study of the biblical text from faith. While thinkers such as Polanyi have advocated for a realignment of theological inquiry to include the subjective or faith element of knowing, we are going further still. We are not just arguing for the faith of the individual scholar, but for *the Faith* which concerns the person of Jesus Christ as he is present in and through his body the church. Pastoral theology, then, can have no other locus in which it is grounded and nurtured than the body of Christ. Not only does this argument demand a Christian social imaginary for Christian theology, but it also requires that the work of theologians must never stray far from the life of local worshiping communities, and their theological writings must be tried and tested in the life of the body. If theology is properly located in the worshiping community, pastoral theology is the nexus of theology proper that concerns itself with the living out of our calling to be Christ's body, with and for the world. Specifically, this means that pastoral theology is shaped in the context of the local gathering of particular people in worship and is accountable to them. It not only bears witness to the church and what the church is called to be and to do, it is also rooted in and can only grow out of the life of the church.

Theology grows out of these local gatherings while also being located in the church throughout space and time (globally and historically), even as the church itself is rooted in the narrative of Jesus Christ that is related to us in and through Scripture and the creeds. As a discipline, theology cannot be isolated from local worshiping communities, nor can it be primarily informed by the social sciences, although it remains vital to directly engage with and learn from these disciplines. Pastoral theology grows out of the church becoming the church, as it is living toward its telos in Christ. Central to that understanding is the recognition that the church is what it is because of God's work, toward it and with it, in Christ and the Spirit.

> While, loosely speaking, pastoral work is what pastors do, this is true only derivatively. Pastors do what they do because of who God is and what God does. Or more precisely, before it is the church's ministry all ministry is first of all God's ministry.[37]

In other words, pastoral theology is about the church—what the church is and what the church is for. The church is not a neutral or empty vessel conveying a timeless message, but a dynamic reality and reordering of space and time toward and in God's engagement with us, in Christ and by the Spirit. Pastoral or practical theology, because it is theology, cannot be dislocated from the active life of the church and its practices. Pastoral theology is grounded in, accountable to, and concerned with enabling the health of local worshiping communities, which represent the concrete instantiations of the body of Christ.[38]

The challenge is how to allow our practices constantly to be challenged, not only by the biblical text and traditional understandings of the text, but also by the practices of the community insofar as they are aligned with and grow out of God's self-revelation in Jesus Christ, even as they reflect engagement with the breadth of learning in other disciplines. This is, indeed, a tall order. Our confidence in this approach must be rooted in God's promise of being present with us (God's real presence). This further emphasizes the interwoven nature of praxis and theory in theological enquiry. Theology is not a neutral or objective discipline, but a discipline that is rooted in the faith of the church.

37. Purves, *Reconstructing Pastoral Theology*, 3. See also Anderson, "Theology for Ministry," 6–21.

38. "Pastoral theology, I believe, must be developed specifically as *Christian* pastoral theology, rooted explicitly and actually within, arising out of, and accountable to the doctrinal or dogmatic content of Christian faith. God, as the principal subject matter, is to be apprehended from within the event—past, present, and coming—of Jesus Christ, and this event, as we shall see, is itself to be understood in a quite definitive way in accordance with the mind of the church as given in the mainstream of Nicene and Reformation theology." Purves, *Reconstructing Pastoral Theology*, xviii.

THE PARAMETERS OF PASTORAL THEOLOGY

Pastoral theology is never static, nor is it simply determined by tradition.[39] It is practiced with the recognition that pastoral theology does not simply look back or cling to tradition but is always moving forward, albeit not under its own energy, but in and through the work of God in Christ and the Spirit.[40] Pastoral theology, then, is to engage with experience, and particularly the experience of the church, in the context of the truth of who God is. This is the great tension that faces pastoral theology and inevitably cultivates humility by making pastoral theology accountable to the church insofar as the church identifies itself with God and God's action in the world.

Pastoral theology, to the extent that it is grounded in the worshiping life of the church, will not only continue to guide, shape, and reform the practices of the church, but will also interface with other disciplines in the context of the Christian social imaginary in which it is situated and toward which it is being drawn, in Christ and by the Spirit. In this context we also draw on the fruit of research in disparate fields: leadership, congregational systems, family systems, cultural and intercultural issues, youth ministry, and children's ministry. There will continue to be subspecialties within the discipline, although each one must be understood in their whole context in an overarchingly theological way.

While pastoral theology must always begin from within the worshiping life of the church—Christ's body in the world—as that place where we begin to know and experience the new world that God is calling us toward, we do not thereby idealize the church, but rather recognize the way in which God in Christ and the Spirit is present in the church, itself *simul justus et peccator.* As such, the church lives in the constant

39. "The work of reformulating these traditions theologically and pastorally therefore involves more than a selective, nostalgic reassertion of tradition. Basic reformulations of Christian faith, in social as well as psychological terms, for communities as well as for individuals, will be required, and that is bound to be painful and contentious for a long time. In particular, the challenges involved in integrating cultural, gender, racial, and other diversity into new modes of consciousness and praxis must be considered an essential piece in contemporary reconstructions of the spiritual tradition. Any spirituality today that seeks to be realistic and truly transformative of persons and communities will need to take seriously these critiques of the dominant tradition from its own disinherited and silenced voices." Hunter, "Five Questions for the Future of Pastoral Theology," 6.

40. "The liturgical act serves the Word intimately because it is *of* God rather than merely *about* God." Kavanagh, *On Liturgical Theology*, 115. Italics added.

tension of two competing narratives: the social imaginary of this world and the social imaginary of the gospel.[41] The church itself is interim: It is the church insofar as it is grounded in the work of God in Christ and the Spirit and as it lives toward the future God has for it.[42] We taste that future reality in worship and particularly in the sacraments of baptism and Eucharist, which remind us that to enter this new realm is not to transition from one narrative to a complementary but slightly different narrative, but rather to pass from death to life.

In order to structure this treatment of pastoral theology as aligned with the life of the body, we have chosen to begin with the order of service for Communion in the *Book of Common Prayer* as it has been, and is, expressed and practiced in many local congregations. While the book is specific to Anglicans, the different elements of the service are widely shared, and our emphasis falls on the basic acts that all Christians share: gathering, hearing (including proclamation), confessing the faith, praying, confession, offering, communing, and sending. We are not doing liturgical theology here, although we intend for it to inform our project. Rather, in this approach we are implying and asserting that pastoral theology happens in the midst of the community that is gathered together to worship God. This is not to claim that God works through the church because of what it is in itself, but to emphasize that he has chosen to work through it. The church in worship is not just a locus for the dissemination of information, nor a stained glass hour where we are able to escape from the worries of life; rather, it is a way of living—a way of inhabiting a social imaginary ordered toward God and the telos God has for his creation that enables us to begin to know what it means to be his people in and for the world.

This book is first of all an invitation to the discipline of pastoral theology, so understood. Along the way it means to show the niches that different subspecialties occupy in the larger ecology of pastoral theology and to reaffirm their importance as it orients them in relation to the whole. In these different areas, as for the enterprise as a whole, we hope

41. At Emory, Gerkin "devotes himself to relating 'the insights and dilemmas of pastoral care to the classic theological disciplines.'" This leads to two basic elements in his pastoral theology: "the postmodern pluralistic society, as the 'cultural context,' in which modern persons live and face problems, and . . . the 'Christian tradition' through which pastoral care practices help troubled persons renew their faith in God as well as overcome problems." Gerkin, *Introduction to Pastoral Care*, 17, quoted in Park, "History and Method," 53.

42. See for example the work of Alexander Schmemann, *For the Life of the World*.

the book provides an edifying place to begin, which is always an important matter for theology in service of Jesus Christ, who is himself the first and the last in all that we do and say.

2

Gathered Together

Our Entry into Common Worship

We begin with the gathering of the community, in part because this is the starting point for common worship and we are following the order of worship as the foundation or locus for pastoral theology, but also because the gathering takes us to the heart of our thesis. Just as the gathering begins with God's initiative, so too pastoral theology is a response to God's engagement with us, and not just an engagement with each person, individually or interiorly, but an engagement with and in the context of the embodied community, the community of faith. To locate the community in relation to Christ is not simply to authenticate the community but to frame the way in which the community serves to help people grow up into Christ together (his body). Here we are picking up a theme, or emphasis on practice, that has been central to pastoral theology since the latter part of the twentieth century, while affirming that it is not practice in a neutral or generic sense but practice that is a response to and aligned with God's consistent engagement with us. To express that another way, we are not arguing for practice that then looks to theory or theology for qualification, but practice that is (and has been) shaped by *Theos*, by God with us. The reflective element, which is central to pastoral theology, involves the intentional reflection on practice by the community in the context of the ways in which God has and does reveal himself to be present to us.

Almighty God, unto whom all hearts are open, all desires known, and from whom no secrets are hid, cleanse the thoughts of our hearts by the inspiration of thy Holy Spirit, that we may perfectly love thee and worthily magnify thy holy Name; through Jesus Christ our Lord.

(Collect for Grace or, in the American Prayer Book, the Collect for Purity)

And so begins the liturgy for the Anglican service of Holy Communion. Week after week, year after year, in large and small groups, the collect marks the gathering of the people of God as they come together to worship God. Bringing our burdens, preoccupations, and concerns, we turn our hearts and minds to God as we enter into his presence. Different denominations have different approaches to gathering people together in worship, but they tend to have one thing in common: a recognition of the gift of being gathered together in the presence of God in and through Jesus Christ.[1] For pastoral leaders there is an acknowledgment that those gathered together come with many different issues and concerns on their hearts: a health issue in the family, estrangement from a friend or family member that is weighing on their hearts, financial concerns that threaten to overwhelm them, employment issues, or maybe just the regular struggle and frustration of trying to get children dressed and ready to go to church. Whatever is happening in our lives, the gathering marks a transition as we are drawn into the presence of God in this time of worship. As Simon Chan suggests, this is not simply a shift in our focus of attention from one thing to another; it is a transition into an altogether different place.[2]

At the heart of Christian worship is our entry into a space and time ordered toward God. With Moses we are climbing Mount Sinai (Exod 19); with the Psalmist we are entering the presence of the Holy One (Ps 15). With Isaiah we stand in the throne room of God. We gather together in a space and time that is structured by a different narrative than that of the public sphere—one which is ordered toward God—indeed, one in which God is present to us. "Who shall ascend the hill of the Lord? And who shall stand in this holy place?" In the Anglican Church the Collect

1. While Christian communities emphasize that the church is gathered in Christ and by the Spirit, in practice many people assume that the gathering together is about us and our initiative.

2. "Churchgoers are beginning a journey . . . they are leaving this world to enter the kingdom of God." Chan, *Liturgical Theology*, 30.

for Grace frames this reality of gathering together: our freedom to stand in the presence of the Almighty God. Because it is entering into the presence of God it is not an alien world for God's creatures, although it will at times feel alien to us as it involves a different ordering of this world.

Many years ago I (Peter) lived in England for several years. It was only after living there for a month or two that I began to realize how different England is from North America (not to mention the differences between the USA and Canada). So many elements of both worlds are the same that it is easy to overlook the deeper differences between the two places. Over time and with some familiarity I began to recognize how significantly different the two worlds are, especially in the nuances of language and the patterns and habits of daily life. A shared language means that we can sometimes overlook or gloss over the significant differences. Different accents and the fact that cars drive on the opposite side of the road are immediate and obvious differences, but it takes time to see the more substantive differences. For many people coming into the church it will immediately feel like a foreign world, but the most immediately visible differences (pews or singing) may serve to mask the more significant differences that mark the church as a place set apart for God. We may not always be aware of how different it is or may be unable to name the differences, yet these differences are integral to how people experience and engage with the community, and they are integral to how the community is shaped. Many times I have seen people crying throughout a worship service. Often they are not able to say why they are crying, nor is it simply an issue of them having been moved by the worship, but somehow they have recognized that there is more happening in this space than is immediately apparent.

To describe worship as the entry into a different space and time is not to suggest that this is an otherworldly or wholly spiritual experience. As physical creatures we exist in the physical realities of this world. But to enter into the presence of God is to enter a physical world that is ordered differently because it is (in at least some ways) aligned with God and God's desires for us rather than the assumptions of the public world. God's space and time is foreign to us not because it is otherworldly but because it is other-ordered, in contrast to the way that human sin and rebellion order our lives and our world (and ourselves) antithetically to God. (We will address the issue of human sin more fully in chapter 8.) To worship is to enter into the presence of the God who is Lord of all of creation and all created beings and who sustains all existence. Worship, then, is not a turning away from the physical world as such, but rather turning away from the disordering of this world to enter into the truth of this world as God's world; that is, all that is true and beautiful and holy. It is not a spiritual escape, but entry into a space and time where the physical and spiritual are being reconciled with each other just as we have been reconciled with God in Jesus Christ.

A central emphasis on gathered community shapes the manner in which we think about pastoral theology in multiple ways. Not only does it challenge the tendency toward understanding pastoral theology as pastoral care that is focused on clergy caring for individuals in the church, it also reframes the way in which we understand the scope of pastoral theology.[3]

Edward Wimberly is very helpful in regard to the first tendency. He challenges the clerical paradigm of care, noting that care in the black church is and has always been a communal ministry, involving members helping each other, and not a task restricted to the pastor of the local congregation.[4] Wimberly also argues for a much broader notion of pastoral care which "exists when the hungry are fed, when the naked are clothed, when the sick are healed, when the prisoners are visited. Therefore it can be concluded that pastoral care has always existed in the black church because the needs of persons are ministered to by others all the time."[5]

Wimberly's framing of pastoral care or pastoral theology implicitly affirms that this involves the whole community, not just the clergy, but that it also encompasses the whole life of the church: Worship, mission, outreach, even administration are part and parcel of the building up of the church which is part of the wider scope of pastoral care and pastoral theology. The one caveat we would offer is that this is not solely about people or families in crisis situations. Indeed, we would hope that pastoral theology is, in this sense, concerned not only with a curative response

3. The church is the frontline for many pastoral care crises, yet there needs to be a much clearer understanding of the church's (and clergy's) role alongside the role of professional caregivers, whether that be psychologists, psychiatrists, or psychotherapists.

4. Moschella and Butler, *Edward Wimberly Reader*, 15.

5. Moschella and Butler, *Edward Wimberly Reader*, 13. Wimberly specifies, "Pastoral care is defined as the bringing to bear upon persons and families in crisis the total caring resources of the church. Although such roles and functions as worship, church administration, preaching, and teaching are not generally considered pastoral care, they become resources for pastoral care when their dominant concern is for the care of individual persons and their families in crisis situations."

to crisis issues but a preventative or formative approach to building up the body.

Here we need a brief excursus to clarify that our entry into a new sphere as we gather to worship is not to idealize the church, nor to imagine it as in some way isolated from the world. The church is an entry into a liminal time and space where the disordered world is confronted with its telos, that is, all things being rightly ordered in relation to their creator. The church is a gathering of people both reconciled and fallen (again, in Luther's expression, *simul justus et peccator*). It is a Christian social imaginary located in and in some ways shaped by a secular social imaginary. We gather, or better, we are gathered together to be able to taste and see what God has done for us, even as we, the gathered, know the ways of the world (often all too well) and are misshapen by the ordering of this world as it presently exists (much more deeply than we often acknowledge).

The Bible begins with the story of creation and goes on to tell the story of God's work faithfully creating, sustaining, shaping, and redeeming the world. Along the way God identifies and grounds his presence in tangible physical particularity. The narrative described in and framed by the biblical text culminates in Jesus Christ and now is embodied to one degree or another in the church, Christ's body, as it gathers in local and particular communities of people in the space and time in which God gives himself to be known. In Jesus of Nazareth we hear the narrative, which finally and fully makes sense of this world and for this world. Colossians 1 bears witness to this. This is the true narrative of this world.

Exodus 25 describes in careful detail the setting up of the tabernacle: "And have them make me a sanctuary, so that I may dwell among them. In accordance with all that I show you concerning the pattern of the tabernacle and of all its furniture, so you shall make it." The particularity of the details frames the way in which God particularizes himself for us. This is not a condition of his presence with the people of Israel but the way in which God chooses to ground that presence. The universal is made particular: God does not remain at a distance but gives himself to us; he ties himself to his creation. God is not a principle, but a person who gives himself to be known in engagement with us. And it is by God's initiative in consistently bringing this narrative to us and bringing us into this narrative that he sustains and provides the space and time for us to come to know him.[6]

The centrality of the narrative of God in Jesus Christ and the way in which it is presented to us bring us face to face with an aspect of Western thought which continues to confuse and distort our understanding. In the modern era, even until today, the majority of the Western world has operated with an epistemology that is grounded in an understanding of cognition as essentially independent of our situation and embodiedness. Indeed, the universalist claims of Western philosophy (and theology) have more often than not operated as though place and therefore particularity is unimportant. This disembodied approach to epistemology has rendered us, or defined us, as autonomous beings capable of free self-determination.[7] The fallout from this disembodied epistemology is insidious, woven into the narrative of the modern Western world in a myriad of ways, as it has an impact on the whole framework in which we understand human being and knowing. The anthropological assumption behind this approach to knowing is that human beings are primarily thinking things.[8] This assumption has shaped our understanding of the church as much if not more than it impacts our understanding of the physical world, precisely because of our tendency to spiritualize the Christian faith.

A spiritualized Christian faith focuses on the universal at the expense of the particular. The particular and local contours of the worshipping community are often seen (in a gnostic manner) as secondary or even window dressing rather than the embodied context in which we together meet God and come to know God. Take, for example, the seeker friendly

6. "The Bible is not simply read aloud in order to convey information, to teach doctrine or ethics or history, though of course it does that too. It is read aloud as the effective sign that all that we do is done as a response to God's living and active word, the word which, as Isaiah says, accomplishes God's purpose in the world, abiding for ever while all flesh withers like the grass. The place of scripture in Christian worship means that both in structure and content God's initiative remains primary, and all that we do remains a matter of response." Wright, "Freedom and Framework," 187.

7. "Liberalism [as the reigning or operating philosophy in the West] is most fundamentally constituted by a pair of deeper anthropological assumptions that give liberal institutions a particular orientation and cast: 1) anthropological individualism and the voluntarist conception of choice, and 2) human separation from and opposition to nature." Deneen, *Why Liberalism Failed*, 31.

8. Hans Boersma references Curtis Freeman in *Contesting Catholicity*, where he "laments 'soul competency'—the radical emphasis on individual conscience . . . [that] has come to dominate Baptist theology." Boersma, "Wafer-Thin Practice," para. 4.

church movement, which assumed that we can shape the worship of the church in a way that is aligned with culture without that impacting the core message of the gospel. In *Renovation of the Church* Kent Carlson and Mike Lueken describe their own struggle to understand why people coming to their seeker friendly church weren't growing up in their faith.[9] They began to realize that the way worship is structured or ordered is essential to the way people understand or take in what is communicated verbally. As the incarnation makes clear, knowing Jesus involves knowing him within a particular context. We cannot know Jesus in a neutral or objective sense, because we only know someone or something within a particular context, in relationship.[10] And this is not and could never be an interior relationship where we know Jesus independent of his own context.

In his project on Cultural Liturgies Jamie Smith challenges the anthropological assumptions which all too often inform Christian worship:

> Protestants designed worship as if believers were little more than brains-on-a-stick. The primary target was the mind; the primary means was a lecture-like sermon; and the primary goal was to deposit the right doctrines and beliefs into our heads so that we could then go out into the world to carry out the mission of God.[11]

While not all Protestants approach worship in this way, there are many churches where worship services consist of a long sermon with a few songs at the beginning to warm people up or to focus their attention (indeed in many churches the opening songs are understood to be the worship). It may not be described quite so overtly, but the assumption is that the sermon is what the gathering is all about. People go to church to hear a good sermon which will challenge them, instruct them, or inspire them as to how they should live out their faith. In the way people speak about church (and decide which church to go to) and in the way the service is structured, the focus is clearly on accessing the universal truths that lie behind the character and context of the local worshiping community. This becomes even more evident in many conservative churches

9. Carlson and Lueken, *Renovation of the Church.*

10. "If Christian Truth is Truth in the form of Personal Being in Jesus Christ, then knowing the Truth must involve a relation in being to it as well as a relation in cognition. . . . Knowing the Truth and being recreated in the Truth are inseparable." Torrance, *School of Faith*, xxxvii.

11. Smith, "Redeeming Ritual," para. 14.

which claim to have a high view of the authority of Scripture, yet the only Scripture that is read during the service is the verse or verses which the preacher includes in the sermon. In this context, the gathering of the community is simply that, a gathering together of a group of individuals in order that they might receive instruction or information which will (hopefully) prove useful or serviceable to their lives.

This approach to worship makes worship primarily about us and what we do rather than about God—encountering and coming to know the God revealed to us in Jesus Christ as we gather or are gathered by the Spirit.[12] But it is also problematic in the way in which it frames our understanding of what it means to be human and how we, as human beings, come to know God. A Cartesian anthropology has taught us that our thinking is independent of our practice (since practice is inevitably local and temporal) yet has the power to determine practice. The working assumption is that if we want to change ourselves, the first thing we need to do is to change how we think about things, and then with a determined effort of the mind we will be able to change our behavior as well.

This is similar to the concern raised by pastoral theologians like Browning who want to emphasize the centrality of practice. And not just practice as a practical approach to thinking about the church, but that practice is central to human knowing and must inform the way in which we understand not only pastoral theology but theology as a whole.

BEHAVIOR SHAPES COGNITION

The relationship between cognition and behavior is a complex one, and there continues to be vigorous debate as to how they are related. There is, however, a broad consensus that the simplistic ways in which we once thought about cognition as determining behavior are wrong. We don't learn as disembodied minds which function independently of our situation and circumstances; rather, we learn through our embodiedness. By embodiedness we don't simply mean that we learn through our five senses, although that is true. What we mean is that the particular space-time situations in which we are located shape who we are in such a way as to provide the foundation from which and in which we learn. Cognition is not independent of our embodiedness, and the mind is not independent of the physical embodied self, but is wholly integrated with the

12. See Torrance, *Worship, Community and the Triune God of Grace.*

body. We learn or we come to "know" over time by being located within a spatial and temporal environment: We come to "know" through and in the midst of our situations. Just as the mind affects what the body does, so too, our located embodiedness and the matrix of relationships that are essential to that embodiedness shape how the mind perceives things. This confirms that the dynamic relation of the body with the mind is much more integrated than we often assume; the mind does not control the body, as though it were an independent entity flipping switches which then cause the body to behave in a particular manner.

One of the marks of modernity is the affirmation of the freedom of the individual. This is characterized by a freedom of rationality to move beyond the constraints of tradition and authority and is associated with a notion of critical thinking as neutral or objective because it may set aside all suppositions or commitments in order to reach a higher or transcendent mode of cognition.[13] While this freedom to transcend our givenness is vital to what it means to be human and to how we understand the central place of cognition, it is a mistake to understand this as freedom for the mind to operate independently of the body.[14] A solipsist notion of freedom where the individual (mind) soars above the world and its surroundings is illogical, even as it is fundamental to popular understanding. It is better to speak of situated freedom, in which tradition, experience, situation, and authority shape the basis by which we are able to move forward or beyond who we are. The transcendence we are arguing for is a relative transcendence—the freedom to move forward is in fact discerned, shaped, and even to some degree directed by the tradition and authority (the narrative) within which we are located.[15]

13. As Deneen notes, the cultural notion of freedom requires the rejection of traditional categories of authority: "The classical and Christian emphasis upon virtue and the cultivation of self-limitation and self-rule relied upon reinforcing norms and social structures arrayed extensively throughout political, social, religious, economic, and familial life. What were viewed as the essential supports for a training in virtue—and hence, preconditions for liberty from tyranny—came to be viewed as sources of oppression, arbitrariness, and limitation." Deneen, *Why Liberalism Failed*, 25.

14. "To a large extent, the defense of freewill has been a central concern of medieval Christian ethics and traditionally depends upon making a sharp metaphysical division between the body and the mind, such that our will can be considered the unfettered activity of a soul which exists independently of the body, a 'ghost in the machine,' as Gilbert Ryle famously put it (Ryle, 1949)." Robertson, "Stoic Fatalism, Determinism, and Acceptance," para. 12.

15. "Therefore a proper method of instruction will have to reckon with an event of communication which is also an event of reconciliation, and with the transcendent operation of the Holy Spirit who enables man to receive truth beyond his natural powers,

OUR GATHERING TOGETHER AS FORMATION

That brings us back to engage again with the gathering of the community in worship. We gather in the presence of God, in response to God, to worship in a context in which God is at work shaping us as his people through Christ and the Holy Spirit. Renewal in the church and renewal in discipleship and formation have to take into account the way in which we are embodied learners or embodied knowers. Learning requires a framework for understanding—not just a cognitive framework, but a cognitive/behavioral framework in which we "know" as much through how we live as through how we think.[16]

In *A Faithful Church*, John Westerhoff and O. C. Edwards offer a helpful distinction between the twentieth-century tendency toward Sunday school models of learning, which focus primarily on conveying information, in contrast to more comprehensive models of learning like an apprenticeship model of learning where learning and formation happen in the context of both instruction and practice.[17] Westerhoff is among a number of scholars who suggest that one of the reasons why people aren't growing up in their faith is because our models of catechesis or discipleship have failed to take into account the way that people learn. When he speaks critically of a Sunday school model of formation, he doesn't simply mean children's programs but is referring much more broadly to a whole approach to learning for both children and adults which is focused on conveying concepts or ideas in order to change the way people think. The trouble is that the Sunday school model operates on the basis of a false notion of what it means to be human and is assuming a distorted understanding of the mind and the relationship of the mind to the body. The mind does not function independently of the person's situation, but is very much integrated with who they are. That

---

and so to be lifted up above himself in communion with God." Torrance, *School of Faith*, xxii–xxiii.

16. "Having fallen prey to the intellectualism of modernity, both Christian worship and Christian pedagogy have underestimated the importance of this body/story nexus—this inextricable link between imagination, narrative, and embodiment—thereby forgetting the ancient Christian sacramental wisdom carried in the historic practices of Christian worship and the embodied legacies of spiritual and monastic disciplines. Failing to appreciate this, we have neglected formational resources that are indigenous to the Christian tradition, as it were; as a result, we have too often pursued flawed models of discipleship and Christian formation that have focused on convincing the intellect rather than recruiting the imagination." Smith, *Imagining the Kingdom*, 73–74.

17. Westerhoff and Edwards, *Faithful Church*.

is not to say that Sunday school or continuing education programs are wrong or fruitless, but that the way we have tended to implement them fails to account for the multiple levels or means by which people learn, so when we put our confidence in these ways of learning in isolation from a more holistic understanding we neglect the many other necessary elements in learning.

Recent endeavors such as Godly Play or the Catechesis of the Good Shepherd have countered this trend with a more holistic approach to learning. The Catechesis of the Good Shepherd is modeled on a Montessori model of learning which invites children into the process of learning in embodied ways. The Sunday school space is crucial and is carefully set up to foster an understanding of how God is present to us, as opposed to many Sunday schools that are set up classroom-style with a circle of child-sized chairs gathered around the teacher. The children are allowed to handle and touch the different elements used in worship not only to gain familiarity with them, but to "know" or enter into the practice of worship. Rather than simply teaching the children the moral principles of the Christian life, the children are invited into the practices of the worshiping community. It is fascinating to see these children joining their parents in worship, where it is apparent that they often know the prayers better than their parents, and they have imbibed a reverence for the practice of worship that opens them up attentively to God's presence.

In Rom 12 Paul uses active language to refer to what we do and how we live: *We are to present our bodies as a "living" sacrifice—this is our spiritual worship*. This is not a focus on the spiritual (the mind) as opposed to the physical, but just the opposite: namely, the physical aligned with the spiritual—with God. (Paul is not working with a dualistic view of mind vs. body or spiritual vs. physical.) Paul goes on, "Do not be conformed to this world." Do not let your lives—your actions, your behavior, your physical self, your thinking—be aligned with this world's ordering or ways of being but "be transformed by the renewing of your minds so that you may discern what is the will of God." What is clear from the letter as a whole is that this is not an endeavor in which we are to find our way to God, but rather our response to the God who in Jesus Christ has come to us and reconciled us to himself. The verbs for conformed and transformed are both in the passive tense. There is a sense in which this is something which happens to us rather than something which we determine on our own. We will either be conformed to this world or be transformed by the Holy Spirit. This is as much something that happens to us as something we choose to do in the context of the situations we participate in and live out of.

Formation in the Christian life, or transformation into the Christian life, cannot happen simply by choosing to think differently. It involves living differently, since thinking and living are always mutually interconnected, so that we learn to live within a different pattern of behavior and a different set of habits: this is the putting on/putting off language of Colossians.

PRACTICAL SENSE

The danger at this point is that it may sound as though we are choosing to side with a behaviorist approach, where the role of cognition is denied or downplayed. For some, any emphasis on behavior or practice shaping cognition implicitly denies the central place of cognition. Yet, polarizing the relationship between practice and cognition begins with an untenable notion of an autonomous intellect which is understood to function independent of its location or situatedness. Instead, we are arguing for a *situated* cognition where cognition is located in the context of our relatedness to the other and to the physical world; it is shaped by and alongside of how our lives are ordered in this world.

Jamie Smith begins *Imagining the Kingdom* by responding to some of the feedback he received for the first book in his Cultural Liturgies series, *Desiring the Kingdom*. Some commentators accused Smith of a certain anti-intellectualism as his emphasis on practice appeared to downplay human cognition. Indeed, an emphasis on knowing primarily in and through practice or participation might appear to deny the central place for cognition. But to reject the notion of an independent mind does not necessarily imply a denial of the central place of cognition. In fact, although his argument is intentionally polemical, Smith is not arguing for practice as the sole element in formation, but for cognition that is coherent with practice: the practical sense.[18]

> "Practical sense" is the know-how that resides in the body, that unique sort of understanding of the world that is identified with a habitus. . . . Practical sense is not an intellectual or mental

18. This is aligned with Aristotle's notion of phronesis or practical wisdom.

> processing of objective inputs; it is more a kind of adept immersion in an environment.[19]

To speak of practical knowing is to acknowledge that there is a basis for our knowing that is not grounded in an independent cognitive capacity or an ability to think independently of our situation and apart from our adaptation within that situation. Rather, cognition is grounded in our conscious and unconscious practices or situated patterns of living. Our unconscious thinking in particular is reflected in our habits. This understanding of practical sense argues for a broader sense of cognition that includes our embodiedness and cannot be separated from our physical situation.

To argue for practical sense is to assert that practices are not an extension or expression of how we think, but are fundamental to how we think. In this regard, N. T. Wright speaks of an apprenticeship approach to formation rather than a classroom approach to formation.[20] For example: If we want to understand how to build a house, it is not enough to simply pick up a set of plans and start building. First, we need a whole set of practices and basic skills with which to understand what it means to build, to be able to see the different elements which need to happen and the order in which they need to happen, as well as to know the building regulations; we need to have an overall sense of the process involved. We need to know how to measure and cut, how to hammer nails and drive screws, and how to use a level and do layout. Once we have this experience we continue to develop in our understanding by being part of a community of people who share building ideas, technologies, and methods. Our practice in building shapes the way that we think and are able to think about building. This is not to suggest a distinction between practical as opposed to theoretical knowledge, as though there were certain things we learn through practice or habit and other things we learn purely through independent thought. Rather, it is to suggest that the basis of all knowledge—how we know and what we know—is grounded in practice. Again, this emphasis on practice is at the heart of the concerns of many pastoral theologians like Browning.

19. Smith, *Imagining the Kingdom*, 141–42. Smith continues, quoting Bourdieu, *Logic of Practice*, 66: "This is why it is not representational: it's not a distanced observation of objects by a body, or images generated on the internal screen of my consciousness. Practical sense is not that sort of knowledge; it is more a kind of proficiency, a mastery—what Bourdieu calls a 'feel for the game.'"

20. Wright, *After You Believe*.

Here we need to note that we are speaking, in the first place, of a broad definition of practice, picking up Alasdair MacIntyre's argument from *After Virtue* where he speaks of practice as

> any coherent and complex form of socially established cooperative human activity through which goods internal to that form of activity are realized in the course of trying to achieve those standards of excellence which are appropriate to, and partially definitive of, that form of activity, with the result that human powers to achieve excellence, and human conceptions of the ends and goods involved, are systematically extended.[21]

Practice includes the structures and patterns of life, our conversations, and our relating to others and to the world in which we live. The narrative structure of our world and our lives in the world is woven into the fabric of our common life and is the basis of our life together, communication, and understanding.[22] Story provides the moral map of our universe. "It is narrative that trains our emotional perceptual apparatus to perceive the world as meaningful."[23] It reflects the *in betweenness* in which we live in this world as both physical and spiritual beings.[24] In this context we can argue that even theoretical knowing is itself grounded in practice; through human activity and engagement we have the framework or situation which provides for knowing. While aligning with MacIntyre's approach, we would also affirm Dykstra and Bass in their qualification of MacIntyre's understanding of practice in relationship to the church: "Our present understanding of practices differs from MacIntyre's account in *After Virtue* in that ours is now theological and thus normed not only

21. MacIntyre, *After Virtue*, 187.

22. "Practices are theory-laden; they embody and enact beliefs. Practices are also deeply formative; they shape belief, religious identity and community. . . . Practices also invite us into spiritual wisdom and transformation." Wolfteich, "Re-Claiming Sabbath as Transforming Practice," 254.

23. Smith, *Imagining the Kingdom*, 108.

24. "As both Merleau-Ponty and Bourdieu suggest, we live at the nexus of body and story—a 'between' space where the aesthetic force of a narrative or poem captures our imagination because it resonates with the bodily attunement that so fundamentally governs our being-in-the-world. . . . We're less convinced by arguments than moved by stories; our being-in-the-world is more aesthetic than deductive, better captured by narrative than analysis. Indeed, the philosopher Alasdair MacIntyre says that stories are so fundamental to our identity that we don't know what to do without one. As he puts it, I can't answer the question, 'What ought I to do?' unless I have already answered a prior question, 'of which story am I a part?'" Smith, *Imagining the Kingdom*, 173–74, quoting MacIntyre, *After Virtue*, 216.

internally but also through the responsive relationship of Christian practices to God."[25]

INTENTION OR DISPOSITION IN KNOWING

In "Practices and the New Ecclesiology: Misplaced Concreteness?" Nicolas Healy challenges what he calls the new ecclesiology, where thinkers like Hauerwas or Hütter argue for a renewed understanding of the centrality of practice.[26]

> Repeated performance of behavior patterns does not, of itself, issue in the right formation of church members nor the acquisition of Christian virtues. Character is indeed formed through practices, but only as they are performed with appropriate intentions and construals. Without such, practices may foster as much as halt the decline of the center and the absorption of the church into the world.[27]

The Protestant concern with putting false confidence in practices is well founded. There are far too many examples of church communities where it seems they trust their traditions more than they trust God, or where well-established practices are never called into question and any sense of reference to God and the ways in which God is present to the world has long since been lost. Lauren Winner's book on the dangers of Christian practice is a reminder that practices can shape us for both good and ill, including some of those practices which are central to the church.[28] Neither Hauerwas nor Hütter is advocating a blanket affirmation of practice for the sake of practice. Indeed, we might say that Healy,

25. Dykstra and Bass, "Theological Understandings of Christian Practices," 21n8.

26. "Hutter has established the practice of theology within the 'public church,' which he describes as a secure and settled community whose authority lies in the Spirit-authorized core practices and doctrines. But the church's stability and authority comes at the expense of a theologically (and sociologically) thin account of the church and of the Spirit. Without further development, his theory seems unable to show how the Spirit might work salvifically in our mis-performance of church practices, or in our performance of non-Christian practices. Nor can his theory help the church respond to those challenges to its established manner of life and thought that come to it, not from modernity and its distortions, but from the in-breaking of the prophetic word and Spirit of God." Healy, "Practices and the New Ecclesiology," 299.

27. Healy, "Practices and the New Ecclesiology," 295.

28. Winner, *Dangers of Christian Practice*. While we would agree with the argument that practices can shape us for good or ill, we are not convinced by Winner's argument that particular practices such as the Eucharist are in themselves distorting.

Hütter, Hauerwas, and others are engaged in a conversation seeking to refine the way in which we might nuance our understanding of the relationship between practice and cognition. Hütter quotes Lindbeck to affirm how practice is oriented in relationship to the story of God's engagement with his people:

> To become a Christian involves learning the story of Israel and Jesus well enough to interpret and experience oneself and one's world in its terms. A religion is above all an external word, a *verbum externum*, that molds and shapes the self and its world, rather than an expression or thematization of a preexisting self or of preconceptual experience.[29]

It is not practice for practice's sake, or practice in the general or neutral sense, but *this* practice and this telos which guides the practice of the church (see chapter 5 on the Confession of the Faith). An emphasis on practice is all very well, but the question is, especially in the context of local worshiping communities, how to discern which practices are formative of the body as Christ's body as they are properly ordered (and intentionally reflected upon) in the church. "It becomes rather too easy to interpret the emphasis upon the church and its practices as if it reflects the view that Christianity is all about being Christian, and the gospel is broadly identifiable with the church's practices and doctrines."[30] While this demands a much more in-depth discussion than we can offer here, suffice it to say that it is practice as it is grounded in God as the initiator and sustainer of the life of the church.[31] What Healy says of Hauerwas is also true of a straightforward emphasis on practice by pastoral theologians: Without an adequate account of the triune God, "the new ecclesiology may seem too reliant upon an overly abstract and thus flawed philosophical and sociological apparatus."[32] What makes these specific practices essential to the Christian life is never the practices in themselves, but that they are grounded in Christ and continually challenged and reformed by Christ, as Christ makes himself known to us by the Spirit and in Scripture. Scripture is the narrative that the Spirit uses to consistently draw the community toward its telos in Christ.

29. Lindbeck, *Nature of Doctrine*, 34, quoted in Hütter, *Suffering Divine Things*, 47.

30. Healy, "Practices and the New Ecclesiology," 302.

31. Dorothy Bass also wants to emphasize divine initiative. Practices such as worship, prayer, and hospitality, to name three of twelve central practices, are human responses to divine action. Bass, *Practicing Our Faith*, xi.

32. Healy, "Practices and the New Ecclesiology," 302.

In addition to locating the practice of the church in the action and initiative of the triune God, there is also the question of human response to that initiative. A singular emphasis on practice fails to account for intention. A person is not passive in engagement in practice, but actively participates and applies these practices with intention. Another way to state this and avoid the pitfall of emphasizing cognition in isolation from practice is to speak of a disposition in receptivity.[33] The church provides the space in which it is possible for us to come to know God. Yet it is possible to participate to some degree in the life of the church without coming to know God. Because the church is itself a liminal space, it holds before us both options: the option to enter into the life of the worshiping community in such a way that we come to know Christ, or to participate in the church without truly coming to know Christ. Indeed, it is too often the case that a local church itself emphasizes practices (both traditional and cultural or seeker friendly) that mislead as much as redirect our lives in Christ. It is not just the intention of the individuals but the intention of the whole community as it consistently seeks to be realigned with God and God's desires for it that leads toward the community's rootedness in Christ. The physical local church is not a gathering of saints but a mix of people who are in many different places, just as the church is also the reconciled world coming to live in relationship—right ordering—with Christ.[34] The church provides the condition for the possibility of coming to know Christ and to live into the relationship with him as it continues to be grounded in God and God's engagement with it.[35]

33. "Both learning and instructing require a disposition which echoes or reflects the nature of the subject-matter involved. No less than any other, Christian communication requires from the learner, not only an attitude of humility and wonder, but a disposition in receptivity corresponding to its material content." Torrance, *School of Faith*, xxv.

34. "Faced with the confused and sinful practices and intentions and construals of our congregations, we need to know how the Holy Spirit, rather than being 'bound' to the church and its practices, can *overcome* the effects of the churches upon their membership, and the membership upon their churches, so that in spite of the church as well as by its help we may be sanctified and brought closer to Christ." Healy, "Practices and the New Ecclesiology," 303.

35. "Here in Ephesians 4:1–16 it becomes apparent that the unity for which Christians must work is not merely pragmatic, a recognition of differences in which we all shrug our shoulders, do our own thing, and allow other people to do theirs, but a deep, rich, many-sided unity which enables the church to grow toward maturity, leaving behind—as in 1 Corinthians 13 but now as a present task!—the immature babyhood which might otherwise remain as a permanent and vulnerable state." Wright, *After You Believe*, 214.

> Here we return to the fact that it is only within the community of God's people that communication can take place, but now we see that this is the community of the reconciled where reconciliation between man and God and man and his fellow is actualised. It is in that community of reconciliation that the learner receives the required disposition toward the Truth, and himself enters into reconciliation with the Truth.[36]

Intention is always grounded in a situated knowing. It is not a linear, two stage process—we do not form people intellectually so that following this they might choose to live out that formation in the world. It is rather an iterative process where we live into this new world in order to then know what it means to continue to choose to live into this new world. Formation is not simply changing the way people think, although it certainly includes that. The question is not whether there is a place for cognition in formation, but what kind of rationality are we speaking about? We too easily put our confidence in a rationality which isolates communication and comprehension from our situatedness.[37]

Again with reference to Rom 12, for the apostle Paul the mind is not independent of the physical self but is wholly integrated with the embodied person as they are located in the physical world. Ellen Charry is helpful at this point in suggesting that it is our experience which grounds our cognition: "Insight and understanding are not the only way we are formed. We also come to understanding by doing: thinking is shaped by experience. Indeed, much cognitive learning remains aloof unless and until it is experienced."[38] This sense of growing into our cognition is helpful especially as Charry takes the next step to frame this in terms of love: "It is not only the case that we must know God in order to love him. It is also the case that in loving we learn what loving is—indeed, how difficult it really is."[39]

To know God is to love God and to love God is to know God in and through our obedience to him, aligning our lives with his. Formation involves allowing the life of the community to be shaped so that it provides

36. Torrance, *School of Faith*, xxxvii.

37. Part of the reason for this is "the complex legacy of dualism and nominalism in Western Christian theology, through which the sensible and intelligible realms, history and eternity, were thrust away from each other, and creaturely forms (language, action, instructions) denied any capacity to indicate the presence and activity of the transcendent God." Webster, *Holy Scripture*, 19–20.

38. Charry, *By the Renewing of Your Minds*, 240.

39. Charry, *By the Renewing of Your Minds*, 240.

the situated context in which we may together come to know God with heart, soul, and mind. To come to know God requires the adaptation of our knowing (practices) and relationship toward him as he has and does make himself known.[40] It is in the ordering of our lives in relationship to God that it becomes possible to truly see him more clearly.

The gathering of the community is nothing less than our entering together into the ordered space and time within which true knowledge of God becomes possible. It is in this context that the gathering of the community becomes the locus out of which pastoral theology or theology arises. We come to understand or know what it means to be a Christian in part by having a framework of patterns and habits of living within which to locate that understanding. Likewise, we hope to shape a pastoral theology which speaks into the life of the church because it is grounded in the way God has and is shaping his people. We intend to help people enter into the new world of the gospel, the new creation in Christ, but not solely by talking them into it. They need to enter the world and experience it, knowing in situ or in practice, in order to come to know God and God's intentions for this world. Knowledge requires relationship,[41] both with that which we are coming to know (most especially when it is another person that we are coming to know, whether that person is divine or human) and with a concrete community or context of understanding. Only in this way can we enter into this story to engage with its character and characters and live into it, so as to begin to know what it is about, and particularly to get to know the One in whom the story finds its center: the God-man.

40. "All knowing involves an *adaptation of our capacities* in accordance with the nature of the object." Torrance, *School of Faith*, xxiv.

41. "In fact we are not really able to know other people except in so far as we enter into reciprocal relations with them through which we ourselves are affected, that is, in friendship. If it is a fundamental principle that we may know something only in accordance with its nature, then we may know it only as we allow its nature to prescribe to us the mode of knowing appropriate to it and to determine for us the way in which we must consciously behave toward it. Personal beings require from us, therefore, personal modes of knowledge and behaviour, that is, the kind of knowledge that comes through a rapprochement or communion of minds characterised by mutual respect, trust and love. It cannot be otherwise with our knowledge of God. If we are really to know God in accordance with his nature as he discloses himself to us, we require to be adapted in our knowing and personal relations toward him—that is why we cannot know God without love, and if we are estranged without being reconciled to him. Knowing God requires cognitive union with him in which our whole being is affected by his love and holiness. It is the pure in heart who see God." Torrance, *Mediation of Christ*, 25–26.

3

Offices and Gifts in the Church

A Meditation on Ephesians 4

From the gathering of the community the question arises, Who will be involved in the worship? Or perhaps better, how will each person who has gathered be involved in worship? Ephesians 4 presents an evocative image of the whole body functioning together with leaders who are understood as serving to facilitate the healthy functioning of the whole body under Christ. Leadership must be perceived as at once authority and service (e.g., *Baptism, Eucharist and Ministry*), and stands in contrast to the ego needs of the leader which too often result in clericalism or the cult of celebrity. This corporate understanding is developed by reflection on Jesus's critique of the Pharisees, and is illustrated in conversation with contemporary works on leadership.

The welcome at the outset of a service of worship demonstrates that an identifying feature of a local church community is not only who is gathered but the variety of people who play roles in leadership or service. Whether we are speaking about a church with a strong emphasis on a set liturgy and the ordained or a church that emphasizes informal liturgies and the participation of a variety of people, there are some basic working assumptions as to how participation is understood, encouraged (or not), and supported. Regardless of denominational affiliation there are myriad ways in which people may contribute to the worshiping life of the community: there are readers of Scripture, those who sing or lead music, those who welcome, and those who teach Sunday school. We might learn a lot about a church and how they understand themselves by watching who is involved and how they are serving. Recently, while visiting one small local church where most of the congregation were elderly, it was a joy to see one recent immigrant family who played key roles in the service. The mother was the lay reader, one son was the crucifer, the other son ran the sound board, while the daughter read two of the readings for the day. Following the service, the congregation followed the family downstairs as they hosted coffee hour for everyone. The elderly congregation were grateful for the family's service since many of them were too old to help out, but the family were also pleased to be serving. What was particularly inspiring was the way in which this family served: The mother had a joyful presence in her leadership and the teenagers all responded graciously when they were thanked for the roles that they played.

Even in large or mega churches, however, finding willing volunteers to fill different roles too often becomes an onerous task: Rotas are set up to make sure that someone is assigned each role each week. Busy with sermon preparation or liturgical planning, pastors often view the task of finding volunteers to fill different roles in the service pragmatically: Who can we find to do the work that needs to get done? The same is true of other ministry initiatives outside of the worship service—how can we find more volunteers to fill these different roles? It is not surprising that this often becomes a self-perpetuating pattern where the individuals who volunteer for different roles—particularly Sunday school—burn out, and it becomes increasingly difficult to find more volunteers willing to step forward. This repeating pattern doesn't simply reveal the need for a more robust recruiting plan, but a fundamental lack of vision or understanding of how the church is called to function or what the church is called to be. While these issues are often understood purely pragmatically, they are in fact key questions in pastoral theology: how the body of Christ is to be understood, how it is to function, and how it is to be built up. The question isn't so much who might take on the different roles in worship as how participation should be understood and supported as part of the calling of the community as a whole.

The image of the church as Christ's body from Eph 4 evokes a striking pattern and vision for the church:

> Speaking the truth in love, we are to grow up in every way into him who is the head, into Christ, from whom the whole body, joined and held together by every joint with which it is equipped, when each part is working properly, makes the body grow so that it builds itself up in love. (Eph 4:15, 16)

Every joint with which it is equipped, every part working properly: this is the image of maturity put forward by Eph 4. Our calling is not primarily to form mature or complete individuals; rather it is a vision of a mature body where each part—each person—is learning how to live together as Christ's body in and for the sake of not just the local church, but also of the world outside of the church. The recent emphasis in many churches on discipleship is commendable, but the language of Ephesians doesn't allow us to see this as a call to cultivating mature individuals, but a mature body. Yes, a mature community requires mature individuals, but no one can become mature in isolation from others. This builds on the practical implications of Eph 2, where we are called to learn to live in reconciliation with one another just as we have been reconciled to God in Christ. Indeed, it suggests that we only come to know what it means to be reconciled to Christ in our being reconciled one to another in the practical and often difficult life of the church community.

Paul's letter to the Ephesians states that God's plan is to reconcile all things in Christ, who is the head over all things. In one of the courses I (Peter) teach, the students are required to work with particular passages in the Letter to the Ephesians. We often end up discussing how understanding the central theme of the unity of the church is vital to interpreting any given passage in the letter. What is more, the building up of the body is not for the sake of the church in itself but is for the sake of God's ultimate purpose of reconciling all things in Christ. Ephesians 1:13 states, "The building up of the body of Christ, the church, is towards the measure of the stature of the fullness of Christ." The space or place to which we are called, and the ultimate goal for the church, is to be a part of what God is doing in bringing all things together under Christ. This *telos*—this mission—should shape everything we do as a community, and it is in this context that we should hear the call to reconciliation in Ephesians chapter 2.

UNITY

Anyone who has been around the church for even a short time will wonder if the author of Ephesians is a little too idealistic. Is this an overly realized eschatology? The church around the world is badly divided and has been from its earliest days.[1] We seem to be far more effective at hurt-

1. "There is a way, however, that Christian division has indeed proven one of the

ing one another and alienating one another than building one another up in love. There is nothing new to this pattern of division.[2] This issue of division is a particularly challenging issue in the context of a project in pastoral theology such as this book, which seeks to defend pastoral theology as a discipline which arises in the milieu of the church.

The Epistles, taken as a whole, bear witness to the many issues which divided the church from its earliest days. Paul, for example, speaks directly to the pride and spiritual elitism which were so evident in the Corinthian church. While the Letter to the Ephesians doesn't describe specific situations of division, the clarion call is for those who are divided against each other (Jew and gentile) to be reconciled. Life with the people of God is almost always messy. We find ourselves hurt or slighted by the comments or actions of others. We are frustrated by the political commitments or interests of different people in the community. We don't like the music that another person in the community finds deeply moving or inspiring. These conflicts in local worshiping communities pale in light of a history of Christian communities warring against one another and at times killing one another.

The damage effected by our divisions is directly exposed and confronted by Jesus's words on witness: "By this they will know that you are my disciples, that you love one another" (John 13:35). Jesus's prayer aligns with the potent images of the church we see in Colossians and Ephesians: a body with every part working together as intended. The credal affirmation that the church is one and holy stands in stark contrast to the reality of the church temporally and spatially divided. How are we supposed to understand this call to (or declaration of) unity and witness in light of the reality we see and experience in the church?[3] A report from a conference in Oxford in 1937 asks this question succinctly:

> What reason for example has the church given the world to believe that it has the secret of true community in Him whom it preaches and professes to serve? The life of the church is deeply

central topics of theological reflection, from Paul to Tertullian to Irenaeus to Cyprian to Augustine." Radner, *Brutal Unity*, 126.

2. Hans Urs von Balthasar aligns the church with the people of Israel in speaking of the church as the fallen spouse of Yahweh, literally as the "Chaste Harlot." Kress, "Simul Justus et Peccator," 264, citing Balthasar, "Casta Meretrix," 203–5.

3. As vital as the question of unity and division in the church is to our discussion, it is a complex question that we can only touch on briefly in this chapter. See the more extended discussion in Radner, *Brutal Unity*; Congar, *Chrétiens désunis*; or Reno, *In the Ruins of the Church*.

> infected with the very ills from which humanity suffers. The division and conflicts of mankind have been reproduced and even justified within its borders. Again and again Christian groups have persecuted and sought to destroy one another, and with equal guilt have persecuted men of other faiths—and this is still happening to-day. Thus a Satanic element has entered the life of the church.[4]

How do we address the disparity between the call to unity and the conflict and division that is the reality of the church, especially if we are speaking of a pastoral theology that arises from the life of the church? There have been many ways in which people have sought to make sense of the contradiction between a biblical affirmation of unity in the church and the reality and experience of division. The Catholic Church has located unity in the figure of the pope, with an emphasis on the unity of the institution. But institutional unity doesn't necessarily lead to the kind of unity Jesus bears witness to, and often simply papers over the deep divides within the church. Since the Reformation, many Protestant churches have chosen to put the primary emphasis on doctrinal unity or doctrinal agreement; in practice, this tends not to strengthen unity but instead results in cascading spirals of division which never seem to end. It also encourages the tendency toward the privatization of faith, with an emphasis on "small[er] local communities of 'true believers.'"[5] This understanding of unity has not only encouraged division, it has also hindered the mission of the church by encouraging exclusivity.[6] Meanwhile, some liberal Protestant churches have argued for a loose affiliation of like-minded people as a more realistic interpretation of unity. The idea that we should simply learn how to put up with one another is, in some

4. "Longer Report on Church and Community," 197, quoted in Radner, *Brutal Unity*, 114.

5. Kress, *Church*, 71–73. "Brad Gregory observes that not only did the Reformation refocus the church on certain doctrines (i.e., *Sola Scriptura*), but doctrine was now all important as a means to establish authority." Gregory suggests "that prior to the Reformation Christianity was embedded in social life, political relations, and the wider culture, whose principal purpose was the sanctification of the baptized through the practice of the Christian faith. . . . Doctrine served Christian unity, but doctrine was not, as it was to become in the Reformation, that which in and of itself constituted Christian unity." Hauerwas, "Which Church? What Unity?," 270n21, citing Gregory, *Unintended Reformation*, 82–84.

6. Somewhat in line with monasticism where the "perfect" assembled are "separated from the masses outside." Kress, "Simul Justus et Peccator," 266, citing Durnbaugh, *Believers' Church*.

ways, a realistic concession to the hard work in moving through difficulties and dealing with conflict, but the biblical witness to unity (in, for example, John 17 and Eph 4) does not allow us to take this easy way out. Not only is this perspective difficult to align with the potent image of a body functioning in unison, it is, as Hauerwas argues, a convenient way to avoid the challenging work of learning to live with one another.[7] At his closing speech for Lambeth 2008, in the face of deep division within the Anglican Communion, Archbishop Rowan Williams reminded the gathered bishops of the weight of the biblical call: "Our unity is not mutual forbearance but being summoned and drawn into the same place before the Father's throne."[8]

One of the most persistent arguments in attempting to align a call to unity with the hard reality of division has been the affirmation that the true church is invisible.[9] To argue that the unity of the church is a spiritual unity appears to solve some of the issues around the evident conflict and division in the church. But in the end this spiritualization of unity also encourages a privatization of the faith. Given the particular struggles faced by the church in the twentieth century, it is not surprising that there was a renewed emphasis on invisible or spiritual unity. This was also echoed in the missional church movement from the middle of the twentieth century where the emphasis shifted to prioritizing the kingdom of God, and the church was seen to be, if anything, a barrier to the kingdom. Menno Simons in some ways anticipated the twentieth-century missional church movement with his concern that using the language of the "body of Christ" would lead to identifying the church with the kingdom of God. Yet arguing in favor of a spiritual unity or the kingdom of God rather than the church fails to address the reality of division among the people of God.

In his commentary on Ephesians, Michael Allen is surely correct when he picks up Peter Leithart's argument and critiques his understanding of the unity of the church; he suggests that Eph 4:4 forces us to affirm

7. Hauerwas, "Which Church? What Unity?," 270.

8. Williams, "Concluding Presidential Address," para. 6.

9. Radner argues that following the 1960s and 1970s, as churches became sidelined, old sectarian and self-protecting ecclesial attitudes reasserted themselves. "And within churches themselves, after all, the intractability of division had led to the current triumph of an age-old Protestant reliance on unity as something existent within a spiritual and invisible realm, one that Catholics were willing to embrace in their own sense of eschatological openness to the mysterious arena of fellowship outside the visible boundaries of the church." Radner, *Brutal Unity*, 109.

that the church is one, at least in some ways, even in the present.[10] It is much easier to remain at arm's length from the people of God or to gather together only with those who agree with our own understanding or commitments. But doing so, or seeing our relationship with God as private, means that we are isolating ourselves from the purposes of God for the whole of creation. Ephesians doesn't allow for an otherworldly image of the church where our only focus is on a spiritual dimension. It allows no room for a church that is just an oasis or escape from an otherwise chaotic world. Instead, Ephesians (and for that matter, the high priestly prayer in John 17) sets the church right in the middle of our world. It locates the church in the midst of God's great plan to unite all things under Christ.[11] In Christ, and by the presence of the Holy Spirit, God the Father has made a new way of living possible. It is life together as the people of God, united in Christ, which is the hope of the world.

The Eastern Orthodox Churches are noted for pointing toward an eschatological view of unity.[12] The unity of the church is the telos toward which we are called, even as we taste this unity in the present. While an emphasis on an eschatological understanding of unity complements the honest acknowledgment of division in the present, it risks positing unity as an unrealized hope or distant dream with little significance for the present. Here, too, it might reinforce a privatization of the faith rather than forcing us to live with the real tension between the call to unity and the reality of division.[13] Perhaps the solution is not to try to locate a fixed or static unity in the present, but instead to allow for the way in which the church participates in and tastes the unity toward which it is called. Here we need to pick up other elements from the Orthodox approach

10. Allen, *Ephesians*, 89–90. Fowl also argues "in the face of the Spirit's already-delivered gift of unity, Christian division simply is a contradiction of the Spirit's unity." Fowl, *Ephesians*, 132, citing Root, "Why Care About the Unity of the Church?," 106–7.

11. Ephesians 1:9, 10—"God has made known to us the mystery of his will, according to his purpose, which he set forth in Christ as a plan for the fullness of time, to unite all things in him [that is Christ], things in heaven and things on earth." And 1:22—"God, the Father, put all things under Christ's feet and gave him as head over all things in the church, which is his body, the fullness of him who fills all in all."

12. In effect, Luther also argued for an eschatological dimension to the *simul*: "Thus our righteousness does not yet exist in fact (in re), but it still exists in hope (in spe). (WA 40 2/23, 18; also 56/274, 8)." Quoted in Kress, "Simul Justus et Peccator," 260.

13. "Eschatologically oriented ecclesiologies slide into unmoored and irresponsible hopes and claims: they become forgetful of the past but therefore also blind to what drives the present and so blind to the character of the Church herself as it now or ever will be as in any way continuous with the present." Radner, *Brutal Unity*, 141.

by noting that this unity is also pneumatic, local, and eucharistic.[14] As the Spirit unites the local gathering of worshipers, they experience the eschatological hope of the unified body. We taste and experience the future unity of the church in a tangible and physical manner in the present, albeit not in a fixed or static sense. Augustine may add an important element here when he suggests that the church's unity is always embodied in the temporal history of the Word, thus locating the church directly in relationship with Christ.[15] It is precisely because we taste the unity to which we are called that we are then enabled and encouraged to work toward it in how we relate to those around us. Indeed, we are compelled toward this unity. How else can we deal with the question of unity in a way that honors the significance of this call while also acknowledging the reality of conflict and division?

Robert Kress has argued that the ecclesial body of Christ is simultaneously, although not equally, holy and sinful. Beginning with Luther's affirmation that the Christian is both justified and sinful (which we have already cited in earlier chapters), Kress notes that Catholic–Lutheran dialogue has moved toward a positive recognition of Luther's understanding of justification. He goes on to suggest that Luther's affirmation should not just be applied to individual Christians, but to the church itself.[16] Kress, while acknowledging that different denominations would understand this affirmation in different ways, suggests that there is a basic acceptance that the church is *simul justus et peccator*.[17] Following the logic of Luther's argument, he suggests that the church is not partially righteous and partially sinful, but is wholly sinful and wholly righteous at the same time.[18] Kress acknowledges that Meyendorff, among other Orthodox

14. Kress cites Evdokimov, *Orthodoxie*, in making this point. Kress, "Simul Justus et Peccator," 268.

15. Radner speaks of Augustine in *Brutal Unity*, 129. Radner goes on to say "Nor, indeed, is the sinful Church as such capable of some resolution to this reality other than the one act of the one Lord who makes one new man on the cross (Eph 2:15–16). In Christ there is peace; in the Church as such, division" (157).

16. Kress dismisses the claim which has often been made about the mixed nature of the church—that the church is holy and its members sinful. Kress, "Simul Justus et Peccator," 270.

17. Kress suggests that Anglican theology, in principle, would have no difficulty in arguing for the mixed nature of the church. Kress, "Simul Justus et Peccator," 265nn45–46, citing Vodopivec, "Ecclesiologia Anglicana," 131–36; and Pawley, "Anglican Views the Council," 117.

18. Kress notes that this aligns with Luther's own understanding that the *simul* applies to both the individual and the church. "God deals so wonderfully with his saints

theologians, argues against an understanding of the church as both holy and sinful, since that would amount to a negation of the full and real presence of Christ and a repudiation of the promises he made to his disciples. And perhaps there is more promise in the Orthodox understanding of the church that allows for eschatological space between the church and Christ. This eschatological framework allows us, with Schmemann, to affirm both the being and the "becoming" of the church.[19] The church lives at the intersection of a world that is turned away from God and the eschatological hope of the whole of creation gathered under the lordship of Christ. A model of the church which sees itself as the idealized community of those who have arrived may appeal by encouraging confidence in the ecclesial body, but it is a false picture of the way in which the church exists in the world.

In *A Brutal Unity* Radner suggests that there is a sense in which conflict and division is right at the center of the church's existence.[20] In fact, might we say that God's power is made evident in weakness precisely through the brokenness of the church? Radner notes that Judas was included in the unity of the disciples: "He is simply 'at one' with the others."[21] In Acts 1:26 Matthias is chosen as a replacement apostle for Judas. This suggests that division has not only been a part of the church since its earliest days, but that Jesus himself recognized and acknowledged the mixed nature of his community of followers: "It is a blasphemy and a horror, yet is it not 'other' to this body."[22] As such, we need a way to think about unity in the present that allows us to hold together the hope and promise of unity with the reality of conflict and division.

While emphasizing the eschatological character of unity and the recognition that unity belongs first and foremost to the work of the Spirit, we are still called to work toward or "maintain" the unity of the Spirit. The contrast between the affirmation that we have been reconciled in Christ

---

that he constantly brings it about in the Church, that the Church is holy and nevertheless not holy, that someone is righteous and at the same time not righteous, that another is blessed and at the same time not blessed (Luther WA 39 1/515)." Quoted in Kress, "Simul Justus et Peccator," 257.

19. Schmemann, "Orthodox Tradition," 13–16, quoted in Kress, "Simul Justus et Peccator," 269.

20. See especially ch. 3, "The Sins of the Church," in Radner, *Brutal Unity*, 121–68.

21. The mystery of the tradition is that it is the church which handed Jesus over: "In Judas, we find the horrendous backdrop of Christian unity in its actual accomplishment: sacrifice for sin." Radner, *Brutal Unity*, 120.

22. Radner, *Brutal Unity*, 118–19.

and the reality of the conflict in which we live in relationship to both the local and the global church means that we live in a tension which compels us toward the hard work of maintaining the unity which the Spirit has given us, even though we only experience this unity in part. Here we might begin to understand and accept that inter- and intra-ecclesial conflict becomes the very tool that the Spirit uses to shape and form us as the people of God.[23] As God's people, we learn to turn toward God and toward one another in a consistent posture of humility and repentance. Allen speaks of Calvin in book 4 of the *Institutes* promoting an active lifestyle of ecclesial repentance rather than a program of presumption and arrogance by the purported elect.[24] Accepting that the church continues to experience division is not a license to affirm the status quo but is instead a call to repentance, in which the church acknowledges its wandering (its history of division, brokenness, and violence) while also holding fast to its calling to live in the unity of the Spirit.

The Letter to the Ephesians suggests that living in this tension is demanding and difficult: "I urge you to walk in a manner worthy of the calling to which you have been called, with all humility and gentleness, with patience, bearing with one another in love, eager to maintain the unity of the Spirit in the bond of peace."[25] In his commentary, Fowl notes that forbearing in love presumes failure, a recognition "that Christians will sin against one another and fail one another." It implicitly calls for a practice of truthful confession and forgiveness.[26] Pastorally, it also means allowing for the ways that God uses conflict to bring about his purposes in the church, rather than avoiding conflict or smoothing over conflict prematurely. It means never living lightly with disagreements with other Christians, because disunity is an affront to the Spirit, yet at the same time allowing conflict in a local worshiping community over an extended period of time to refine us as God's people.

This understanding of unity demands that we be shaped by humility in our engagement with others, including in the posture of the church toward the world. Rather than taking comfort in the belief that we are

23. Radner says of Augustine: "The Church can rightly 'endure' her erring (and perhaps only nominal) members, for thereby she grows in charity and faith itself." Radner, *Brutal Unity*, 129.

24. Allen, *Ephesians*, 92.

25. We can say this without assuming that Paul's stress on unity "indicates that there was a particular fractiousness in the Ephesian church." Fowl, *Ephesians*, 127.

26. Fowl, *Ephesians*, 131.

the "in" crowd or that we have arrived, with humility we recognize the compulsion to live into the unity of Christ with the church and toward the world. This openness toward the world and the recognition that the world is in the church and the church is in the world means that life in the church will always be messy. J. N. D. Kelly has argued for the contrite admission of guilt on behalf of the church as the starting point in ecumenism, and we might also argue this as the starting point in mission.[27] Indeed our witness to the world is not the unity that we have achieved but the unity that we are living toward, a unity which we experience only in Christ's relationship to the church. "The fact that conflict is part and parcel of Christian unity means that the unity of a church is not one based on agreements, but rather one that assumes disagreements should not lead to division but rather should be a testimony to the existence of a reconciling people."[28] The church is a little like a piece of clay thrown on a potter's wheel. Misshapen, muddy, not particularly pretty, but all the while God is shaping something beautiful, even if there are points when only the potter can see the beauty in what he is shaping. This process points toward God and God's care and attention in shaping something beautiful out of something that was, and often is, a mess.

Thinking about pastoral theology that grows out of the life of the church means that we can never simply begin with an inductive understanding that grows out of reflection on the practices of local worshiping communities, but must work with an understanding that holds together practical reflection and is rooted in responsive engagement with the biblical text (see chapter 4) and the traditions of the church (particularly the creeds, as we will discuss in chapter 5).[29] For the fracturing and division

27. Kress, "Simul Justus et Peccator," 265, citing Kelly, "Punto di visto anglicano sulla Constituzione," 1211.

28. Hauerwas, "Which Church? What Unity?," 272.

29. Bonnie Miller-McLemore is one of many recent voices in pastoral theology arguing for a shift toward looking to the local community rather than shaping our theology in reference to Scripture and tradition. She supports her argument using phrases like "imposed on believers" and "no sensitivity to their own experience" to describe the practice of beginning with theology: "Pastoral theologians essentially turned from formal scriptural interpretation and Christian proclamation toward the vivid color and textures of clinical cases. In place of a transcendent doctrinal theology, traditionally imposed on believers in their crises with little or no sensitivity to their own experience or religious understandings, pastoral theologians found theological meaning in lived moments of human anguish and joy. In contrast to religious generalities deduced from scripture and church dogma, religious truth in pastoral theology was deeply inductive." Miller-McLemore, "Living Human Web," 311. While the practice and implementation of theology has often been abused, focusing solely on the local situations of believers

of the church to end, the head must be restored as the whole world comes to acknowledge the lordship of Christ.

JESUS GIVES GIFTS TO THE CHURCH

One theme throughout chapter 4 of Ephesians is that the church grows up as it is shaped by God. After stating that we are to maintain the unity of the Spirit, the chapter goes on to speak of the gifts that Jesus gives to the church so that the church might grow up together with every part working properly. Jesus gave gifts to the church—apostles, prophets, evangelists, shepherds, teachers. This giving of gifts echoes 1 Cor 12 or Rom 12. In Corinthians and Romans we are told that the Spirit pours out gifts on the church—everyone is given something: There is no gift that is more important than any other and no person who is more important than any other. Every person is vital to the health of the whole. But these gifts are not ours to use however we choose or to use for our own benefit or advantage. They are of the Spirit and are given to the church to be used for the church, for the body of Christ as it is built up.

One of Paul's targets in 1 Corinthians is the tendency in the Corinthian community for spiritual gifts to divide the community rather than building it up. Some people in that community suggested that certain gifts showed that some people were more spiritual than others. Too often having a particular gift is seen to elevate the person with that gift: It is viewed as conferring status upon the gifted individual. We live in a culture which speaks of "gifted people" and puts enormous value on the cult of the celebrity. It is not surprising that in the church we often do the same thing. Those who have certain more visible gifts are acknowledged for their roles in the church or seen as more spiritual. Meanwhile those who don't have the more visible gifts can at times step back, believing that they have no particular contribution to make. In contrast, Corinthians speaks of gifts given by the Spirit for the sake of the body.

Here in Eph 4, though, Christ is the giver of gifts. And what is particularly fascinating is that these are not so much gifts which are given to individuals, as individuals who themselves have been given to the church as gifts.[30] This is not an encouragement for leaders to see themselves as

---

is to affirm who we understand ourselves to be rather than responding to our call in Christ. Instead of allowing us to address issues of division within the church, it will multiply them.

30. "In Ephesians the emphasis is not on the individuals or groups who receive

God's gift to the church, but rather that it is Christ himself who is building up the body, and who does so through the different people who are brought together in that body. It is not so much about possessing a gift or being gifted as it is about being given by God for the unity of the church. These gifts are used by Christ to effect the unity of the Spirit.

LAY EMPOWERMENT AND ALTERNATIVE LEADERSHIP

If one had to identify the great and lasting pastoral accomplishment of the Reformation other than the use of the vernacular, it might be the consensus view that ministry is by the whole people of God, as expressed in Luther's idea of the priesthood of all believers. This is a retrieval of the emphasis on the whole people of God in Eph 4 and on the body as the sacred priesthood in 1 Pet 2. Another way to express this idea is that in the latter days the prophetic word is now uttered by the whole people, namely that "Jesus is Lord" (see the Pentecost account in Acts 2 with Joel 2 in the background). This ecclesiological baseline has been reclaimed in recent times in terms such as the "whole people of God," "teach each a ministry," and "total ministry."[31] In our final chapter we will see how this is an example of innovation in the North American church with its origin in the global missionary movement. Here one might discuss alternative ways to discern and train ordained leaders, the use of lay pastors or "minor orders," the rediscovery of the diaconate, and more shared models of oversight, etc.

Apposite in this section is the literature on governance. While it can focus and challenge members of church councils, such literature often assumes secular notions of rapid change and the personality of the leader, both of which bear investigation and challenge. It is ironic that the study of leadership has reached for ideas like vocation, service, and mission at the very same moment that the church has second-guessed them in favor of leadership. Here secular assumptions about self-fulfillment, career, and power dynamics are despoiled and transformed.

'apostleship' as a gift. Rather, apostles, prophets, evangelists, pastors and teachers are *themselves* the gifts given by the ascended Christ through the Spirit." Fowl, *Ephesians*, 140.

31. For example, Bishop Gordon's Teach Each a Ministry work in Alaska. But the unanswered question is whether local clergy actually conduce to this outcome.

Administration is also a ministry of ordering that enables the gospel. The question is how to appropriate the wisdom of secular literature on the subject while adapting it for the church's purposes.[32] The implied contrast to pastoral ministry must be overcome, since a well-run congregation is indeed a means of empowering lay ministry.

CULTIVATING APPRENTICES IN MINISTRY

We have already spoken about a pedagogy which focuses on a practical approach to learning—an emphasis on apprenticeship rather than classroom learning. In the church this implies that central to our life together is the need to encourage, foster, and challenge one another to learn how to get along with one another and to work together for the building up of the body. One of the most effective ways to see this happen is to invite others to share in the ministry of the body. In one church that I (Peter) was a part of, people who were exploring becoming part of the church were first invited to a welcome dinner or BBQ and then almost immediately invited to take on a role in serving in the community. Rather than feeling as though unrealistic expectations were being made of them, most people were grateful to be asked. The church intentionally cultivated an understanding that there was a place and a role for everyone in the community. In this approach the church was careful not to just try to slot people into the area of greatest need. Rather, as part of this process the leadership in the church would sit down and have a conversation with each new person to see who they were, what gifts they brought, and how they might best serve in the community. Too often leaders put the focus on programs and work hard to find people to sustain those programs rather than putting the focus on each person and using the programs to help people learn to exercise their gifts. In principle we recognize that programs should serve people, but too often in practice volunteers are recruited to simply keep programs functioning.

This approach to ministry only works where there is a basic commitment on the part of key leaders to cultivate attentiveness to others in the community. In the *Weight of Glory*, C. S. Lewis speaks of seeing others as God sees them: unique and precious to him.[33] In ministry, that also

32. See for example Welch, *Church Administration.*

33. Lewis, *Weight of Glory*, 7: "To please God . . . to be a real ingredient in the divine happiness . . . to be loved by God, not merely pitied, but delighted in as an artist delights

means paying attention to what God is doing in different people's lives.[34] Eric Abrahamson spoke of the tendency in the business world for a new leader to come into a company and attempt to build it up by bringing in new people and new resources. Thus they look for people based on defined need, rather than looking first to the people, to understand who they are and what they bring. Instead, Abrahamson argues for creative recombination, where a leader will look at who is already there and what resources are available and then work to put those people and resources together in ways that enable healthier functioning.[35] If this applies to a business setting, how much more to the church? The ordained need to pay attention to who God has brought together in a local community and learn how to invite people into ministry opportunities, guarding others from taking on more than they can handle, while honoring the people who are already there. Leaders also need to learn how to let programs die, rather than simply trying to find willing persons to fill the slots. If ministry leaders burn out, it can take years before they are ready to take on something else.

Max DePree suggests that leadership is "abandoning oneself to the strength of others."[36] That doesn't mean abdicating the role of leadership or giving people ministry responsibilities without support or guidance, but leading by giving others opportunities to minister, and giving others the space to grow into ministry—even, and perhaps especially, at those times when it might be easier and faster to do the work yourself. Inevitably, this will be messy and uncomfortable because other people won't do things the same way we would have them done, and it will certainly involve allowing people to make mistakes. In healthy ministry situations there is not only room for failure but an expectation that failure is part of the learning process as we grow up together as the body.

The best way for people to learn ministry and for them to grow into being part of the body is to learn in apprentice fashion alongside someone who has some experience and skill. This doesn't mean simply

---

in his work or a father in a son—it seems impossible, a weight or burden of glory which our thoughts can hardly sustain. But so it is."

34. Matthew 9:36–38—"When he saw the crowds, he had compassion for them, because they were harassed and helpless, like sheep without a shepherd. Then he said to his disciples, 'The harvest is plentiful, but the laborers are few; therefore ask the Lord of the harvest to send out laborers into his harvest.'"

35. See Abrahamson, "Using Creative Recombination to Manage Change," 33–41.

36. DePree, *Leadership Is an Art*, 89.

giving people opportunities (although it does include that). Rather, it involves the more demanding work of mentoring and investing in people along the way. Giving people ministry responsibilities without walking alongside them and showing them how it is done is a little like throwing a person into the water and telling them that they need to learn how to swim. It might work in some instances but is just as likely to result in traumatic experiences. If we are to prioritize apprenticeship learning in ministry, it means that in everything we do, especially in new initiatives, we need to not only involve others, but walk alongside them. In one church I (Peter) was a part of this was one of the ways in which children and youth were integrated into community. They were given roles in the service and then mentored by adults into those roles. Not only were the children and young people delighted to take part in service, it helped to foster intergenerational relationships within the community.

LEADERSHIP IN CHRIST'S BODY

In Eph 4, the gifts listed all have to do with leadership in the church: Some are apostles, some prophets, some evangelists, and some pastors and teachers, which brings us back to the question of leadership. As we noted earlier, more vital than the question of who leads different aspects of the service is the fundamental understanding of the role of leaders. This is perhaps one of the most pressing and difficult questions in pastoral theology—the leader's place in the body. The faith and order paper *Baptism, Eucharist and Ministry* affirms that while ordination is a setting apart of a leader, the leadership role is not therefore a possession of the ordained person.[37] This raises an important distinction: Is the priest or pastor's role to establish and exercise their leadership as the primary authority within the community, or is the priest or pastor's role to serve the body by facilitating the whole body working together? To separate these two questions is to assume a division between ontology and function. As *Baptism, Eucharist and Ministry* suggests, we are to hold both together at the same time with the recognition that the ordained minister acts within the collegial body for the sake of that body.

> Authority cannot be exercised without regard for the community. The apostles paid heed to the experience and the judgment of the faithful. On the other hand, the authority of ordained

37. "Ordained Ministry and Authority," in *Baptism, Eucharist and Ministry*, 20.

> ministers must not be so reduced as to make them dependent on the common opinion of the community. Their authority lies in their responsibility to express the will of God in the community.[38]

Although different denominations have different approaches to pastoral or priestly leadership, the witness of Eph 4 serves as a framework for us all. Likewise, while we would be foolish not to draw on the tremendous range of secular or popular resources available on questions of leadership, we do so in the recognition that this is not, primarily, a pragmatic or practical concern, but a theological one. While secular leadership resources can be very helpful to leaders in the church, they need to be interpreted and discerned in the context of a biblical and theological frame.

The idea that we might be a gift to others is one that could be seen as arrogant or humbling: arrogant, if we believe that we are God's gift to the church; humbling in the sense that God has called us to live in service to others, especially those who are different than we are or who see things differently than we do. While some leaders in the church use their position of authority to lord it over those who come to them for help, the majority of leaders learn humility as they seek to walk alongside those in need. When we are truly attentive to the pastoral needs of others and the pain and struggles they are dealing with, it leads almost inevitably to prayer as we call out to God for both wisdom and healing. The mystery of God's grace in these situations is that God is directly and intimately involved through us—through one another—teaching and enabling us to live in peace and unity with one another: the potter shaping the clay. Our role—our place—is to participate in what God is doing in the church and through the church for the world.

In Eph 4 the gifts of leadership are singled out so that we might know the role or place of leadership in the midst of a healthy body—a healthy church community.

> It is crucial to keep in mind that whatever else one wants to say about them, "apostles," "prophets," "evangelists," "pastors" and "teachers" are offices or ministries given by Christ through the Spirit to enable the church to grow into the unity that is already

38. "Ordained Ministry and Authority," in *Baptism, Eucharist and Ministry*, 20.

given to the church in 4:3. These offices or ministries are gifts for a purpose.[39]

Gifts of leadership are to equip the saints for *diakonia*—for works of service. *Diakonia* is a helpful word because it means both ministry and service. Rather than suggesting that the work of leadership is distinct from works of service, it suggests that gifts of leadership are primarily gifts of service, just as they are also ministry gifts.[40] Those with gifts of leadership are to serve in the building up of the body. Consider verse 12—"to equip the saints [that is, every Christian] for the work of ministry, for building up the body of Christ, until all of us come to the unity of faith." It has been observed that in some versions of the Bible this verse is translated with a comma between saints and "for the work" as though each is a coordinating preposition. As a result it seems to read, "Leaders and teachers in the church are to do three things: 1. equip the saints, 2. do the work of the ministry, and 3. build up the body of Christ." In the context of the whole Letter to the Ephesians witnessing to the body functioning together, it makes more sense to read it without the comma: So the leaders and teachers in the church are to equip every Christian to do the work of ministry in order that the body of Christ might be built up.

The challenge for someone called to leadership is to exercise authority in the community for the sake of the body. This may seem straightforward as a concept, but in practice it is very difficult to maintain. Anyone with significant experience who is honest with themselves will recognize the two parallel temptations of a leader. On the one hand there is the temptation to exercise authority independently, suggesting that we are doing this for the sake of others, when in fact it may have more to do with implementing our own agenda or trying to bypass potential opposition. The other temptation is to fail to exercise authority for fear of opposition or conflict. Not only does this result in long term problems in the health of a local community, it also tends to act as a barrier to the work that God is doing. As we noted above, God has shown a pattern of using conflict or difficulty as the very instrument of effecting his change in a community. The failure to exercise authority may be an avoidance tactic, while too forcefully exercising authority can mask conflict instead of allowing God

39. Fowl, *Ephesians*, 140.

40. "The term *ordained ministry* refers to persons who have received a charism and whom the church appoints for service by ordination through the invocation of the Spirit and the laying on of hands." "The Church and the Ordained Ministry," in *Baptism, Eucharist and Ministry*, 17.

to use it redemptively. A leader is called to recognize and live with this tension of working through differences while avoiding the dual temptation to exercise authority too quickly or too slowly, being too blunt or too laissez faire. Recognizing and living with the messiness of conflict is one of God's great gifts to those called to leadership because it inevitably fosters a humility which consistently reminds us that we must always be in prayer seeking God's counsel and forgiveness if we are to follow his call. The leader's job is not to exercise authority unilaterally, but to seek to faithfully attend to God's will for the community.[41] It is in being attentive to God and what God is doing in a community that a leader is both humbled and set free to speak and lead with conviction.[42]

The priority of service is further emphasized when we recognize that the center of gravity for the body is to be turned outward instead of inward. A focus on Christ turns the community outward since our service to Christ's body is ordered toward service to Christ and his purposes for the whole of creation.

> In order to fulfil its mission, the church needs persons who are publicly and continually responsible for pointing to its fundamental dependence on Jesus Christ, and thereby provide, within a multiplicity of gifts, a focus of its unity. The ministry of such persons, who since very early times have been ordained, is constitutive for the life and witness of the church.[43]

With Christ as the head of the body, the ordained person serves the body by facilitating its working together rather than taking on primary responsibility for ministry by themselves.

DISORDERED DESIRES IN LEADERSHIP

This raises the specter of clericalism, which has taken on particularly ominous tones in the Catholic Church over the past few decades. By clericalism we mean a disordered understanding of ordained leadership

41. "Ordained Ministry and Authority," in *Baptism, Eucharist and Ministry*, 20.

42. Basil responded to Emperor Valens about the call of the bishop: "In all else we are meek, the most humble of all. But when it concerns God, and people rise up against Him, then we, counting everything else as naught, look to Him alone. Then fire, sword, wild beasts and iron rods that rend the body, serve to fill us with joy, rather than fear." Orthodox Church in America, "Saint Basil the Great," para. 22.

43. "The Church and the Ordained Ministry," in *Baptism, Eucharist and Ministry*, 17.

that perceives ordination as a license to exercise power in the church without a healthy understanding of one's relationship both to the body and to Christ, the head of the body. Lest we think of clericalism as an issue only within the Catholic Church or other episcopal churches, we need to note that a tendency toward elevating leaders in an unhealthy fashion has existed from the beginning of the church, when Jesus's first followers were arguing over which of them was the greatest, and even before that, in regard to the spiritual leadership of the Jewish community (Ezek 34). While the excesses of clericalism might be more evident in a hierarchical church, the root issue of spiritual elitism in which the priest or pastor is seen as somehow above others is evident in many different ecclesial traditions, just as Jesus criticized the Jewish religious leaders for this attitude. In nondenominational churches which have eschewed more formal structures there is particular danger in locating authority in a charismatic figure.[44]

The Mars Hill podcast series produced by *Christianity Today* is a sobering exposé of the many ways in which authority can be abused. The charisma of the leader was used to elevate him above the community and gave him an authority that was difficult to challenge. If anyone in the church called his leadership into question he quickly and deliberately forced them out of the community. He personally invited people into positions of leadership who then had a sense of obligation to him. Both the lead pastor and other leaders in the community justified this behavior by pointing out the positive things that were happening in people's lives as evidence of God's blessing on them, and therefore affirmation of their work. To further complicate matters, both the lead pastor and the church cultivated an attitude of exclusivity, which allowed them to ignore voices from outside of their own community challenging the way leadership was exercised.[45] While this form of charismatic leadership, which is common in some Protestant denominations, is not usually defined as clericalism, its distortions and the way power is used and abused are very similar. One of the terrible truths and legacies of the church is that too many leaders are guilty of abusing those under their care in a variety of ways.

44. "As Max Weber pointed out, in times of confusion and destruction, authority shifts to the personality of the 'charismatic leader', who appears to understand the movement of history and offers the guidance that established structures no longer provide." Hitchcock, "Liturgy and Ritual," para. 44, citing Weber, *Theory of Social and Economic Organization*, 361.

45. Cosper, *Rise and Fall of Mars Hill*.

Diane Langberg discusses her journey in understanding the prevalence of abuse in the church:

> Slowly, I began to understand that power, deception, and abuse were all tangled up together. People who were highly esteemed and seen as godly were in fact deceiving themselves and others in order to commit and conceal ungodly deeds. As time went on, I saw entire systems do the same thing. Systemic abuse, an utterly foreign concept to me at the time, became clearer as I discovered that sometimes the people of God unite to "protect" God's name by both committing and concealing actions that look nothing like God. God's people were breaking his heart.[46]

In Mark 12 there is a fascinating encounter where the Pharisees and Sadducees are trying to expose Jesus as a fraud. Jesus's harsh criticism of them might lead us to believe that they were hypocrites in an obvious and public way. Indeed, they have often been described as the archetypal hypocritical or corrupt leaders whom everyone despised (which allows us to caricature and dismiss them). In fact, they were venerated and held in awe as wise, devout leaders in the faith.[47] Jesus's witness suggests that when a scribe showed up at a special meal or event they were welcomed with open arms; it was a great honor to have a scribe present. And if a scribe walked through the marketplace, people stopped what they were doing to acknowledge the scribe and greet him with respect.

We cannot get a sense of Jesus's encounter with the scribes unless we recognize that the scribes, like most spiritual leaders, took their roles very seriously. The scribe in post-exilic Israel would be like the person described in Ps 119—one who loves the law, delights in the word, and meditates on it day and night. They were experts in biblical interpretation and were committed to watching over, guiding, and helping others as part of preserving the faith for the faithful. Yet, Jesus warns his followers to "beware of the scribes" who love to be treated with honor and respect (Luke 20:46). And with that simple warning he exposes their false motivations. In spite of their stated intention to honor the great commandment, they aren't in fact doing so—they aren't seeking to love God with all of their heart, soul, mind, and strength. They, along with almost everyone around them, believed that they were faithful. But Jesus revealed the primary desires of their hearts: to receive honor and respect for themselves.

46. Langberg, *Redeeming Power*, x.

47. Paul bears witness to this in Phil 3:5, 6 when he notes that he was a faithful Pharisee.

The evidence of their displaced allegiance is brought to light in how they treat their neighbors and, especially, the most vulnerable among them: "They devour widows' houses" (Luke 20:47).

The desire to be respected, admired, and liked is second nature to us. And there are some healthy aspects to these desires. The problem is, like the scribes, we often seek to have our desires met or filled in ways that will never bring satisfaction. Accolades or recognition don't leave us satisfied but leave us wanting more. The assumption of privilege invites the exercise of authority in abusive ways and reveals a naïve understanding of the dynamics of power and the abuse of power, particularly spiritual authority, within the church.

That craving for more is rooted in desire, and as Jamie Smith argues in *You Are What You Love*, our desires order and shape our lives—we worship what we love, so our loves shape who we are, what we value, and how we think. When our desires are disordered, they inevitably misshape our thinking and actions. To make it worse, our disordered desires don't just impact us, but also wreak havoc and destruction in our families and in our communities. In *Mere Christianity* C. S. Lewis noted that human history is "the long terrible story of man trying to find something other than God which will make him happy."[48]

What is particularly germane in the contentious age in which we live is that these disordered desires and the fact that we don't acknowledge our underlying commitments prevent us from learning from one another. This is one of the reasons why we so often talk past each other. In his book *Learn or Die*, Edward Hess (a professor at the University of Virginia) argues that our ego is a huge liability to our learning and our growing up. He contends that ego gets in the way of empathy and listening, both of which are critical skills for learning. Indeed, arrogance and insecurity are often two sides of the same coin. Unfortunately, more often than not, we are the last to recognize that we have a problem with our ego. And distorted egos wreak all kinds of havoc. "Clericalism, whether fostered by priests themselves or by lay persons, leads to an excision in the ecclesial body that supports and helps to perpetuate many of the evils that we are condemning today," as Pope Francis wrote in his "Letter to the People of God" on the abuse crisis in the Catholic Church. "To say 'no' to abuse is to say an emphatic 'no' to all forms of clericalism."[49] The

48. Lewis, *Mere Christianity*, 49.

49. Francis, "Letter of His Holiness Pope Francis to the People of God," para. 7.

destructive power of our egos cannot be unmasked until we are willing to acknowledge the underlying and distorted desires that fuel the ego.

The scribes are examples to us, not because they are archetypal hypocrites and thus easy targets for us to avoid but because they were doing everything right except the one thing that is most important of all. The scribes claimed to be and believed themselves to be the kind of people who were seeking God. But underneath their stated commitment to focus on and obey God was something quite different—they were seeking fulfillment through honor and recognition—they just didn't realize or acknowledge it.

In his conversation with the scribes, Jesus exposed that their biblical learning and expertise was in fact leading them and others away from God rather than toward God. They invested a lot of time and effort in becoming competent biblical scholars, but in the end it was clear that they didn't comprehend what they were studying, as evidenced in their not recognizing the God they believed they were worshiping when that God was right in front of them.

Blind to the way their desires were disordered, these religious leaders ended up working against God and against God's purposes to the point that they were desperate to get rid of Jesus. And that was exactly what Jesus tried to warn them about in the parable of the vineyard at the beginning of Mark 12. This parable frames the conversation with the Jewish leaders while simultaneously locating Jesus in his relationship to the Father. But the Scribes and the Pharisees could not see what was right in front of them; their hermeneutic, shaped by the way their desires were ordered, wouldn't allow them to see Jesus or hear what he was telling them. The long list of Christian leaders in the news who have crashed and burned is a potent reminder that we face the same dangers of disordered desires today.

Clericalism in the church and stories of Jesus's disciples jockeying for recognition remind us why questions of leadership in the church need a robust theological framework. More particularly, it demands a healthy understanding of the body of Christ and how the body is meant to work together. Over and over again we see leaders who are able to abuse their authority precisely because they have not allowed themselves to be accountable to others. Ephesians 4 helps to frame an understanding of leadership in the context of serving the body. The gifts which the Spirit gives do not elevate people or set them apart, but enable them to serve the body. The priest or pastor is not a superhero leader who is able to do it all without help, but a leader who recognizes their own strengths and weaknesses, as well as the gifts of others in the community, and is practicing the skills of working with and within the community to enable the whole body to function as one body.

4

The Real Presence of the Word in the Community

It may seem obvious that the questions "where is God?" and "what is God doing?" are at the very heart of pastoral theology. Yet, in the twentieth century, following the work of Anton Boisen and development of the Clinical Pastoral Education model, the focus on a psychotherapeutic approach left little room for God or for God's initiative in pastoral care. Charles Gerkin, who in his early years was influenced by Boisen, sought to recover an emphasis on pastoral care that begins with God, not only as the theoretical basis for pastoral care or pastoral theology but with attention to the presence and action of God: "Pastoral care, indeed all human care, is finally dependent upon the care of God and our human pastoral care is given sustenance and strength by its participation in that healing, redeeming care that only God can give."[1] In one sense we are following in Gerkin's footsteps in seeking to recover a pastoral theology that is theological because it begins with God.[2] Yet, we also want to go beyond Gerkin in giving specific content to the way in which we speak about God's presence with us. In this chapter we explore God's real presence in the biblical word. With the practice of hearing the word read and preached, an assumption of real presence in the word (Boersma,

1. Gerkin, "On the Art of Caring," 407.

2. "Following Thomas Oden, Gerkin attempts a 'post-modern, post-Freudian, neo-classical approach to Christian pastoral care,' in which pastoral counseling recovers its theological roots, without disavowing modern clinical experience gained through a psychotherapeutic paradigm." Park, "History and Method," 56. See Oden, *Care of Souls in the Classical Tradition*, 37.

Vanhoozer, Wilken), drawing from but not servile toward historical criticism, is required. The resulting concept of active divine self-communication is worked out in conversation with Barth, Buttrick, Craddock, and other contemporary authors.

LAYING OUT THE ROOT PROBLEM

The biblical text is central to the life of the Christian community—*we are people of the word*—and that is a problem not only because we have lost confidence in the biblical text, but also because we don't even recognize our loss of confidence. How can we be *people of the word* when we don't know the word we are of? Commentators have noted how the only biblical passages read in many conservative congregations are snippets or a verse or two that are incorporated into the sermon, often simply applied as proof texts to bolster the preacher's argument. In more liturgical churches the Revised Common Lectionary was intended, in part, to include more Scripture than the Common Lectionary, at least on Sunday mornings, to make up for the fact that most people weren't reading Scripture throughout the week. Yet in these same churches there hasn't been an increase in the amount of Scripture read or the community's familiarity with Scripture. Instead, the lectionary is often ignored or viewed as a grab bag of options from which preachers can choose which readings to include in the service. Rather than working with a vision of helping the community engage with Scripture, the concern has been to avoid boring the congregation. Paring down the readings may avoid numbing the congregation, but it doesn't address the fact that we simply don't know or have confidence in the Bible.[3] Or to express that another way, we have lost confidence in the text because we don't know what the text is or how to value it.

What makes this lack of confidence in the text confusing is that there has been much energy expended in academic circles on carefully studying the text. During much of the modern era there has been a proliferation of techniques and approaches to reading the biblical text. Many of these approaches have enabled us to look more closely and carefully at Scripture. We've learned to ask all kinds of questions about the text and its setting, and the information gained as to origins, context, and

3. Long, referring to Fosdick's pastoral approach to preaching, notes, "Boredom becomes a homiletical deadly sin." Long, *Witness of Preaching*, 32.

content is vast and complex. And yet, this increase in knowledge has not led to an increase in confidence in or valuing of the text, but instead the opposite—a shift away from text altogether. It is particularly sobering to recognize that some of the efforts to take the Bible seriously have been the very instruments which have served to undermine our confidence in it. In a similar vein, claiming the inerrancy of Scripture with the intent of upholding the authority of Scripture tends to emphasize the other-worldliness of the text, which leaves us with the mistaken impression that the text is not relevant to real life issues, and affirms the idea that the inspiration of the Holy Spirit is solely retrospective rather than a recognition of God's real presence *now*.

We are heirs of the tradition represented in the writings of Spinoza and Hobbes where the possibility of a transcendent God who engages directly with us is ruled out a priori. Not only do we read Scripture with no real confidence that God might engage with us through that reading, but when we think about God's presence, the God we have in mind is either spiritualized or immanentized, with little or no capacity to engage in the physical world other than to offer occasional words of comfort with little content or context. Meanwhile, the *spiritual but not religious* movement, which is the fastest growing expression of faith in North America, puts the emphasis on our personal or inner experience of the divine. But this god is not the God revealed to us in and through the biblical text, or the history of the church, or even the person of Jesus Christ, but is rather the immanent spirit who speaks to our hearts and inevitably affirms what we already hold to be true. It is no surprise that the Jesus often spoken of in our churches looks more like one of us than like the Jesus of Nazareth to whom the text bears witness. In Charles Taylor's words, we have buffered ourselves against the possibility that the transcendent God might truly encounter us.

Among those who desire to take their faith seriously, it is not unusual for some to suggest that it doesn't feel as though God is present when they read Scripture. But what should it look or feel like: a warm feeling, an intuition, a spiritual experience? In the evangelical para-church settings I (Peter) was part of in university, a "Quiet Time" involving prayer and reading was encouraged as part of the discipline of a faithful Christian. But it seemed more of a duty to perform than a practice through which to cultivate a relationship with God. It was meant to be accompanied by a desire to spend time with God, but most people would still have found it difficult to define what it means to speak of God's presence in and through Scripture, and the emphasis on one's personal (read: private) relationship with God meant that the corresponding understanding of reading and responding to the text corporately was seen as secondary, or as an optional extra to our "personal" walk. This resulted in a lopsided understanding of the reading of Scripture, where it was too easy to see it as a duty performed by "faithful" Christians rather than an essential part of living the Christian life. And our own reading of Scripture lacked the engagement with other voices that is essential to a healthy reading of the text. We might also mention the incipient Marcionism which continues to plague evangelical circles, with the result that devotional readings of the text often focus on the Epistles and the reader is primarily looking for helpful advice on how they might live, with little or no ability to contextualize that advice. The claim of God's presence in Scripture remained vague or ethereal, and indeed, the whole approach left little room for being convicted by the Spirit. There was little sense of what an encounter with God might produce or form in our lives.

REAL PRESENCE

In *Scripture as Real Presence*, Hans Boersma engages with a breadth of patristic writers advocating for a robust understanding of the way in which God is present in and through Scripture. He brings Origen and Chrysostom, with their respective Alexandrian allegorical and Antiochian literal readings, into dialogue.[4] For both ancient writers, the question isn't whether God is present in the text, but the way in which God is present. Speaking of Abraham's encounter at the Oaks of Mamre, Origen emphasizes that the narrative describes a face-to-face encounter with God; the story allows us to see God. Chrysostom speaks of Abraham's response to the God who has become immanent in time and space, with the emphasis on God's presence in this world. Origen bows to the divinity of Christ, while Chrysostom praises his humanity. Boersma suggests that rather than representing conflicting views, "the two are complementary expressions of the mystery of God's ultimate *synkatabasis* (condescension) in Jesus Christ."[5] Both assume God's real presence to us in the narrative.

4. Boersma makes it clear that this is not a hard and fast divide, as both writers incorporate elements of literal and allegorical approaches in their handling of the text.

5. Boersma, *Scripture as Real Presence*, 61. Boersma translates *synkatabasis* as condescension—not in the derogatory sense of diminishing but in the sense of Phil 2 and the self-humbling of Christ.

In the academy, for a time people assumed that the best observer of Scripture was detached and neutral—a person who was able to put aside the lenses they brought to the text, including faith, in order to conduct a careful and thorough examination without bias or prejudice.[6] That assumption has been unmasked as simplistic, since there is no such thing as an unbiased or neutral approach, but there remains a tendency to examine the text from above. It is as though the careful student of the Bible is one who sees the biblical text laid out like a cadaver on an examination table so as to pull, prod, and dissect it. Hand in hand with this approach is the tendency to separate out the different pieces of the text in order to see each part more clearly. As Wilken suggests, this approach makes it very difficult for us to hear the story:

> If the Bible is dismembered to serve an exotic theological program and biblical texts are deployed willy-nilly . . . the Scriptures will remain a closed book and it will not be possible "to find the truth in them." Without a grasp of the plot that holds everything together, the Bible is as vacuous as a mosaic in which the tiles have been arbitrarily rearranged.[7]

Careful scientific methods and techniques can tell us all kinds of things about a life lived; we find bones once broken, diseases survived, perhaps even the wear and tear of overuse. Yet in the midst of all the information gleaned, there is no basis for knowing the cadaver as a living being. There is no *personal* encounter; there is a disjuncture between the living person and the physical remains. Any conclusions arrived at would not necessarily align with the understandings of those who knew and loved the person, who have shared the story or narrative of this person. Rather than truly revealing the text, such an "objective" or scientific reading fails to account for the relationship which is essential for seeing, hearing, and responding to what the narrative relates.

This is not to argue for a spiritualizing of interpretation, where we emphasize the subjective over the objective or bypass modern critical scholarship. Neither does this support a retreat from contemporary cultural issues, as though readers might isolate themselves from current matters or concerns. Rather, it calls into question the distance that a solely historical reading of the text places between it and our current

6. Much of this section is taken from my blog: Robinson, "Theological Interpretation of Scripture."

7. Wilken, *Spirit of Early Christian Thought*, 67–68.

situation—a distance that reflects a lack of understanding of the God who speaks to us in and through the text. The *retrieval* of the work of the earliest interpreters of the text is vital to this endeavor, not least because of the variety of ways in which they approached the text—figural, tropological, allegorical, and literal. As such, they give a breadth and depth to the reading of the text that challenges our own narrow readings. In his engagement with Gregory of Nyssa, Boersma also notes the indispensable place for virtue in reading the text:

> He doesn't treat virtue as just part of the application of the text that follows after we've carefully articulated its meaning. Saint Gregory knows of no such gap between exegesis and application. Rather, he regards virtue as (1) a prerequisite for good reading, (2) the proper contents of the biblical text, and (3) the aim of the exegetical process.[8]

We tend to be wary of an emphasis on virtue as crucial to encountering God in the text for fear that it undercuts grace by making obedience a condition for God revealing himself to us.[9] In our efforts to get to the authentic meaning of the text we can forget that aligning our lives with God allows a context to make sense of the text in light of who God is.[10] As Boersma makes clear, for Gregory, God himself gives us virtue, so rather than a precondition to encountering God, entering into virtue is entailed in knowing God.[11] It isn't that we must follow certain steps in order to be rewarded by God revealing himself to us, but that knowing God involves

8. Boersma, *Scripture as Real Presence*, 19–20.

9. Boersma goes on to note that Gregory avoids moralism or self-help religion by his pervasive Christology and his doctrine of participation.

10. "Some have doubted. And then in turn there were some who sought to refute doubt with reasons. As a matter of fact, the connection was actually this: first of all they tried to demonstrate the truth of Christianity with reasons or by advancing reasons in relation to Christianity. And these reasons fostered doubt and doubt became the stronger. The demonstration of Christianity really lies in *imitation*. This was taken away. Then the need for 'reasons' was felt . . . and thus doubt arose and lived on reasons. It was not observed that the more reasons one advances, the more one nourishes doubt and the stronger it becomes, that offering doubt reasons in order to kill it is just like offering the tasty food it likes best of all to a hungry monster one wishes to eliminate." Kierkegaard, *For Self-Examination*, 68.

11. To Gregory, to participate in virtue is to participate in God, for God is virtue, and "since it is our aim to share more deeply in the life of God, virtue is also the very aim of biblical interpretation." Boersma, *Scripture as Real Presence*, 20.

ordering our lives in response to him.[12] It is as we journey with God that we begin to know God and delight in the gift of God's word with us.[13]

The call for virtue as essential to our encountering God in the text is not solely or even primarily about individual virtue, but rather about a community of virtue. As communities together learn what it means to live in Christ, they are enabled to see Christ more clearly both in the text and in their midst. This applies not just to the local community in isolation, but the church extended throughout space and time. In order for individuals to come to know Christ more deeply, they must be participating in a social imaginary that both challenges the preconceptions that hinder our encounter with God and allows for the reformation of our practices in such a way as to align hearts and minds with Christ, making space for God. The church is to be the Christian social imaginary—the ordered space that sustains the possibility of knowing and responding to God in his word as we grow up together in knowing God.

God consistently makes himself known to us in active encounter. The initiative always lies with God. Yet, this is an initiative that demands our response. Our hearts must be trained in order to see, hear, and respond to God. In order to grow into our relationship with God we must allow our lives to be aligned with him and his desires for us.[14] It is in that alignment that space is created both within us and in our communities in which we might come to know God.

Today there is widespread recognition of the impossibility of a neutral, objective approach to the reading of Scripture. One result of this has been a proliferation of different interpretive approaches: feminist readings, liberation readings, post-colonial readings. While we should acknowledge that everyone brings to the text their own particular assumptions and their own particular theological frameworks which inevitably shape the way in which they read the text, these "advocacy" approaches can lead to the assumption that all such approaches are legitimate in their own right. The result is a cacophony of voices where the emphasis is on the reader rather than the text. In describing literary approaches to

12. Bonhoeffer wrote, "Only [one] who believes is obedient and only [one] who is obedient believes." Bonhoeffer, *Cost of Discipleship*, 63. This is not to say that obedience is a prerequisite for belief, but that obedience is belief.

13. "The soul watered by sacred Scripture grows fat and bears fruit in due season, which is the orthodox faith, and so is it adorned with its evergreen leaves, with actions pleasing to God, I mean." John of Damascus, "Orthodox Faith," 8.

14. Rom 12:1, 2.

hermeneutics, Tremper Longman suggests that reader-centered theories assume that meaning resides in the reader rather than the text.[15] Instead of arguing for the legitimacy of each person's own reading of the text, we would emphasize that engagement with Scripture is engagement with God. The issue isn't our confidence in the text, as though the text exists as a thing in itself, but confidence in the God who reveals himself to us in and through the text. *The word is living and active* precisely because it is God's living word to us.

What lies at the heart of our understanding of and approach to the text is theology proper: We come to know the God revealed to us in Jesus Christ and through the Holy Spirit in the text which bears witness to this God. "Those who approach the Bible as Scripture must not abstract it from the Father who ultimately authors it, the Son to whom it witnesses, and the Spirit who inspired and illumines it," writes Kevin Vanhoozer.[16] This is not simply a reaction against the modern tendency to begin from a position of philosophical naturalism. Rather, it is a claim about the biblical text in light of the way this God engages with us in and through it. And it centers around the confidence that God in Jesus Christ continues to engage with us through the Holy Spirit and in the text.

As Hans Boersma's reflections on Origen and Chrysostom indicate, the earliest interpreters struggled to make sense out of reading the text because they were seeking to make sense of who this God is who has revealed himself to us in Jesus Christ. In contrast, in our modern world we examine the text to see how it resonates or connects with us in our situations. Our interpretative lens determines in advance the limits of what the text might mean. As the scholar Tad Guzie put it, "Scientific exegesis begins with a text which speaks of a mystery: patristic spiritual exegesis begins with the mystery spoken of in the text."[17] As such, the early interpreters' basic posture in relationship to the text was one of reverent attention to the God who has made himself present to us in the text and continues to do so to foster our knowing of him. Hughes Old, commenting on the Didache (early catechetical teaching), said, "The worshipping congregation" understood Christ to be present with them "by means of the teaching and preaching of the word of God. . . . The *Didache* teaches a doctrine of the real presence which is kerygmatic

15. Longman, *Literary Approaches to Biblical Interpretation*, 38.

16. Vanhoozer, "Interpreting Scripture," 212.

17. Guzie, "Patristic Hermeneutics and the Meaning of Tradition," 649.

rather than eucharistic."[18] An understanding of "real presence" in the word points to the confidence that it is God who speaks into our lives and our world to show himself to us, and in the light of who he is, he also shows us who we are.

The crux of the problem is that in postmodernity we have been conditioned only to accept authority that aligns with what we already value or believe. This is further complicated because the Bible is a narrative which is in conflict with the operating narratives of our world. The gospel does not simply help us make sense of our situation or guide us further along our path toward a distant spiritual existence or future realm, but rather draws us into a new way of understanding ourselves and our world. It is a *metanoia*: a change in our orientation and the direction we are traveling.

In light of the transformation into which the text invites us, we can see how an emphasis on relevance can be so misleading. Relevance is often understood as our being able to make use of the gospel in our own context: The gospel thereby becomes a tool in our lives for our own self-realization instead of a call to the radical reordering of our lives.[19] And this brings us to consider the place of preaching—not as *the* central component of worship, nor even as an isolated element in worship, but as an integral aspect of God's real encounter with us through Scripture.

THE PIVOT AND THE PREACHER

Both preacher and listener are to stand under Scripture. We approach the text as its servants rather than its masters, whether we come as a reader or a preacher. Preaching does not merely follow after the reading of Scripture, but is better understood as part and parcel of the community learning to indwell Scripture. The preacher, on behalf of the community, leads the response to and engagement with Scripture; what must inform our understanding of the biblical text and preaching are basic theological assumptions about God and how God engages with us and with the church in all of its complexity, as well as the place and role of the reader and teacher.

18. Old, *Reading and Preaching Scriptures in Worship*, 265, quoted in Robinson, *Art and Craft of Biblical Preaching*, 42.

19. "Pastoral preaching can end up downsizing the gospel, giving aid to the narcissistic notion that the purpose of the Christian faith is to make us happy and comfortable, reinforcing selfishness and undermining the call of the gospel to move out of ourselves and toward others in service." Long, *Witness of Preaching*, 32.

The historical critical method has encouraged an understanding that we are over the text, so that the text is something to be prodded, grasped and manipulated in order to understand it. It should be no surprise that in this context, preaching is understood to have two stages, with the preacher as interpretative mediator (biblical expert) between the text and the community. The preacher interprets the text, and then translates the text again for the listening community. Preachers need to be both experts in the text and experts in reading the community. While there is significant truth to this process, it tends toward a false paradigm of what is actually involved in the practice of preaching, since it fails to allow for God's essential role in his self-communication.

The preacher's task is to understand themselves, their community, and their calling in the light of who God is and what God is doing, including an understanding of God's presence with the community. This shifts us from an understanding of the preacher as the interpreter of the text and the community to an understanding of the preacher as one who goes to the text and goes to God on behalf of and together with the community. He or she serves not as a mediator interceding with a distant God, but as one who has been given the time and energy to turn to God on behalf of the community. It is not the preacher's task, nor is it within the preacher's capability, to make God relevant to their listeners, as though God were at a remove. Rather, it is essential to understand and operate out of the assumption that God is always the initiator. The preacher's task is to align themselves with what God is already doing, rather than attempting to do God's work for him. Preaching, then, is to engage with God in the context of this text—this narrative—to indwell Christ in order that we might be able to more fully live, together, into this world. We read and engage with the text in, for, and with the church—including the global church and the chorus of witnesses who go before us.

My (Peter's) father served as a pastor and preacher for most of his life. He recounted a story of a woman who introduced herself by saying, "You don't remember me do you?" Faced with a direct question he had to respond, "No, I don't think I do." The woman went on to explain how she had been present twenty years earlier for a worship service where my father had preached. My father (no surprise) had no idea what he had said in that sermon. The woman said that she had been through very difficult situations, but throughout it all she had continued to struggle with what she had heard in the sermon that day. She said, "It took a long time, but eventually God used that sermon to bring me back to the Christian faith."

It is one of the mercies of God that preachers never fully know what God might be doing in a person's heart as they hear the word preached.

AUTHORITY

David Buttrick offers an evocative description of a little church in Indiana that had a huge pulpit towering over the congregation: "It towered over pews so that preachers . . . stand nearly a full storey above the people, tossing down the Word of God like tablets from Mt. Sinai."[20] In a huge cathedral a towering pulpit might be an essential aid for allowing the preacher to engage their listeners, but in a tiny country church it reflects a different set of assumptions. An elevated pulpit is not so much a practical way for the preacher to be able to communicate; rather, it represents the place and authority of the biblical text and preaching in the life of the community. The assumption is that we are speaking about the "place" of the biblical narrative, in worship, that the community stands under scripture. This ministry of the word is essential to the social imaginary that is shaped in and through the worshiping community.[21]

In the nineteenth century the great evangelical Anglican pastor Charles Simeon described the authority of a preacher as an authority grounded in their calling:

> Ministers are ambassadors for God, and speak in Christ's stead. If they preach what is founded on the Scriptures, their word, *as far as it is agreeable to the mind of God*, is to be considered as God's. . . . We ought therefore to receive the preacher's word as the word of God himself. With what humility then ought we to attend to it! What judgments may we not expect if we slight it![22]

20. Buttrick, "Preaching Today," 3.

21. "The ministry of the Word involves far more than ideas. Thanks to a host of postmodern prophets, we are more aware than ever of the power of language to shape human thinking and experience. Language creates a 'world,' that is, a cultural framework in which we live and move and process our experience. *Preaching, teaching, and evangelism are the means by which the gospel becomes that all-encompassing framework that allows us to think and experience truth, goodness, and beauty in light of the history of Jesus Christ.* The ministry of the Word involves more than communicating a few truths; it involves transmitting a whole way of thinking and experiencing. Preaching and teaching should be 'evangelistic,' then, in the sense of enabling people to indwell the gospel (=*evangel*) as the primary framework for all that they say and do." Vanhoozer, *Drama of Doctrine*, 74.

22. Simeon, "Directions How to Hear Sermons," 346–47.

This view of authority seems utterly foreign to most of us today. Traditional conceptions of authority (public and private) have been displaced or rejected in all spheres of life, and the place and significance of the church in society has changed. One of the marks of postmodernism and the shift toward the autonomy of the individual has been to locate authority primarily with the individual and whoever or whatever they choose to accept as authoritative for themselves. In addition, any notion of the preacher as an authority has been further eroded by the very public failures of far too many spiritual leaders.

"Is there even a place for preaching today?" It isn't just lay people who ask that question. It is a part of the existential landscape for any preacher and has led to a quest for alternatives. In some churches the sermon has been replaced by interviews or group discussions. In other churches, rather than preaching, the focus has shifted to storytelling, with the assumption that meaning should not be imposed but that each person must be free to interpret and apply the story for themselves. In many mainline churches the expectation (in some cases the unspoken rule) is for only a short, five-minute personal reflection by the pastor or priest, taking care to make sure that the reflection does not touch on sensitive topics. In most cases, either deliberately or by default, authority now rests with the listeners:

> In the early 2000s, the advisory committee of my small congregation in Massachusetts told me to keep my sermons to 10 minutes, tell funny stories and leave people feeling great about themselves. The unspoken message in such instructions is clear: give us the comforting, amusing fare we want or we'll get our spiritual leadership from someone else.[23]

Lest we yearn for an earlier era and a more robust acceptance of authority, we need to acknowledge that this change is partly a response to unhealthy or abusive authority. It is not a recent development. Fifty years ago, Fred Craddock's *As One Without Authority* (1971) marked a significant shift in the way preachers were thinking about the form of the sermon.[24] Craddock began by addressing the problems facing the preacher in an age where people no longer accept religious authority, or for that matter are skeptical of all authority. Critiquing the traditional

23. MacDonald, "Congregations Gone Wild," 9.

24. The shift marked by Craddock's book has become known as the New Homiletic or a shift toward narrative preaching. Narrative preaching in this case does not suggest storytelling but the recognition of the place of narrative in epistemology.

approach to preaching (the three-point expository sermon), he suggested that one of the reasons much preaching is ineffective is that listeners have changed. They are, in many cases, more sophisticated and less open to a traditional authoritative mode of preaching. Craddock argues for an inductive rather than a deductive approach to preaching. Instead of simply offering a thesis and then exploring and defending the thesis in three or more relatively balanced points, the sermon should begin with questions which will get the listener's attention because they are pertinent to their concerns. In speaking of the deductive approach, Craddock asks why preachers feel compelled to give away their sermons in the first moments, and suggests it is like starting a joke with the punch line. The preacher has no inherent or positional authority. If they want people's attention, they must first give them a reason to listen.

FOCUS ON THE TEXT OR ON THE LISTENER

Buttrick argues that the twentieth century was marked by two approaches to preaching, with one approach focusing on the listeners and the other focusing on the biblical text. He identifies the first approach with Harry Emerson Fosdick.[25] Almost one hundred years ago Fosdick wrote an article in *Harper's* magazine which asked why preaching was having so little impact on people's lives. He suggested that most preachers were failing to make a connection with the lives of their listeners and that they should begin there rather than beginning with the biblical text. Buttrick's contention is that those who have followed Fosdick end up offering sermons that do little more than help people feel better about themselves. This pastoral approach to preaching, he suggests, is little more than therapeutic personalism and fosters designer religion tailored to the needs of the individual. The way Fosdick framed the issues and the solution he offered encouraged and fostered an approach to preaching that has only accelerated the loss of any confidence in preaching.

We have learned our lessons well from the tradition fostered by Fosdick. When churches face decline or are struggling to attract new people, the natural response of many church leaders is to suggest that they need to do a better job of connecting with people. Concerns for

25. "Is God, the holy God of Israel, nothing more than a free therapist for individual problems? . . . Most North American pulpits, following Fosdick and fanned by the existentialist Fifties, have tumbled into a narrow personalism." Buttrick, "Preaching Today," 6.

relevance preoccupy many, if not most, clergy gatherings, usually to the detriment of the congregations they serve.

Several years ago, a friend recounted their experience at a local church. They had developed a friendship with the pastor and occasionally shared dinner on a Saturday evening. Too often at church the next morning they would hear elements of their conversation with the pastor not only as anecdotes but as the essence of the sermon. Rather than a flattering homiletical approach or evidence of laziness on the part of the preacher, it was justified as a way of paying attention to the context. The danger in preaching sermons that put the primary focus on connecting with listeners or designing services to be more relevant or seeker friendly is that we treat people as consumers. This in turn fosters an environment where faith is perceived as a path to self-realization: Church or faith is there to meet our felt needs. It is no surprise then, that people stop showing up when conflict arises or when they disagree with what has been communicated. Their commitment to the church depends on the perceived benefit: They haven't been converted, nor are they fundamentally open to conversion. They have heard and responded to a modified gospel which affirms who they already understand themselves to be. Sermons that begin with the question of relevance do not invite others into the gospel and its radically different way of living in the world; instead they offer a simple variation on or complement to the culture's social imaginary.

Yet, before we dismiss Fosdick, we need to note that underlying his approach to preaching is the recognition that listeners won't listen if they don't find anything personal in the sermon. Here Fosdick's insight is vital. Preachers who don't pay attention to their listeners won't have any listeners. Paying attention to the listeners and their situations is crucial for the preacher who desires to share the gospel.

Ronald Allen's book *Hearing the Sermon* explores the place of the listener using Aristotle's categories of *ethos*, *logos*, and *pathos* to show how listeners hear in distinct ways as they attend to relation, content, and feeling:

> Some parishioners were engaged in a sermon mainly because they knew, loved, and respected the preacher (*ethos*). These folk speak of "connecting" with a sermon or a preacher and use relational language, regardless of what kind of question is posed. An equal number of parishioners were captivated by a sermon based on its biblical or theological content (*logos*). These listeners "think through" the sermon and are impatient when the

> preacher takes a long time to get to "the point" or keeps rambling on after it is made. Another almost equal third of respondents were engaged when feelings were elicited by a sermon (*pathos*). Those whose mode of processing is that of pathos speak of what "moves" or "touches" them in the sermon.[26]

These three types of listeners are represented by extended transcripts from respondents plus commentary from psychology, rhetoric, and theology. The message is clear: One style of preaching (i.e., narrative preaching that gives its nod to ethos and pathos but little to *logos*) will not cut it over time.[27]

Preachers don't preach into a vacuum, but into particular contexts where different approaches will prove more or less effective, depending on their listeners.

As a result, Fosdick gives voice to a vital question: Why do so many people attend church and listen to sermons but not see any real change in their lives? In *As One Without Authority*, Craddock argues that we should be just as concerned with what a sermon does as with what a sermon says.[28] Fosdick's pastoral sensitivity and insight helped him raise a question every pastoral leader or teacher faces on a regular basis: Is the gospel making a difference in people's lives?[29] Week after week the preacher is faced with this question while preparing sermons and receiving feedback from their congregations. And yet, it is a dangerous trap to begin to measure progress in terms of the differences we can observe. It is difficult not to succumb to the pressure to simply make a connection with our listeners, perhaps by telling good stories which resonate with and confirm their experiences, or seeking to offer helpful advice that listeners might apply to their day-to-day lives.

Craddock's argument in *As One Without Authority* has been dismissed by many who seek to affirm a high view of preaching, since at first blush the emphasis on the listener appears to advocate relevance over faithfulness. Instead of putting our confidence in Scripture, the focus shifts to the preacher's ability to communicate. By contrast, these critics maintain, we need to primarily focus on faithfulness to the biblical text. This is an argument for classic expository preaching, where the preacher carefully and faithfully unpacks the text for the listener. It is true that

26. Rudy-Froese, review of *Hearing the Sermon*, 96.

27. Rudy-Froese, review of *Hearing the Sermon*, 96.

28. Craddock, *As One Without Authority*, 5–6.

29. Buttrick, "Preaching Today," 5.

far too many preachers are so focused on *connecting* with their listeners that it becomes difficult to find much about the Bible, or in some cases, even a mention of God in their sermons. Yet, as we have already noted, it is sobering to see how many churches claiming to hold a high view of Scripture have little if any reading of the Bible during the worship service. Some pastors who prioritize "biblical" preaching believe they are being biblically faithful but are oblivious to their own hermeneutic of interpretation.[30]

Buttrick may identify Fosdick's approach as little more than therapeutic emotionalism, but he is just as critical of the opposite approach, which he labels biblical positivism and identifies with Karl Barth.[31] Buttrick clearly has in mind what is often called biblical preaching, where the preacher carefully unpacks the text to extract from it principles and guidelines or doctrine. Critics of this biblical approach to preaching suggest that it does more to expose the unexamined lenses of the preacher than evidencing faithfulness to the text. As John Knox argues,

> The difference between biblical and unbiblical preaching has little to do with the structure of the sermon and whether it is topical or expository in form. The difference lies deeper than that. If it is possible . . . to preach a quite unbiblical sermon on a biblical text, it is also possible to preach a quite biblical sermon on no text at all.[32]

What is often called biblically faithful preaching is too often shaped by a hermeneutic that sets the preacher up as the biblical expert and renders the Bible inaccessible for the lay person. In turn, an emphasis on the Bible as divinely inerrant, meant to affirm the authority of the text in our lives, has to the contrary sustained an understanding of the text as wholly other than this world, with little direct import for our day-to-day living. Divine inerrancy assumes that the Bible is otherworldly, even in some ways docetic, and represents a spiritual reality that can never wholly align with this world.

30. "Some clergy do well in biblical courses and yet are so unconscious of their homiletical methodology and theology that they deliver sermons actually contradictory to the understanding of the Bible they otherwise profess." Achtemeier, "Artful Dialogue," 18.

31. Buttrick, "Preaching Today," 7–8.

32. Knox, *Integrity of Preaching*, 19, quoted by Rice, *What's the Shape of Narrative Preaching?*, 24.

While the three-point sermon might appear to be a helpful tool allowing the preacher to organize and communicate their thoughts in a straightforward manner, when used exclusively it teaches the listener an enlightenment epistemology which isolates a purely cognitive knowing as opposed to a more grounded or situated knowing. When it is used as the sole approach to constructing sermons it conveys the notion that we go to the text to have our thinking informed, rather than going with the expectation that God will encounter us and call us to repentance. As a result, in spite of an expressed desire to be faithful to the text, it encourages the listener to adopt a posture of standing over the text; the text is seen as a resource to be mined for information or guidance which can subsequently be applied to our lives. Over time, it is inevitable that communities of listeners adapt to the forms of sermon used by the preacher, particularly if they consistently stick with one form, and in turn they tend to judge the quality of sermons (and their importance) by how well they follow or fit an accepted or "traditional" form within their community.

The suggestion that we must choose between preaching that moves us emotionally (or helps us help ourselves) and preaching that communicates the text point by point but is concerned only with changing our thinking is a false dichotomy.[33] Most preachers would confirm that preaching must be both biblical and relevant. Nonetheless, preachers seeking to be biblically faithful and those seeking to be relevant often dismiss one another. While it does seem as though much of the preaching in the twentieth century could be identified with one pole or the other, Buttrick himself has polarized the issues and has missed the basis and impetus of Barth's position. Barth was not in the first instance calling us toward a biblical literalism or fundamentalism but was in fact challenging the implicit deism that characterized so much of twentieth-century theology, which operated with the understanding of an absentee God. For Barth, Scripture is the central means by which God actively communicates himself to us.

Revelation, for Barth, is nothing less than an event: an encounter with the living God. God has not given us the Bible as an objective and passive body of revelation which we might pick up and examine at our

33. "Biblical preaching, Knox says, has four characteristics: (1) it stays close to the essential biblical ideas; (2) it is 'centrally concerned with the central biblical event, the event of Christ'; (3) it 'answers to and nourishes the essential life of the church'; (4) 'True preaching is itself an event—and an event of a particular kind. In it the revelation of God in Christ is actually recurring.'" Rice, *What's the Shape of Narrative Preaching?*, 24, quoting from Knox, *Integrity of Preaching*, 23.

leisure. Nor is it a body of revelation in which the onus is on us to read it correctly. The preacher is not simply invited to pick up the Bible and try to figure out how to communicate God's self-revelation in a way that makes sense to people in a particular time and place. Rather, preaching is to enter into the process of God's self-communication. Confidence comes from knowing who God is and how God works in the world. The essential secret is not mastering certain techniques, but being mastered by certain convictions, or living better into the reality that Jesus is Lord. Properly understood, Barth's position allows for the complexity of reception while the emphasis or focus remains on God as the initiator and sustainer of his self-communication. Indeed, God knows us well enough to know how to communicate himself to us.

A polemical response to Craddock or Fosdick misses the deeper issues they were grappling with and assumes a narrow view of faithfulness. Underneath the concern with relevance is a more practical concern—is the gospel good news? Is it liberating the captives, opening the eyes of the blind, feeding the hungry? Is the gospel enabling people to live into the kingdom of light—the kingdom of the Son whom the Father loves? These are all vital questions, not only because they prioritize the mission of the church but because they align with the mission of God.

The kind of sermons we preach implicitly teaches our listeners about the kind of God we believe in. Far too many preachers emphasize biblical faithfulness in their preaching but speak of God in the third person. Preaching about God in the third person assumes the absence of God and encourages the listener to look to the sermon as a resource for self-improvement. The operative hermeneutic in this approach, grounded in a particular understanding of biblical criticism, goes unacknowledged or is glossed over even while asserting that the preacher is being faithful to the text.

> Behind the concept and the act of preaching there lies a doctrine of God, a conviction about his being, his action, and his purpose. The kind of God we believe in determines the kind of sermons we preach.[34]

We cannot sustain a habit of preaching without proper theological confidence.

> A healthy doctrine of preaching springs from a healthy theology. . . . Begin with an inadequate or feeble doctrine of God and

34. Stott, *Between Two Worlds*, 64.

> the pulpit utterance will be feeble. . . . Ours is not a silent God, a God who sits, sphinx-like, looking out unblinking on a world in agony.[35]

Ultimately, our confidence in preaching does not come from our skills or our abilities or even from our hard work, as important as those are, but from the God who makes himself present to us. This again is a question of "real presence." As Fleming Rutledge asks, Is God the subject of all the verbs?[36]

Preaching is not an either/or. We do not need to simply focus on the text and allow the text to speak; nor do we need to become so caught up in how we communicate that we put all our focus on how to say what we want to say. The preacher does not pick up the text as though it exists as a passive body of information that must be brought alive by the preacher, but instead she enters into the process of God's self-communication. She becomes part of that process of the word becoming embodied in this world. And who she is and what she is in a particular cultural context becomes part of how God communicates the truth of himself to people in a particular time and place. As such, our primary concern is not to make the text relevant or to try to bridge the gap between then and now. Nor is the primary task to endeavor to apply the text to our current situation, but rather, to listen to the voice of the Spirit who opens our hearts and minds to turn and listen to the God who continues to speak in a coherent and consistent manner into our lives and world through Scripture.

35. Coggan, *Sacrament of the Word*, 31.

36. Rutledge, *Crucifixion*, 280.

5

The Confession of the Faith

We come now to the creed. In the Anglican order of service the recitation of the creed comes after the reading of Scripture. Some might argue that this chapter should have come at the beginning since it affirms a central claim of our approach to pastoral theology: Our emphasis is on the agency of the God revealed to us in Jesus Christ, where the church is the confessing community whose own narrative life is continually realigned with who this God is and has shown himself to be. Yet, in the order of service the creed follows the reading of Scripture as an appropriate response to Scripture. It is the church's witness to the voice of Scripture as it has sought to understand and respond to that voice in the midst of learning to live out the gospel. This is the nexus out of which pastoral theology arises, and in some ways it provides a methodology for pastoral theology. The historic creeds were pastorally motivated in a way apropos for our own situation. Torrance maintains that Nicene Faith is "significative" as it communicates who God is and how he invites us into relationship.[1] Pastoral theology is not theological because it grapples with questions about God, but because it is rooted in the credal (and ecclesial) affirmation of the particular ways in which this God has made himself known to us. This may seem like an abstract affirmation when many churches seldom if ever recite the creed, while others see the claims of the creed as outmoded or compromised. And perhaps this is exactly our concern: that to be theological, pastoral theology depends on Christian communities that are learning to live into the truth of who they are in

1. Torrance, *Space, Time, and Incarnation*, 1–2.

Jesus Christ. The language of participation expresses the same reality in a way consistent with Reformation thought.

> In these last days he has spoken to us by his Son, whom he appointed the heir of all things, through whom also he created the world. He is the radiance of the glory of God and the exact imprint of his nature, and he upholds the universe by the word of his power. (Hebrews 1:2–3)

> Since then we have a great high priest who has passed through the heavens, Jesus, the Son of God, let us hold fast our confession. For we do not have a high priest who is unable to sympathize with our weaknesses, but one who in every respect has been tempted as we are, yet without sin. Let us then with confidence draw near to the throne of grace, that we may receive mercy and find grace to help in time of need. (Hebrews 4:14–16)

In the midst of the liminal days at the end of World War II, Dorothy Sayers lays out a clarion call for the robust recovery of Christian dogma in her book *Creed or Chaos?* She argues that in light of the failure of other philosophies and in spite of a continued wariness toward the claims of Christian dogma, there is a compelling case for the renewal of Christian dogma, particularly as found in the creeds: "The rival philosophies of humanism, enlightened self-interest, and mechanical progress have broken down badly. . . . no good whatever will be done by a retreat into personal piety or by mere exhortation to a 'recall to prayer.'"[2] It is sobering to recognize the many similarities between the time when Sayers was writing and our own era. Although we may not be engaged in a world war, the many global conflicts and wars seem very close. Then there are the environmental issues we are facing, including everything from global warming to the accumulation of plastic in our oceans. All of this as we slowly move beyond a global pandemic that has killed so many people and turned everyone's life upside down. In a similar manner, with so many different voices offering competing truth claims we have learned not to trust anyone.

Sayers might be a little too dogmatic for some today who would counter her concerns by citing the polarization that we currently see in political dogma; there are far too many examples of people gathering around a particular creed or cause while ignoring or remaining blind

2. Sayers, *Creed or Chaos?*, 29.

to alternate perspectives. Dogma has become conflated with dogmatism, closed-mindedness, inflexibility, insensitivity, and a lack of empathy or understanding for the needs and concerns of others. As a result, the new creed or dogmatism that is broadly accepted culturally is a principle of privatization in which there is a primary commitment to avoid imposing our truth claims on others. That is, except for the truth claims which are the privilege of wealthy Western countries and which arise from the cultural social imaginary of autonomous individualism with the assumption that the only person I can trust is me.

Trusting in myself and my own view of the world works relatively well when we are able to insulate ourselves from situations or events in the world around us. It doesn't work as well when circumstances leave us without a buffer or we are regularly confronted by a variety of events beyond our control. At that point we inevitably start to seek some other source of hope or safety. It would be a mistake, however, to see the creeds primarily in terms of dogmatic claims or positions that we might cling to. We are not invited to put our confidence in the creeds, but to put our confidence in the One to whom the creed directs our attention; this is not just for each of us individually, but is a call for the church as community to order its life as the body of Christ. In that context, Sayers's call to respond to the creeds remains prescient both in her time and today. She was not offering a general call for political dogma, but a task for the church: *Creed and Chaos?* summons the church to renew its commitment to the God witnessed to in the creeds.

Sayers engages two common concerns with the creeds. First, they make claims that seem to have no relevance in our day-to-day lives. Secondly, the dogmatic nature of these claims is an affront to human sensibilities insofar as they claim to be speaking of *the* truth in a universal sense rather than my own authentic perspective. These concerns are further exacerbated by a failure to understand the place and purpose of the creeds in the life of the church. "Teachers and preachers never, I think, make it sufficiently clear that dogmas are not a set of arbitrary regulations invented *a priori* by a committee of theologians enjoying a bout of all-in dialectical wrestling."[3] The creeds, and particularly the Nicene Creed, arose in the midst of fierce debates, not over theoretical questions but over pastoral concerns. Our understanding of and hope in the salvific work of God in Christ and its implications for our day-to-day lives are

3. Sayers, *Creed or Chaos?*, 35.

wholly interwoven with who we understand God to be and how God relates to us and with us. When (Peter) I am meeting with a family who is planning a funeral for a loved one, the promise of a "god somewhere up in heaven" is a distraction rather than a comfort. Perhaps a distraction is all that some people need in the immediacy of death and the pressures of planning a funeral, but in the long journey of mourning, it is through confidence in the character and person of God that we begin to know the comfort that sustains us. Confusing platitudes such as "God needed her more than you do" reveal more about our discomfort with death than any confidence in the love of God. It is precisely here, in the face of death, that Christian confidence in the God finally and fully revealed to us in Jesus Christ not only offers reassurance, but liberates us from vague platitudes about God. In this context, it is worth remembering that the conciliar arguments were not arenas for intellectual sparring, but focal points in the struggle to make sense of the claims of the Bible, and especially the claims of the incarnation in the context of our daily lives.

The dogma that Sayers argues for, in the light of the creeds of the church, has at its center questions about "who or what Christ is, and why His authority should be accepted."[4] And central to the claims about Christ is who he is as the God/man:

> If Christ was only man, then He is entirely irrelevant to any thought about God; if He is only God, then He is entirely irrelevant to any experience of human life. It is, in the strictest sense, necessary to the salvation of relevance that a man should believe rightly the Incarnation of Our Lord Jesus Christ.[5]

For Sayers, it is incumbent on preachers and teachers of the faith to engage with the creeds in order that their people should gradually come to some understanding and knowledge of the reality of which the creeds speak. She argues that most people are surprised to discover that the creeds contain any statements that bear a practical and comprehensible meaning, even though that was the primary intent of the conciliar formulation. In this chapter we argue, in line with Sayers, that the *theology* in pastoral theology is grounded in claims about God that are affirmed particularly in the Nicene Creed, and that these claims fundamentally shape what it means to do theology pastorally.[6]

4. Sayers, *Creed or Chaos?*, 32.
5. Sayers, *Creed or Chaos?*, 32.
6. George Hunsinger offers a very helpful framework for understanding different

THE NICENE FAITH

It would be interesting to survey Christians across denominations to see what they understand by the phrase "the Nicene Faith," or even to see if the creeds retain a central place in their self-definition. Many Protestant churches do not use the creeds in their worship, and even those who include a recitation of the creed in their approved liturgies often omit it in practice. We have moved a long way away from people like St. Augustine who believed that memorizing the creed should be an integral part of baptismal catechesis as it served to help internalize the truth of God and God's ways.[7] To many people, the creeds seem to be overly abstract, out-of-date, unnecessary, and perhaps sexist or mythological in language.

Meanwhile, some who are familiar with the history of the creeds might ask what we mean when we speak of the Nicene Creed. Are we referring to the creed that was affirmed at the Council of Nicaea in 325, or the creed that was affirmed at the Council of Constantinople in 381, or some other variation that was used at different points? This *apparent* lack of clarity is then used to diminish or negate the significance of the Nicene Creed in the present life of the church. Yet, J. N. D. Kelly advises that the early church wasn't concerned about variations in the creed.[8] Instead, they were able to speak of the Nicene Creed in reference to both early and later versions because the significance of the claims that were made in the original are also reflected in later versions. Thus, the Nicene–Constantinopolitan creed was still referred to as the Nicene Creed. Kelly goes on to argue that the Nicene Creed was a way of speaking of the Nicene Faith rather than a reference to the exact wording of the creed as it was written down at the council of Nicaea in 325. His concern is to highlight the importance that was attached to the Nicene teaching and the creed's controversial keywords, rather than the specific text of the creed confirmed at Nicaea.[9] Those keywords were an affirmation that the Son is *homoousion* with the Father and the corresponding declaration

approaches to Christology in "Salvator Mundi." Using Hunsinger's model, we are arguing in this chapter for a high Christology.

7. Jones, "Beliefs, Desires, Practices," 196.

8. "The whole style of the creed, its graceful balance and smooth flow, convey the impression of a liturgical piece which had emerged naturally in the life and worship of the Church, rather than of a conciliar artifact. C [the Constantinopolitan creed] was probably already in existence when the council took it up, although it is likely that the fathers touched it up here and there to suit their purposes." Kelly, "Nicene Creed," 34.

9. Kelly, "Nicene Creed," 34.

that the incarnate Son was and is truly and fully God.[10] These claims in turn are essential to the way in which we understand how God engages with us and makes it possible for us to engage with him.[11]

This affirmation leads to a second question: Is the creed simply a conciliar document that was primarily a reflection of theological debates at a particular point in history, or is it essential to the liturgical life of the church? The credal claims about the incarnation and the person of Jesus Christ are crucial for understanding and engaging with who God is and how God, in turn, engages with us. The redemption effected by God in Jesus Christ, which is basic to the creed, articulates the effective working out of God's commitment to engage with his creation in such a manner that his creation might come to know and live in response to him. This is of immediate import to the Christian faith. The God who created the world is the same God who has redeemed the world in Jesus Christ, and in fact, that Jesus Christ is that same God.

> Thus it is the faith and understanding of the Christian Church that in Jesus Christ God Himself in His own Being has come into our world and is actively present as personal Agent within our physical and historical existence. As both God of God and Man of man Jesus Christ is the actual Mediator between God and man and man and God in all things, even in regard to space-time relations. He constitutes in Himself the rational and personal Medium in whom God meets man in his creaturely reality and brings man, without having to leave his creaturely reality, into communion with Himself.[12]

This claim concerning the person and work of Jesus Christ corrects the tendency in some churches to isolate the cross from the life of Christ. In some contexts, an exclusive focus on the cross (with the intention of upholding the significance of the cross) has meant that the wider context of the incarnation is ignored or downplayed. Likewise, when we have isolated the death on the cross from the life of Christ, we will fail to see the affirmation of the created order—the material world—or to see God's intentions for his creation. We end up with abstract notions of forensic

10. The statement in the Apostles' Creed that Jesus is Lord is also an affirmation of the deity of Jesus, albeit not as clearly as the *homoousion*.

11. "The *homoousion* is the core confession of the church that has guarded the mystery of the incarnation, without which there would be no Christian faith, and apart from which there is no ground for understanding the mission of God." Purves, *Reconstructing Pastoral Theology*, 24.

12. Torrance, *Space, Time, and Incarnation*, 52.

justification. The incarnation is thereby perceived as instrumental rather than essential to the cross; the cross is understood as a divine act that could have happened regardless of whatever form God assumed in the incarnation.

A primary focus on what has been accomplished on the cross (the retrospective work of Christ) leads us to ignore Christ's role in the present, interceding for us at the right hand of the Father (the prospective work of Christ).[13] This leaves no room for the ongoing mediating work of Christ as our high priest.[14] This not only distorts the way we interpret the significance of the cross but also reinforces a view of God as living in an altogether separate realm.

It is the claim of the mediating work of Christ (both retrospective and prospective), which the creed presents us with that lies at the heart of our argument for a pastoral theology that is theological. Pastoral theology that intends to be relevant and appropriate to the real struggles and concerns of individuals and communities must be rooted in who God is for us. This, indeed, is the issue that Irenaeus and later Gregory of Nazianzus were arguing for when they said that the unassumed is the unhealed. It is precisely because God in Jesus Christ took on our humanity that God is able to heal and restore our humanity. The trend toward pastoral theology that is shaped by the social sciences and the praxis of local communities intends to offer practical theology that will help people make sense out of their lives. Yet, with a closed immanent frame, as we look for help to make sense of our lives, it allows us no other options but to look to our own situations and experiences. We are left trying to sort out what seems best to us as we try to be supportive and caring of others.

13. Working with the categories of John McLeod Campbell, Trevor Hart argues for retrospective and prospective elements to the salvific work of Christ. He does so in the context of the Protestant tendency to focus solely on the retrospective aspect of redemption in a desire to emphasize the objective nature of redemption—that this is what God has done for us. The retrospective aspect is that Christ dealt with the reality of sin and guilt on the cross, putting to death the old humanity. Alongside of the retrospective is the prospective: "The establishing of humanity in a new relationship with God, the exaltation of humanity to a previously unknown glory" (74). In Jesus, humanity is brought into a relationship with God which is where we are now called to live. In both retrospective and prospective aspects, the true humanity of Christ is key. Christ's humanity is vital both in what has already been accomplished as well as what is being and will be accomplished. As the book of Hebrews makes clear, it is because Christ is fully human that he is able to become our substitute and deal with our sinful condition. Hart, "Humankind in Christ," 67–84.

14. See Heb 4.

It is not surprising that abstract notions of redemption, too often defended in conservative churches, are in view when progressive voices in the church call for the church to move beyond the historic creeds and the traditions of the church. Yet what is being rejected is itself a distorted understanding of the creeds. The redemptive work realized in the cross finds its foundation precisely in the specificity of the incarnation.[15]

Many years ago I (Peter) was part of a small group in the congregation in which I was serving as the pastor. One woman, who had been a part of this group for at least four or five years and had been a part of the church for much longer, said, "I get it, Jesus was actually human." I am not sure of all that she meant by that statement, but it was clear that, at least in part, she was coming to recognize that the humanity of Jesus is essential to his salvific work. While she had understood the idea that God has come among us in Jesus for our salvation, she didn't understand that the way God has effected salvation is through his assumption of our humanity. This woman had an adult son who was severely handicapped. For much of her life she had struggled with the question of why God was letting this happen to them. Her understanding of the humanity of Jesus didn't fully answer that question for her, but it began to give her a basis for making sense of the way in which God has entered into the reality of human existence. This recognition provided her with a new sense of hope and confidence in the way in which God is truly a part of our world.

Pastoral care that assumes that the work of Christ is only prospective has little to offer in helping us navigate our current struggles and issues. At the same time, when an emphasis on the incarnation excises the cross, pastoral care inevitably shifts toward the idea of enabling individuals to realize their own identity, even while it is not clear exactly what that might mean. The incarnation is not a simple affirmation of the intrinsic value of our humanity, but is a declaration that the love of God and the judgment of God are one and the same: love and judgment most fully made visible in the cross of the incarnate one.

Theological claims are not simply doctrinal positions supported by biblical texts that we do our best to defend. They are, rather, ways of speaking about the God who has created us and who has called us to live

15. Stephen Chester makes this same point in relationship to Luther: "That Christ's presence within faith is central to what Luther understands Paul to mean by faith makes it impossible for Luther to construe justification and union with Christ as contrasting categories. To be justified requires union with Christ, since it is only united with him that his righteousness is received, and to be united with Christ requires justification since it is in justifying faith that Christ is present." Chester, "Apocalyptic Union," 393.

in response to his desires for us. Theological claims guide us into a way of living from God and ordered toward God. True pastoral care rooted in the life of the good shepherd means aligning our lives with God and what God has expressed concerning who he is and what his desires for us are, as we enter into the strange new world of the gospel.

This emphasis on the integrity of God's action in Jesus Christ with the person of Jesus Christ is echoed by Rowan Williams in "The Nicene Heritage," where he speaks of "the recognition that what Christians understand as divine agency has features that can only be made sense of if the divine life is agreed to be such as to make *that* kind of action (as seen in the history of creation, covenant, redemption) natural to it."[16] In the incarnation, what we see is not simply a mediated image of God, but who God truly is, even as we accept that this is not all there is to say about God. "This is not to claim a conceptual grasp of what it's *like* to be God, only to try and guarantee that what's said of God allows for the full implications of how we encounter the freedom or creative resource that does not come from a pattern of circumstance in the universe, any set of finite causes."[17] This requires an understanding of God as irreducibly manifold act—as being concretely what God is eternally, necessarily and only in this manifoldness, which is in turn to affirm the continuity of the work (and persons) of Christ and the Spirit with the One who sustains the universe.

The Nicene Creed affirms that in Jesus Christ we not only see who God is, but how God acts, in order that we might know God in and through what God has done and is doing for us. The incarnation is not a temporary episode but the basis by which God continues to be present to us through the Son and the Spirit, and it is this which is reflected and affirmed in the creed. As T. F. Torrance contends, the language of the creed is not merely symbolic but is "essentially significative, employing conceptual forms of thought that are intended to refer us to God in a direct and cognitive way."[18] God gives himself to us to be known by us even as God remains other than his creation. So when we speak of the

16. Williams, "Nicene Heritage," 46–47.

17. Williams, "Nicene Heritage," 47.

18. Torrance, *Space, Time, and Incarnation*, 1. "The Nicene Fathers were convinced that the disciplined statements they made in formulating the Creed were rightly and properly related to what they signified, i.e. through a basic conceptuality that did not vary with the many forms of man's own devising but was controlled by the reality intended." Torrance, *Space, Time, and Incarnation*, 2.

transcendence of God we are not referring to a spatial distancing of God from his creation, as though God dwells in an altogether separate space. Rather, the creed is affirming exactly the opposite: that "God Himself in His own being is actively present with us as personal Agent within the space and time of our world."[19] God is free to engage with us without that engagement altering who God is in God's self. God is not constrained by what we might say about him, but is able to engage with us immediately and intimately, without that changing who God is.

Kelly goes on to suggest that the significance of the affirmation made at Nicaea was not understood or accepted by many at that time. Debates within the church continued; it was, as it were, something the church had to grow into. The earlier Origenist view of God was of "a holy Triad, of an ineffable Godhead with two subordinate and, in the last resort, disparate hypostases."[20] Kelly submits that it took the next four or five decades for the affirmation of Nicaea stating that the Son is truly and fully God (and the subsequent affirmation of the deity of the Holy Spirit) to become the accepted view of the church.[21]

> The Son and the Spirit were "one in being" (as we now translate *homoousion*) with the Father, and the Godhead was an indivisible unity expressing itself in three eternal modes differing only in their relations. The Nicene creed, in its original form N[Nicaea] and its more mature development C[Constantinople], symbolised this far-reaching revolution.[22]

This claim, unacceptable and nonsensical to many in the fourth century, continues to be a stumbling block to many today, albeit in a

19. Torrance, *Space, Time, and Incarnation*, 1.

20. "Prior to Nicaea the accepted Christian doctrine of God was an Origenistic one of a holy Triad, of an ineffable Godhead with two subordinate and, in the last resort, disparate hypostases; but after Nicaea the pressure group which pushed through the introduction of the *homoousion* dragged, if you will forgive the crude metaphor, these two inferior hypostases within the divine essence. During the four or five decades following Nicaea the predominant view in the church continued to be Origenistic, pluralistic; that applies as much to an orthodox leader such as Cyril of Jerusalem as to Eusebius of Caesarea and Arians of right and left wing. But once the creed of Constantinople both reaffirmed and supplemented the Nicene creed proper, there could be no future for such pluralism." Kelly, "Nicene Creed," 38.

21. D. H. Williams argues that advocates continued to defend the creed and to explain its biblical foundations to fellow Catholics throughout the mid-fourth century in the face of groups (and councils) who sought to challenge the creed and its terminology. Williams, "Monarchianism and Photinus of Sirmium," 187–206.

22. Kelly, "Nicene Creed," 38–39.

different context. The complex debates around the creeds and the claims they make about God leave some people wondering what the creeds have to do with our daily lives. Our intent here is not to explore these questions in depth, but to reiterate the point which Sayers raises with regard to the relevance of the creeds today. The "turn to the subject" has resulted in our defining relevance based on whether we are able to understand and determine value for ourselves. Something has relevance if it satisfies our perception of value. But a broader understanding of relevance is shaped by whether or not something has significance for our personal and social settings, regardless of whether we are able to recognize or understand its import. The claims of the creed concerning Jesus Christ are definitive for what it means to be human, whether or not we accept or acknowledge those claims.

In *A Secular Age* Charles Taylor argues that our secular culture has ruled out the possibility of a transcendent God who engages with us, and our culture continues to buffer itself against that possibility. In the immanent frame we have constructed a social imaginary (a way of seeing and living in the world) which allows no room for a transcendent God.[23] In *Almost Christian*, Kenda Dean reflects something of the same sentiment. She notes that North Americans prefer a god of convenience; where "Christianity is not a big deal, . . . God requires little, and the church is a helpful social institution filled with nice people."[24] Dean's suggestion might be seen as a call for us to take God more seriously, yet there are all kinds of ways in which the buffering that Taylor speaks of plays out in unfortunate ways. Take for example the prosperity gospel, which appears to put confidence in God as intervening in our situations if we pray in the right manner. The problem is, the God we expect to intervene bears more resemblance to a genie in a bottle than to the God revealed to us in Jesus Christ. As a result many people have walked away from their faith because God didn't answer their prayers in the way that they expected and hoped for. We might also look to the close relationship between the Republican Party and the evangelical church in the United States, where there appears to be a desire to take God seriously, particularly with regard

23. "We overlook that what ultimately upends faith is the loss of the plausibility of transcendence and the presumption that our world is only a natural and material place. In the age of authenticity, the self is buffered, the world is disenchanted, and God is always on the verge of being reduced to a psychologically created imaginary friend." Root, *Faith Formation*, 100.

24. Dean, *Almost Christian*, 12.

to moral issues, yet churches and individuals are selective as to which moral issues they believe matter to God. In more progressive churches, an antipathy toward conversion is often rooted in a rejection of the *homoousion*—the claim that Jesus Christ truly is God. The buffering that Taylor refers to, in which we are not able to hold our understanding of the transcendent God together with the God who is present to us in Christ and the Spirit, plays out in all kinds of practical ways.

Our rejection of the claims of the Nicene Creed and the incarnation are often not an issue of relevance but of expediency.[25] We prefer a god who is there for us when we need him rather than a God who has a claim on the whole of our lives. We live in a world that has a priori ruled out the possibility of a transcendent God, never mind a transcendent God who is present and active in our lives and our world. The immanent frame of our culture is the counternarrative to the narrative of the Nicene Faith.

The Nicene Creed, in the light of incarnation, affirms that God is indeed present to us and makes himself known to us even as he remains the holy other.[26] The creed is the declaration that Jesus Christ is the reality of this world and, as such, the only true basis for relevance in this world.[27] Theological claims guide us into a way of living from God and ordered toward God. At issue here is not whether we recite the creed regularly in worship, although that certainly has its place in a community that needs to hear again and again the central claims of the gospel narrative, but whether we are learning to see and know ourselves, the world, and God in the light of and in relationship to this same God who created and redeemed this world in Jesus Christ.[28]

25. N. T. Wright says something along these lines when he speaks of the Gospel of Judas: "This became almost comically clear in the early comments on the translation and publication of the ancient gnostic tract which has been named *The Gospel of Judas*. The editors of the newly discovered text made it clear that for them this wasn't just an interesting historical document, but rather a vital clue to a more exciting form of Christianity than dull, boring old orthodoxy. The canonical Jesus instructed his followers to deny themselves and take up their cross. The gnostic Jesus tells you to discover yourself and follow your own star." Wright, *Creation, Power and Truth*, 16.

26. "God is the transcendent Creator of the whole realm of space and stands in a creative not a spatial or a temporal relation, to it." Torrance, *Space, Time, and Incarnation*, 3.

27. The church in itself has no claim to be the locus of relevance or truth for this world but only insofar as it is "in Christ."

28. "One of the purposes of official ritual is to preserve the beliefs of the worshipping community during times when there is a danger of losing sight of those beliefs, to keep them intact until such times as they are rediscovered. Thus a concomitant danger in unauthorized liturgies is that the principle '*Lex orandi est lex credendi*' can be cited

It is helpful that Kelly also notes that the creed affirmed at Constantinople in 381, while aligned with the fundamental shift of Nicaea, reflected a gradual refinement that resulted from its use in the context of worship. In other words, although the creed may not have been officially used in worship until the sixth century or later, it was already being refined and polished in the context of the worshiping life of the church. That confirms that even as the councils continued to engage with and gradually accept the central affirmations of the Nicene Creed, worshiping communities were recognizing and responding to the faith represented by the creed in their worship, in the social imaginary of the church community.

In "Debate on the Liturgy," Alexander Schmemann argues for the essential and dynamic relationship between the liturgy (practices of the church) and the creeds (confession of faith).[29] The two are organically related and interdependent: The law of what is prayed is the law of what is believed—*lex orandi lex credendi*. The creeds arise out of the practices of the worshiping community just as the faith of the community informs and transforms those practices.[30]

Kelly argues that the Nicene Faith represents a turning point at which the church moved forward in its understanding not only of who God is, but of how God engages with us and, by implication, who we are and who we are called to be in relation to God. Today, in a manner similar to the early days of the church, we need to relearn in life and practice the significance of the incarnation in terms of what it says about who God is and what God is doing in this world. Central to our calling as people of the faith is learning how to live according to the Nicene scriptural narrative rather than the narrative of the closed immanent frame of a secular age. In that sense, to be a Christian is not simply to assent to a set of beliefs but to enter into the Nicene Faith; it is to live in this world

---

to prove that omissions, such as that of the Creed itself, reveal that such particular doctrines are no longer the teachings of the Church. Among practicing Catholics, it appears that even the concept of God is now weak and confused, encompassing everything from Chalcedonian orthodoxy through deism to a kind of self-deifying pantheism." Hitchcock, "Liturgy and Ritual," para 20.

29. We will explore this relationship in the chapter on the Eucharist.

30. This "implies an organic and essential interdependence in which one element, the faith, although source and cause of the other, the liturgy, essentially needs the other as its own self-understanding and self-fulfillment. It is, to be sure, faith that gives birth to, and 'shapes,' liturgy, but it is liturgy, that by fulfilling and expressing faith, 'bears testimony' to faith and becomes thus its true and adequate expression and norm: *lex orandi est lex credendi*." Schmemann, "Debate on the Liturgy," 218.

in response to and relationship with the God who has revealed himself to us in Jesus Christ. The Nicene Faith relates the heart of the biblical narrative and invites us to enter into this narrative in order to come to know and understand ourselves in the context of this God. Struggling with the Nicene Creed, learning how to live into the world it reflects (as narrated in Scripture), and learning how to respond to the God it gives voice to is at the heart of what it means to be a Christian community.

MY FAITH OR THE FAITH

A follow-up question to our earlier survey of Christians across denominations might ask what we mean when we speak of faith. If Andrew Root is correct, a majority of respondents in the Western world would speak of faith as an individual's commitments, or a set of claims or ideas.[31] Indeed, the assumption would be (in line with Schleiermacher's *Christian Faith*) that faith is the universal subjective dimension of human beings.[32] Schleiermacher's emphasis on the subjective or experiential aspect to faith is not at issue so much as the way in which the focus has shifted to prioritize the individual's experience. Today, to have faith is to believe certain things and to be committed to certain ideas or beliefs, with the emphasis on the individual's faith or commitment to that set of ideas. The focus is on the importance of an individual's faith rather than what or who they have faith in; thus faith is assumed to be primarily an element of meaningful *individual* existence.

This understanding of individual faith has been further complicated by the presumed conflict between faith and reason. In the modern age, the church has often encouraged an understanding of faith in opposition to reason. We speak of *blind* faith in positive terms, with an assumption that we must simply believe even if all the evidence somehow points in the opposite direction. If we do this, however, we fail to recognize that we are operating with a narrow cognitive approach to faith. We have simply changed the boundaries in a manner which effectively spiritualizes the

31. "While these charismatic evangelicals continued talking about a personal relationship with Jesus and seeking ecstatic experiences in worship, they nevertheless made faith formation about commitment to the idea of Jesus, stripping formation, ironically, of its transcendent encounter with divine action, making conversion an epistemological shift rather than an ontological encounter." Root, *Faith Formation*, 80.

32. There are distinct echoes of Schleiermacher in some of the ideas put forward by Emerging Church movement leaders such as Rob Bell. See Bell, *Love Wins*.

faith and isolates it from the church historically and globally.[33] This conservative approach is not far removed from some progressive voices, such as those from the Emerging Church movement who believe that the key in making faith real and relevant is to disconnect it from the historic creeds and focus on interior personal experience.[34] What we may not realize is that the retreat into a notion of faith as a personal and private commitment is at the same time a retreat from the universal significance of Jesus Christ, revealing as he does God's way of acting in the world and God's purposes for the world.[35]

The other way of speaking of faith is not to focus on an individual and their level of conviction, but to think of "the faith" as an objective dimension of this world. In this case the focus is on the content of faith: what, or in a Christian context, who it is. This faith is not a choice between cognitive assent to a traditional set of dogmas or an interior faith that reflects our personal level of conviction. Rather, it is an understanding of faith that has to do with personal encounter with Christ, not in an interior spiritualized manner, but in the ways in which God has made himself known to us and continues to encounter us in Jesus Christ and by the Holy Spirit. "Jesus does not simply proclaim the Gospel; he is its substantial content."[36]

The crucial claim here is that faith has both corporate and individual dimensions, and that it is not only cognitive but also involves the ordering of our lives. This can be related to the question of the practice of baptism. The debates around infant or believer's baptism are far too complex to be explored in any detail here, yet they often reflect our understanding of faith as either corporate or individual. But life in the community of the church and participation in the life, death, and resurrection of Christ involves both the actions and commitments of the individual as well as the life in Christ that we are entering into.[37] The central place of the

33. We may also speak of a "heavenly hope," by which we mean a future reality that is disconnected from our current experience.

34. McKnight, "Five Streams of the Emerging Church," 34–36.

35. We might think of Calvin's "spectacles of faith" which allow us to see the world for what it truly is.

36. Hart, "Humankind in Christ," 70.

37. "Baptism is both God's gift and our human response to that gift. It looks towards a growth into the measure of the stature of the fullness of Christ (Eph. 4:13). The necessity of faith for the reception of the salvation embodied and set forth in baptism is acknowledged by all churches. Personal commitment is necessary for responsible membership in the body of Christ." "Baptism and Faith," in *Baptism, Eucharist and Ministry*, 3.

creed as the baptismal covenant gives expression to the comprehensive and Christ-centered nature of the faith into which the newly baptized Christian is entering.[38]

Experience is vital to faith, but it is not an individual's experience in isolation but the wider experience of the church that frames our knowing of God. To have faith is to live in the context of *the Faith* so that the contours and boundaries it offers shape our knowing of God (providing a social imaginary in which we might come to know God). Here we might follow Augustine or Anselm in suggesting that to know God we must love God. The shared and inherited life of the church gives shape to this loving of him. Or we might learn from a philosopher such as Wittgenstein, or more recently Charles Taylor, in insisting that knowing (or faith) is always located in a context: a community, or a social imaginary.[39] We love him in a distinct form of life in a particular place and time. Or we might turn to Karl Barth, who not only identifies revelation with the presence of Christ with us, but then links reconciliation and revelation. We know and love him as he speaks and acts personally on our behalf.

What is missing from the popular affirmation of personal faith is a sense and context for understanding Christian faith as encounter with Jesus, the Son of God and the second person of the Trinity; that faith is not adherence to certain truth claims about Jesus (or a private interior relationship with Jesus) but is more properly to come to know and love Jesus, who is made present to us through the Holy Spirit in the context of the church, the body of Christ.[40] And here we have in mind a church whose own narrative is shaped by the creeds.

38. "Christian baptism is rooted in the ministry of Jesus of Nazareth, in his death and in his resurrection. It is incorporation into Christ, who is the crucified and risen Lord; it is entry into the New Covenant between God and God's people." "The Institution of Baptism," in *Baptism, Eucharist and Ministry*, 1.

39. "God's intervention in history, and in particular the Incarnation, was intended to transform us, through making us partakers of the communion which God already is and lives. It was meant to effect our 'deification' (theosis). In this crucial sense, salvation is thwarted to the extent that we treat God as an impersonal being, or as merely the creator of an impersonal order to which we have to adjust. Salvation is only effected by, one might say is, our being in communion with God through the community of humans in communion, viz., the church." Taylor, *Secular Age*, 278–79.

40. This is where Schleiermacher (and more recent advocates like Rob Bell) are correct in insisting on personal encounter. The problem is to suggest that this personal encounter is with someone or something other than the God spoken of in the context of the Nicene Faith.

There are, then, two remedial moves that we need to make in speaking about what faith is. The first, which is counterintuitive in our individualistic era, is to shift the focus away from an individual's conviction or commitment. As important as *personal* faith is, the understanding of faith as my commitment or my level of conviction is rooted in a post-Cartesian anthropology rather than reflecting a Nicene or biblical approach to faith. Personal faith and commitment are central to the Christian faith, but when it becomes *primary*, the focus shifts to who we are rather than toward the one in whom we have faith: the person Jesus Christ about whom the strong claims of the creed are made.

The second move, which follows on the first, is to emphasize *the faith* as a reality which we enter into, rather than an individual internal conviction. Faith is a particular way of living, an ordering of life in the world, and living into that reality. Again, it has concrete, corporate, and inherited dimensions, all consistent with what we have said of a social imaginary.

PARTICIPATION IN CHRIST

Recent scholarship on Luther, for example among the Finnish school, has sought to recover Luther's understanding of faith as located in direct relationship with Christ. Faith is not just an objective belief in Christ or what Christ has done but something which enables us to dwell with him. In this relationship we participate in Christ and in his relationship with the Father. By grace we share with Christ as he takes our humanity into the presence of the Father; this is "the faith." Indeed, faith is first and foremost Christ's own responsive relationship to the Father in the incarnation, crucifixion, resurrection, and ascension. The New Testament scholar Michael Gorman, who has written extensively about participation in Christ, argues that "faith is the narrative posture of obedient self-offering to God. In this regard, faith truly is sharing the faith of Jesus (Rom 3:26)."[41] It is our sharing in the faith of Jesus in the context of his pneumatized body.

This understanding of faith resonates with Paul's language of being "in Christ." Since the work of E. P. Sanders there has been among Pauline

41. Gorman, *Cruciformity*, 154, quoted in Root, *Faith Formation*, 123.

scholars a groundswell in the recovery of the notion of participation as central to Paul's theology and particularly his soteriology.[42]

> It is nearly impossible to engage Paul seriously today without recognizing the centrality of participation to his lived experience ("spirituality") and his theology. Participation is not merely one aspect of Pauline theology and spirituality, or a supplement to something more fundamental; rather, it is at the very heart of Paul's thinking and living. Pauline soteriology is inherently participatory and transformative.[43]

In the midst of this renewal in the language of participation there remains for some a significant unease with it, in part for fear that participation might suggest a type of Neoplatonist absorption.[44] There is also a concern that the notion of participation fails to maintain the distinction between God and his creation.[45] It is vital to recognize and affirm that any notion of participation only makes sense within the understanding of God as established by the Nicene Faith. That participation is not a sharing of essence, but entry into relationship with Christ by the Spirit.[46] This is not participation in some divine substance, or a commodity of salvation, but participation in the relationship which Jesus Christ enjoys with the Father. This is consistent with the classic Reformation emphasis

42. For a survey of work on Paul's understanding of participation, see Macaskill, *Union with Christ in the New Testament.*

43. Gorman, "Paul's Corporate Cruciform, Missional *Theosis*," 181.

44. "Habets captures the general unease many feel: contemporary western scholars (particularly Protestant scholars) are regularly concerned with the problem of 'a pan(en)theistic concept of union in which the believer becomes dissolved into the essence of the divine nature so that he or she ceases to exist as a distinct entity.'" Blackwell, *Christosis*, 108, citing Habets, "'Reformed Theosis?,'" 494.

45. Union with God does not collapse the distinction between God and humanity. "Since Jesus Christ freely and graciously establishes the union and always remains Lord of it, no such synthesis could possibly take place, because if it did Jesus Christ would cease to be the Lord that he is. Yet, union with Christ *can* occur precisely because it takes place as an event of divine lordship and human obedience." Neder, *Participation in Christ*, 3.

46. For both Irenaeus and Cyril the work of Christ and the Spirit is basic to participation. This is no abstract notion of union but a union grounded in the personal presence of the Triune God. Blackwell, *Christosis*, 106.

Of Cyril: "[Believers] do not participate in the divine in some abstract manner but through the personal presence of Christ through the Spirit, somatically and spiritually. Just as the vivifying and sanctifying presence of the Spirit was lost through the sin of the first Adam, Christ as the second Adam has restored the presence of the Spirit to humanity, returning incorruption and sanctification to them again." Blackwell, *Christosis*, 252.

on justification, insofar as we are invited into this relationship by God's gracious initiative.

In dialogue with E. P. Sanders, Richard Hays argues that it is vital to speak of participation in concrete rather than abstract terms. He suggests that participation in Christ may be understood in a variety of ways: "belonging to a family; political or military solidarity with Christ (as in Romans 6); participating in the *ekklēsia*; and living within the Christ story ('narrative participation')."[47] In reference to the creed we might say that speaking the creed together and recognizing it as part of our worship involves the latter two categories: participating in the *ekklēsia* and living with the Christ story. Participation in Christ is not about a private interior or "spiritual" encounter, but it is living into Christ's body at the same time as that body, in Christ and by the Spirit, lives into the biblical narrative.

CONCLUSION

The contours of the debates have changed significantly since the fourth century, but the primary question has not: In what way can we speak of, come to know, and bear witness to this God who has not only identified himself with our space and time in the incarnation, but continues to engage with us in order to reconcile and draw the whole of creation toward his telos for it? The early church was seeking to defend the transcendence of God while also affirming the full deity of Christ and the Spirit—God with us. Today we need to address the cultural assumptions of the immanent frame which make no allowance for God's engagement with us, except perhaps in a pantheistic manner. The creed signifies the distinctiveness of *the faith* and clarifies that it is about God and not about human attempts to make sense of the gods or to bear witness to the gods. It has to do with this God, the One who makes himself known to us as the creating and redeeming God in and through Jesus Christ. This is not a theoretical or abstract question, but is the basis by which we can learn to live in the present in the light of the new life—the new creation, which God has established in Jesus Christ.

In *Worship, Community and the Triune God of Grace*, James Torrance provides a practical example of what we are contending for in

47. Gorman, "Paul's Corporate Cruciform, Missional *Theosis*," references Hays, "What Is 'Real Participation in Christ'?," 336–51.

this chapter as he argues for a renewal of our understanding of worship. Torrance explores what it means for Christians to worship in the context of the God to which the Nicene Faith witnesses. Worship always begins with God, and not just with God as the object of worship, but as the One who in Jesus Christ leads us in worship. Torrance contrasts two types of worship: Trinitarian worship beginning with a Nicene understanding of God, and Unitarian worship beginning with a focus on us and what we are doing. He further suggests that Unitarian worship comes in two forms: the Harnack (Hick) Model, which rejects traditional theological claims concerning the person and deity of Jesus Christ while offering a moralistic view of the Christian faith (guidelines on how to live a good, meaningful, or wholesome life), and the "Existential Present-day Experience Model," which he identifies with the evangelical church.[48] The deity of Christ is affirmed in this latter model, but Christ's work is understood solely in a retrospective manner. As a result, we operate with an understanding of a God who is largely absent. In both types of Unitarian approach, worship becomes about us and what we do rather than about God and what God is doing.[49]

While James Torrance focuses his argument specifically on worship, it is clearly applicable to the whole of the Christian life. To speak about the Christian faith (or the Nicene Faith) as a particular way of understanding and inhabiting the world in light of the incarnation and what it has revealed and declares to us about God is to enter into a possibility grounded in the person and work of Christ, both historically and in the present. Instead of understanding pastoral work as something which we do, we understand that pastoral work and therefore pastoral theology always begins with what God is doing. It is to participate in God's own reconciling of the world to himself, in that Jesus has reconciled us to God and continues to intercede for us at the right hand of the Father. To speak of the Christian faith as the Nicene Faith is to recognize or acknowledge the significance of the shift (the turning) point that was affirmed at the Council of Nicaea and further refined at the Council of Constantinople.

The church, then, is that community learning to live in the world in light of the presence and action of God: "God" not in a generic or pantheistic sense of the divine, but *this* God, revealed to us in Jesus Christ, who has reconciled us to himself. Here the call is for the church to be

48. Torrance, *Worship, Community and the Triune God of Grace*, 25–27.

49. Torrance, *Worship, Community and the Triune God of Grace*, 28–34.

the church, to know who she is called to be and will one day be, and to live toward that calling. As creatures of this world who are also creatures of God, we continue to live in the tension between a closed immanent frame which allows no space for God and a social imaginary that is being shaped in response to the incarnation, cross, resurrection, and ascension. This tension is acutely felt in the church itself, which inhabits both the social imaginary of this world and its eschatological calling in Jesus Christ.

Learning to live into the Nicene Faith has immediate implications for how we live in the world as well. We will address the question of mission in a later chapter, but we need to say something briefly here. Our primary witness to the world is that we are communities learning to live into the Nicene Faith in a world that has buffered itself against any possibility of God's presence and action in our midst. To bear witness is not simply to speak about God (although it includes that); it is to live in the light of *the faith* in the midst of our different contexts. When communities bear witness to the transcendent God through prayer, acts of service, caring for the poor, and acts of justice, it becomes possible for those who are living within a closed immanent frame to come to know and respond to God. This includes both those outside of the church and those within the church. We bear witness by feeding the hungry, caring for the poor, and seeking justice for the oppressed, and the act of bearing witness is itself essential to the church in knowing and living into a social imaginary that allows space and place for God. We participate in God's own ministry to the world and come to know God in and through participating in the ministry of Jesus Christ to the world.

6

Responding to God's Gracious Word

"Lord, Teach Us to Pray"

A NOTE AT THE OUTSET: The next three chapters, dealing with prayer, confessing and absolving sins, and bringing our offerings to God, are entitled "responding." This is deliberate, since we on our own have nothing worthy to bring. It is only in grateful response to God's gracious initiative that we can do so. This finds expression in the service as a result of the fact that the word of God, conveying the good news, has preceded our gathered worship. The symbol here is the intercessions or "Prayers of the People." In distinctively Christian prayer, Jesus shares with us his intimacy with his Father. Diverse Christian spiritual traditions share the goals of shaping our hearts, consecrating the world as God's, and getting us ready to listen to God.

Coventry Cathedral was bombed out. In spite of its roof being destroyed, the small congregation huddled together to receive communion. Collapsed, yet open to the sky, with the worshipers left only to suffer and continue. The image of this famous photo came back to my (George's) mind when the Reverend Fleming Rutledge offered it as an illustration of the church in Ephesians: glorious, flattened, at prayer. I had actually been in a similar scene two decades earlier. A recently ordained friend had come to visit us at the seminary in central Tanzania. There was still, overlooking the town, the ruins of an old church, once set apart for expatriates, but now reduced to rubble. There our friend celebrated his first Eucharist, with the state of the church in our mutual home lurking in the back of our minds. Over time, it occurred to us that the image held, not just for the church out there but for us, too, who as individuals and a body make up the church. A church inherited, marred by us, open nonetheless, where communion continues to be offered in spite of ourselves. We come to know ourselves better over the years, we who are more the unlikely locus of the orison than its agent.

Jesus was praying and when he had finished one of his disciples said to him, "Lord, teach us to pray." (Luke 11:1)

Teach us to pray. It is a strange thing to ask, at least for someone who has grown up in a Jewish community, regularly attending synagogue. The people of Israel prayed in their homes, gathered every Sabbath to pray, and regularly traveled to the temple on pilgrimage. Jesus's disciples surely grew up praying—it would have been a normal part of their life together—and yet this disciple asks, "Lord, teach us to pray." The context suggests that this disciple observed something different in the way Jesus was praying. What was it that caught their imagination? Something in the way Jesus prayed was different than the prayers of other Jews, and was different enough that this disciple, who had been praying his whole life, now asks Jesus to teach his followers how to pray: Lord, teach us to pray.

Calling out to God or "the powers that be" is something that comes naturally to human beings when we are overwhelmed by circumstances or faced with the limitations of our own ability to change our situation. A plethora of various prayer practices or meditation techniques are promoted in a variety of traditions and contexts, all of which endorse the benefits of prayer. Across these different faith practices, prayer is broadly understood to calm our spirits, help realign our hearts and minds, and allow us to call out to a higher power. But, like that disciple, we too are compelled to ask what is unique in Jesus praying to his Father.

While worship is prayer in the broader sense, the time set aside for the Prayers of the People focuses the community on praying together even as it effectively teaches us how to pray. How do we speak to God to share our hopes, dreams, fears, and needs? While we may tend to focus on techniques or practices of prayer, the primary question we should ask is, To whom are we praying? When the disciple asks Jesus "teach us to pray," he is surely recognizing that Jesus's prayer conveys something about his relationship to the One he is praying to. The Prayers of the People, in much the same way, are not just about our efforts to get the attention of the divine, but also teach us about the One to whom we pray, and thus, what Christian prayer to God consists of.

A pastoral example may be of help here. I (George) once called upon a parishioner who had recently lost her husband to cancer. She described standing in the parking lot of the hospital and calling out to God. But it seemed to her that her prayer was lost in the vast night sky with its thousand stars. What assurance did she have that her prayer would get to a God somewhere infinitely high and distant? She had the instinct to cry out to God in her distress, but the question of who, where, and how plagued her intercession and lament.

The distinctly Christian understanding of prayer answers precisely these questions. Jesus gives to his disciples his prayer to the Father because he has invited them into his relationship with his Father. Jesus responds to his disciple with what we call "the Lord's Prayer," the prayer that Jesus gives also to us. Many books have been written on the Lord's Prayer as a model from which we might break down and describe the various classical elements of prayer, including adoration, confession, supplication, and thanksgiving. All of these are important elements in prayer, and the pattern of the Lord's Prayer is a rich resource for us in learning how to incorporate these different elements of prayer into our prayers. But the Lord's Prayer needs first to be understood in the context of the disciple's request "teach us to pray." Jesus' prayer is not simply giving us a pattern or technique by which we might pray and by which we might confidently appeal to God. Jesus' prayer does not evince or evoke a strategy by which we might win God's attention or favor. It is, rather, a practice of prayer that *begins with*, and bears witness to, *the relation of the Son to the Father*.

PRAYING IN THE CONTEXT OF THE TRINITY

Jesus's prayer in Gethsemane carries echoes of the earlier garden in Eden where Adam and Eve walked with God. Here we come to the heart of the understanding of the prayer which the disciples heard, and then saw, in Jesus. It is prayer, not as a reflection of human endeavors to get the attention of God or the gods, but rather, prayer as relationship—as fellowship with the God who comes to us. This aligns with the history of the prayers of the people of Israel. In the context of God's covenantal relationship with them, prayer is always a response to the voice of the God of Israel, his call and presence with his people. Likewise, our prayer as Christians is not about human efforts to call out to God or to gain his attention, but our response to the God who is present with us. So the answer to the woman crying out to the night sky is this: We know where our prayer reaches and how we may find God because we know Christ, who dwells at the right hand of the Father making intercession for us.

This understanding of prayer needs to be qualified in light of the biblical witness to the work of the Son and the Spirit. In prayer we enter into Jesus' own relationship to his Father. The Lord's Prayer has been part of the core of the formation of new Christians—of catechism—throughout Christian history. Jesus addresses God as his "Abba," his dear Father, which reveals their relationship of intimacy and unity; as such this is a constitutive element of what would become the doctrine of God as Trinity. The promise of the gospel is that we are given a share of Jesus' intimacy with his dear Father. The intercessions of the people vividly illustrate this, since they are made on the way to communion, wherein we are invited into the holy of holies at the pinnacle of the service, there to recite the Lord's Prayer itself.

We come to see what is involved in the claim that we are "participating" in the divine life.[1] We are not co-equals—that is reserved for Christ. We are not absorbed into God—we remain creatures, even in heaven. We do not gain power, but like Mary, surrender our wills, which in turn are empowered for good by God (the tradition of Christian prayer has always looked nervously on the high claims of mysticism and the low claims of quietism). As for us, the best we can do is groan—what a wonderful way to take the air out of any pretentious description of our spiritual capacities (Rom 8:26), or of elaborate schemas or theorizing on prayer (against the Gnostics). In this living relationship we are encouraged to wrestle like Jacob, complain like Job, doubt like Thomas, and be redeemed and recommissioned like Peter.

Here we do well to recall, as we noted in chapter 4, that the work of Christ is both retrospective and prospective.[2] It includes what God has already accomplished for us in the life, death, and resurrection of Jesus Christ and what Christ continues to do for us in the ascension, in the present. We are given a share of Jesus's relation to the Father so that we might address, in spite of our incapacity, our heavenly Father in the power of the Spirit. The Letter to the Hebrews puts a particular emphasis

1. See Charles Williams's *Descent of the Dove* and Peter Leithart on coinherence in *Traces of the Trinity*.

2. Hart, "Humankind in Christ."

on the mediating work of Christ, not only in his work on the cross but in his ongoing representation and intercession for us at the right hand of the Father. So here we see that our praying is to participate in the ascended Christ's relationship to the Father.

This understanding of prayer in the Son is further qualified by the work of the Holy Spirit and is altogether consistent with Paul's description of Christian life as prayer in Rom 8:26–30. The Spirit intercedes for us in groans too deep for words. The Spirit takes the initiative, praying through us, as it were, to the Father, because we are co-heirs with the Son as adopted children, so as to be further conformed to him. There are two elements to consider here. The first is that the work of the Spirit gives voice to the deepest impulses of our hearts, and the second is that it is the work of the Spirit which brings us to know and understand the person of Christ. To speak of prayer, then, is to speak of the movement of the Holy Spirit in our very hearts. We know when something is the work of the Holy Spirit and not some other spirit because the Paraclete is sent by Jesus Christ and is always consistent with what Jesus taught.[3] There is no mission of the Spirit apart from that of the Son; the works of the persons of the Trinity are indivisible, as Augustine taught.[4] But this same Spirit who is the comforter does not simply comfort us, but throws us into the wilderness, would have us identify with the least and the lost, disturbs the lukewarm within the church, and foretells God's plucking up and planting in the world at large. The image of a fireplace in which the fire may be lit is an evocative one.[5] The fire burns and consumes yet brings heat and light at the same time; it is a powerful force. And so, the Spirit is at once a Spirit of order and also a Spirit of freedom. This points to an ordered freedom, and an order that conduces to freeing persons, sometimes even from those things that we don't really want to be free from.

Scholars have noted the parallels between the Lord's Prayer and Jesus' prayer in the garden of Gethsemane, where Jesus entreats the Father while also praying "thy will be done."[6] This does not signify resignation to powerlessness in the face of Jesus' circumstances, nor is it aligned with

3. John 16:9–11, 14.

4. "Opera Trinitatis indivisa sunt." Augustine, *Homilies on the Gospel of John*, 7:132.

5. Charles Hummel's book about renewal and the charismatic movement employs this image; Hummel, *Fire in the Fireplace*.

6. For example, see Neumann, "Thy Will Be Done," 161–82. On the theme of abiding with Jesus at the foot of the cross, see Bonhoeffer on Christian life in the modern age in the letter from Bonhoeffer to Eberhard Bethge, Tegel, July 21, 1944, in *Letters and Papers from Prison*, 485–87. See also his *Lord's Prayer*.

his mother's words at the Cana wedding where she says, "Do whatever he tells you." It affirms the will of the Father as good and perfect and true: It is a prayer for God's good and perfect will to be acted out in this world and in our lives. Our affirmation of trust and confidence in God reflects the obedience of the Son to the Father, not as a rote obedience, but rather as an act of faith grounded in the love of the Father. Jesus not only shows us this trust in his prayer "thy will be done"; he also effects this trust for us. As the One who intercedes for us he trusts in the Father on our behalf. When words fail us or we lack the confidence to entrust ourselves into the hands of God, it is Jesus who goes before us and opens the way for us to follow in his prayer to the Father in his confidence in the Father's love. So prayer is wholly trinitarian, not in the sense that the doctrine may be reduced to a human experience of praying, but on the contrary, because what we experience must be understood anew and more profoundly in relation to the divine life itself.

A cross-cultural example may reinforce the same point. When the first Protestant missionaries arrived in Buganda in the later nineteenth century, the hearers were amazed by the gospel. The news of the incarnation of the Son did not amaze them so much—they were accustomed to gods appearing, and even turning themselves into other forms. But they had a traditional belief in the Creator, and so the news that the Father, safely ensconced in heaven, would care about the misery of his creatures down on this blighted planet so much as to send his own Son was amazing to them. In other words, they would have had a clear sense of the God high and distant in the night sky, but it was amazing to them to know that the Son had descended, suffered, and ascended so as to convey their prayers to the Father, who had a care for their troubles. The idea that Christian prayer is accompanied by the assurance of being heard because of the relation of the Son to the Father was both amazing and compelling to them. So it is for us, if we put the matter clearly.

We can offer here an aside about the implications of our distinctive understanding of prayer. In the first place, Christian theology is not about human efforts to make sense of the divine or the powers that be, but to bear witness to what God shows us of himself. Christian prayer, rooted as it is in Jesus's relationship with the Father, lays the foundation for how we might think about pastoral theology as well. Just as the Lord's Prayer is not first and foremost about different techniques for prayer but is grounded in the Son's relationship with the Father, so too pastoral theology is not first and foremost about different ministry techniques, but is about our participation in the Son's relationship with the Father. This means that while pastoral theology should explore all the sacred and secular resources available to it, it begins with and grows out of the Christian narrative as it is embodied in the worshiping community.

THE PROBLEM WITH PRAYER

Taking our requests and supplications to God is in part acknowledging that there are things which are beyond our control (more than we usually admit). And here we come to one of the primary difficulties we have with prayer. We pour out our hearts, sharing our fears, worries, and needs, but God often seems to remain silent. Shortly after the English evangelist David Watson was diagnosed with cancer in the early 1980s, he believed he had been healed through prayer, as did many of his supporters who had prayed and fasted fervently in the hope of a complete healing. How could God not answer their prayers when David's life and ministry were making such a difference in so many people's lives? But the healing was not to be. When David died of cancer a year later (only fifty years old and at the prime of his ministry), many of his followers experienced a crisis of faith, as they wondered why God did not answer their prayer. So we, too, struggle when our prayers for someone we love appear to go unanswered. It is very natural to believe that if we ask in the right way or with the right intention God will answer our prayer: "Ask whatever you wish and it will be done for you" (John 15:7). To pray is to hope and trust that God will answer our prayers, particularly if we are praying for a worthwhile cause or a worthy person. With our focus on our present needs or fears we don't realize that we can too easily shift from trusting God for who God is to trusting God for what we want or what we believe is the right thing for him to do.

It is not surprising that, as we mature in our Christian faith, we often find ourselves taking fewer requests to God. Either we are unsure of what we should ask for or our prayer life dries up altogether as we begin to assume that God does not intervene to answer prayer. We recognize our own foolishness or selfishness in praying for a parking spot in a busy location. Yet, Jesus teaches us to pray even for our daily bread and encourages us to turn to him with all of our needs. This suggests that by taking everything—our deepest longings, needs, and fears—to God, we are not only acknowledging our utter dependence on God, we are also giving ourselves a reality check—reminding ourselves of the way things really are: "Every good and perfect gift is from above, coming down from the Father of Lights" (Jas 1:17). Likewise, such an understanding of prayer is on the alert against a subtle works-righteousness, even as it is confident that all that is impossible for us is possible for God. When Christians are disappointed that urgent prayer requests are not answered, and when philosophers of religion wonder if such intercession can change God's mind,[7] we realize their disappointment is more about the need for transforming renewal of our minds (Rom 12) than about God's nature and sovereign action. So intercessory prayer involves the vulnerability of sharing our deepest desires with God and truly trusting both desires and results into his hands.

There is a dialectic of "already" and "not yet" which is constitutive of all Christian existence.[8] It provides another way to articulate how we are to think about "results" in prayer.[9] We can apply the terms to ministries explicitly directed to healing. They take the New Testament exhortations seriously and fly in the face of post-modern resistance, which often hides an implicit dualism. But hope for healing must be seen in a wider framework, itself consistent with the Christian social imaginary for which we have been arguing. Healing of mind and body and spirit are inseparable. God can heal by the extra-ordinary means of prayer and the ordinary means of medicine—he is Lord of both. But healing, which is temporary now, is always a sign to be understood against the horizon of the promise of full and final healing in the kingdom. To ask whether someone was healed does not press the question far enough. Otherwise we approach a results-oriented, humanly evaluated, prosperity prone perspective. The "result" is loving submission to the Lord, whose will for us is wholeness and peace now and forever. Healing "already" is a sign of a more comprehensive healing we see "not yet." Appeal to the kingdom should not presume to shorten God's arm to heal now if it is his will. In both cases the church exists to witness to the Healer who is the prime actor and agent.

7. Farrer, *Lord I Believe.*

8. The terms are from Cullmann, *Christ and Time.*

9. A famous author on inner healing is Agnes Sanford, *Healing Gifts of the Spirit.*

GIVING THANKS

This brings us to the practice of giving thanks, which is, after all, what the word *Eucharist* itself means in Greek. Thanksgiving is often included in models of prayer based on the Lord's Prayer, but is more clearly emphasized by Paul as he teaches the early church in Phil 4: "Do not worry about anything, but in everything by prayer and supplication with thanksgiving let your requests be made known to God."[10] Giving thanks begins with taking the time to remember what God has already done. Among other things, it involves the practice of looking at ourselves, the world, and God with a renewed perspective.

We all know that it is important to teach our children to say thank you. We do this not so that other people will notice how polite our wonderful children are, but so that the children will develop a healthy perspective on how much they have been given. Thanksgiving reorients our focus: it helps us to take our eyes off the pit in front of us and look back and see how much we have already been given. Giving thanks to God is even more critical, not because God needs our thanks, but because we need to acknowledge God, "at all times and places," as the *Book of Common Prayer* says in the Eucharist.[11] Giving thanks helps to form trust in the character of God and his heart for us and the world, as we see him in light of what he has already done. It reminds us that God is faithful, loving, and attentive. It opens our eyes to his overwhelming goodness, visible in what he has done and is doing for us. Our confidence becomes rooted in God because of what he has done, rather than confidence in what we own or possess or have control over.

Paul writes his Letter to the Philippians from prison. He doesn't know if he is going to be set free or sentenced to death. The church he is writing to is facing opposition and hardship from many different quarters. They are struggling. In fact, there is division in the church because of the struggles that they are facing. Paul is not saying "pray and then God will do the right thing, or God will make everything better." Instead in Phil 4:11, 12 he says, "I've learned to be content, satisfied, whether I have a lot or little." Rather than putting his confidence in what he has or doesn't have and rather than putting his confidence in the hope that everything will work out the way he wants it to, he has put his confidence in God—in

10. Or later in Ephesians: "Giving thanks to God the Father at all times and for everything in the name of our Lord Jesus Christ" (Eph 5:20).

11. *Book of Common Prayer* (1979), 131.

Jesus. And this is the point: His freedom to trust Jesus is grounded in his coming to know Jesus and living into what Jesus has already done for him. This is what the practice of praying with thanksgiving does—it puts our focus and attention where it should be. It is our reality check, as it frees us from our narrow preoccupations and anxiety to see the world in light of God and God's goodness. The antidote to anxiety is prayer, and particularly praise and thanksgiving, precisely because in prayer we are able to see God more clearly.

Prayer comprises both the celebration and repentance (turning) of Easter and Lent, as the stories of Israel and Jesus did so before. In our age, as we lean toward affirming self-worth and emphasizing self-reliance, we do well to realize that for a great teacher on prayer like Bernard, the word *spirituality* means primarily contrition.[12] This is another of the traditional types of prayer. Often the advice of a spiritual guide will direct us to see better the log in our own eye, or to understand and acknowledge, even in our seeming humility, the urge to stand up in the synagogue and say we are not like others. The goal is paschal, which is to say eucharistic: We worship the risen Christ who shows his wounded hands and blesses us who have scattered in the moment of truth. These two are in him inseparable. We see the same truth, for example, in St. Teresa of Avila, who understood that a deeper sense of her own sinfulness was a sign of nearing the mystical "Interior Castle." This was not a morbid self-loathing, since it was paired with a yet deeper sense of herself as a recipient of grace. It is the overwhelming and abundant grace of God that leads us to prayer, and in prayer to contrition and repentance. (And herein lies the answer to the question whether there is such a thing as becoming an expert in prayer.)[13] The paschal inter-connection of contrition and joy once again takes us back to the answer for the bereaved parishioner crying out into the night sky.

THE PRAYER OF THE BODY: SOME ON BEHALF OF ALL

The intercessions in the Eucharist are called the Prayers of the People, and emphasize the corporate nature of prayer. Yet at the same time, much (if not more) energy is committed to advice for the prayer lives

12. On this see the anthology of Bernard of Clairvaux, *Honey and Salt.*

13. Bloom, *Beginning to Pray.*

of individuals. While Jesus enjoins us to go into our room and pray in secret, there is always an interaction between the one and the many. Even the hermit prays for the ecclesial body as a whole, and the medieval anchorite hunkered down immediately adjacent to the church. Even in secret in our room we remain part of the body. The Prayers of the People are both corporate and individual. The priest (or lay leader) collects the prayer and so gives voice to what each and all have said. Yet as the priest prays, everyone is also offering up their own prayers to the Father.

This same principle of logic of the remnant "on behalf of all" is at work in the following examples: parish prayer groups or house churches, sodalities of catholic devotion, friends praying for a missionary, an Ultreya (a reunion group of the renewal movement Cursillo), a campus para-church group, an advance team for a Faith Alive weekend, the pioneers of a prospective church plant, a monastic Third Order, diocesan intercessors, etc. Such groups may have a more or less formal structure, and may more or less resemble "minor orders" that existed in the history of the church. They may be for a season or lifelong, but they all share the potential to be a focused source of renewal for the body. Some serve a particular vocation within a congregation, while others thrive in the interstices of structured church life. They share the potential for flexibility and the likelihood of lay leadership at its best, discerned and encouraged by the clergy. This "mediating" category of some-for-all between the individual and the whole parish or diocese often is key for the vitality of the church (even as congregations themselves partake of the "one and the many").

THE SANCTIFICATION OF TIME

The old adage that prayer is as much caught as it is taught implies that we are all apprentices in this life at whose center is prayer. We are taught as much by practice as instruction, as much by our colleagues as in our solitude. Invited to participate in Jesus's prayer to the Father, and so his life co-inherent with the Father, we are given an earnest and a foretaste of the kingdom. But our vocation is in this epoch. We are as creatures placed by his will in a specific place and time, who are subject to hunger, temptation, and being wronged. It is here that we experience his lordship over all and eternally. Like Paul with his thorn in the flesh (2 Cor 12), formation in prayer is never without suffering. The life of prayer, under testing, by his grace, makes his lordship palpable.

We also should consider forms of prayer that consciously offer to the Lord our times, and in so doing sanctify them.[14] We have in mind first the seasons of the church's year that recall and so are a kind of sacrament of his "sorrowful, joyful, and glorious mysteries." And likewise we bring that same sacred history to bear on our days, when we mark out mornings, midday, evenings, and night by the word of God. For Anglicans, the sanctification of the day and the night is borrowed from the rich monastic tradition and shared with the whole body of the faithful.[15]

Prayer as the consecration of our times to the Lord requires a word about the Sabbath. Oliver O'Donovan would have us think of it as one of the original sacraments of the Christian life.[16] We could also offer an account of the range of practices in response to the commandment. What matters most for the spiritual life is the framework of our common lives of prayer, which both supports and challenges our active—or over-active—lives. One may note that in our time, characterized by hyperactivity, anxiety, and pervasive trauma, Sabbath may play a greater role in pastoral care and evangelism, and in so doing will lead us quietly to a more rooted ecclesiology.[17]

THE PRACTICES OF PRAYER: SPIRITUALITY

We are now in a position to answer more concrete questions about some of the practices of prayer in the lives of Christians. Having set the topic in a very specific doctrinal and ecclesial matrix should protect against any notion that there should be a determined method or technology of prayer. A good place to begin is with what is usually described as Christian spirituality, a subject of great popularity in the past generation. By spirituality we mean a wide range of religious attitudes and practices

14. See Hatchett, *Sanctifying Life, Time, and Space.*

15. It is worth noting the remarkable book about depression by Kathryn Greene-McCreight, *Darkness Is My Only Companion*, in which she speaks of relying on the body of the faithful saying the Office when she couldn't. While Morning and Evening Prayer is often thought of as an individual discipline, and often was such for Anglican clergy, it also has this corporate dimension.

16. O'Donovan, *On the Thirty-Nine Articles.*

17. This transformation is today inseparable from letting go of social media technology. On this see Byung-Chul Han, *Burnout Society.*

toward God. In the contemporary scene the word is sometimes used in contrast to religion, especially in its institutional aspects.[18] Where does spirituality fit into the picture of the Christian life? We best understand it as all the things humans do in order *to get ready* to address, and be addressed, by God.[19] If we are anxious or garrulous, then quiet and the gathering of oneself is required. Here we have in mind, for example, the recent rediscovery and popularity of Centering Prayer (whose roots are in the late medieval *Cloud of Unknowing*). We may also note the place of repetition in the retrieval of the Jesus Prayer from the Orthodox Church. The goal was to find a way to "pray without ceasing" (1 Thess 5:16), by means of the identification of praying with breathing. This pursuit of an understanding of praying as encompassing one's life, including the bodily and the non-discursive, is important (although the claim to have rediscovered the "uncreated light" therein is more dubious).[20] We find here a ready answer to the popular question of borrowing practices from Eastern religions: for example, yoga. These may be judged helpful or not by the pragmatic measure of whether they serve to get us ready to hear God's word and respond in prayer.

The most popular literature which aims to get us ready to pray has focused on the meditative quietness and self-recollection of the desert. A key figure in this retrieval and popularization was Henri Nouwen, who at once appealed to the intersection with psychology yet wished to distinguish prayer from this. Christian contemplation as a return to the desert involved recognizing the spirits within us and dealing with God's absence. Nouwen also connected spirituality to the foolishness of play for ministry with the disabled, and to an empathic awareness of one's wounds. Others writing in his wake are best understood as pursuing a discipline of getting ready to pray,[21] or offering a kind of apology for contemplative prayer which touts its benefits.[22] (As a seminary student of Nouwen's, I [George] was consoled to learn of his lifelong struggle with

18. Historically, however, this is exactly what it referred to, in contrast to the ordering affairs of the world; so Shakespeare's usage.

19. Here we borrow from a point in Jenson's *Systematic Theology*, vol. 2, ch. 29.

20. Anonymous, *Way of a Pilgrim*.

21. The movement has branched into many roads; consider for example the Shalem Institute, which has sideroads into ecology, reconciliation, etc.

22. Interest in biofeedback and prayer goes back to the 1970s, but now has burgeoned into "neurotheology."

his own hyperactivity and talkativeness—like the rest of us, we pursued by grace a quiet in contrast to his nature!)

PRACTICES OF PRAYER: SUITED TO PERSONALITY

Let us also consider the various types, styles, and seasons of prayer. Different approaches to prayer tend to focus on the types of prayer or offer resources to support and encourage the practice of prayer. We can compare *spiritual direction*,[23] with its roots in Catholic asceticism, in contrast with more Protestant-friendly forms of spiritual friendship which rarely use the traditional ascetical vocabulary.[24] The language of spirituality has inclined toward the former; thus one can see many Reformed seminarians flocking to courses on the Ignatian exercises (in addition to the eclecticism of our time). We have already noted that the traditional *types of prayer* are rehearsed (adoration, confession, petition, supplication).[25] This implies the goal of a balanced and holistic life of prayer, one that reflects the whole of the corporate spiritual life—Lent to Easter. In a parallel way, styles of prayer can be delineated, sometimes correlated to schools of monastic life, along with advice about their suitability for different personality types.[26] Yet another genre is that of *private eucharistic preparation*, which encourages self-examination and penitence.[27] We can understand literature about the saints and the *Sanctoral* Cycle,[28] as a resource of encouragement from the lives of those with extraordinary charisms of prayer.[29] These are all aids, all of which must be employed according to the adage about confession—"all can, some should, none must."

23. Bishop Michael Smith reminded me (George) of the useful differentiation of direction from counseling and therapy in chapter 3 of Kenneth Leech's *Soul Friend*; the latter addresses emotional distress and social adaptation only from a secular framework.

24. We may hope for a renewal of interest in the Puritans and Pietists as guides in prayer.

25. In many cases, behind these distinctions are categories of Psalms, the prayer and songbook of Israel, with its laments, praise, pilgrimage, penitence psalms, etc.

26. Thornton, *English Spirituality*.

27. Classically for Catholic Anglicans, Cobb and Olsen, *St. Augustine's Prayer Book*.

28. But not for Catholics alone, *vide* Foxe.

29. A brief word may be said about the place of exorcism. Interest in the demonic is related to curiosity about the occult, not least among the poorly catechized or the mentally imbalanced. Still, forces of evil are real. One does best to point out that demonic influences are not isolated in dramatic phenomena, but may be found, for example, in the corporate boardroom of a pharma company strategizing the continued distribution of opioids. The wise pastor does well to eliminate explanations readier at

THE "EXILIC," THE BODILY, THE ECUMENICAL, THE FORMAL AND INFORMAL

Finally we have more general comments about the spiritual life. Let us begin with a historical observation. The Prayers of the People, following the psalms, the reading of Scripture, and a sermon, can be traced back continuously to the piety of the exilic synagogue. What do these exilic roots mean? The Jews prayed for their own survival in a far land amid the gentiles, and yet they also heard Isaiah tell them they were a light to those nations on behalf of the Lord of all the world, and Jeremiah tell them to pray for the welfare of their captor neighbors (Jer 29). Prayer for the safety of our fellow Christians throughout the world, for preservation but also for the welfare and justice of the cities of this world in which we sojourn—these goals, too, are deep in the memory of the Prayers of the People. We will cite names, sometimes long lists of them, praying for those in the church and those who are not. Intercession can be liberative, and yet we remain aware that we are resident aliens.[30] It is inherently missional.

We can also note that a sacramental religion like ours will be embodied in its prayers. We encourage physical posture as part of the practice of prayer. We use oil on the heads of the sick. Some find that beads, icons, or movement conduce to a stance of prayer. And we recognize and support the setting aside of particular spaces for prayer. Human beings are spatial creatures, and how we design and inhabit space is essential to the life of prayer. These are in the penumbra of the sacramental, which even itself should be an effectual sign of the presence of the Lord in and with the faithful.[31] These spaces, too, are to be evaluated to the extent that they do not focus attention upon themselves, but rather upon our neighbors and upon the world which is God's.

Here we do well to recall that, insofar as all can pray for any, prayer is by its nature ecumenical. We can gather as Christians across denominational lines for informal prayer, or in occasions of civic interest. Sometimes, as with the Taizé movement, a deliberately ecumenical and yet ordered life of prayer has a uniquely powerful effect, for example among the young. Likewise we do well if the laity claim their full place of leadership in intercession in the congregation, both in groups and in the

hand of psychopathology, and then to use standard resources like the house blessing, since prayer in the name of Jesus is intrinsically exorcistic.

30. Hauerwas and Willimon, *Resident Aliens*.

31. This is interestingly highly pertinent to Pentecostal expressions of the faith.

liturgy. The latter reminds the body that the calling of common prayer is theirs. If they want help in this ministry of leading prayer, there are many additional resources for Prayers of the People on special themes, and litanies of many kinds.[32] Lay people with artistic or authorial gifts can be drawn into the work of composing prayers.[33]

Occasions for such special prayers are the seasons of the lives of the faithful. Prayer should accompany graduation, the quinceañera, parishioners moving away, an engagement, a new responsibility in work or society, an anniversary, and of course, sickness and recovery. The life-cycle, in this extended sense as well as the background sense of it as an expression of the baptismal life, affords to prayer crucial settings, and hence connections, to the lives of parishioners.[34]

Up until this point most of what we have discussed has been available to a range of traditions (and in fact there is great interest in things spiritual in evangelical corners). Let us close with a word in a more specifically eucharistic mode about the location of the Prayers of the People, both backward and forward. They follow the reading of the word of God, the sermon, and the creed, and so we are reminded of the trinitarian and gracious assumptions of the prayer of the body. In the ancient church, prayer was offered for the catechumens before they were ushered out, and so prayer is inseparable from formation. In prayer, by the movement of the Holy Spirit, the sinews of the body are built up, and it grows into full maturity (Eph 4:13, 15–16). As to the intercessions themselves, they usually have a structure of set petitions, with space for congregants to add their own contributions aloud or silently. It is important to note that the set and the extemporaneous live happily next to one another. Both have a natural place in the ecology of Christian prayer. In fact, the set is often best understood as a means of freeing worshipers to offer their own prayers. These are more a matter of personal preference and personality type than of theological weight.[35]

32. See, e.g., Rowthorn, *Wideness of God's Mercy.*

33. The *Book of Common Prayer* allows such creativity, as it cites but does not require the use of the forms provided. However, the structure of prayer—for the world, the church, those in need, for blessings, and in thanksgiving for those who have died—is a venerable one and worth emulation.

34. Here may be added the regular round of prayer, the saying of grace at meals, and prayer before sleep (Tallis's Round!), by which time is by grace sanctified.

35. In the third century eucharistic prayer of Hippolytus, the bishop was to pray "in words something like these": the line between set and improvised prayers was quite permeable.

7

Responding to God's Gracious Word

Confession and Absolution

According to the Christian social imaginary, and unlike therapeutic resolution, pronouncement of absolution effects forgiveness from outside ourselves. It opens onto a discussion of justification. In its wake, we can see how the range of secular therapies can contribute to the Christian life of sanctification.

Almighty God, to you all hearts are open, all desires known, and from you no secrets are hid: Cleanse the thoughts of our hearts by the inspiration of your Holy Spirit, that we may perfectly love you, and worthily magnify your holy Name; through Christ our Lord. Amen. (Collect for Purity)

"We confess that we have sinned against You in thought, word and deed . . ."

"Almighty God have mercy upon you, forgive you all your sins through our Lord Jesus Christ . . ."

It was an hour's drive from my (George's) seminary, though it felt much longer, traversing as it did several decades of memories of my life. It had been several years since my return to faith—that chaotic and creative time many of us associate with our college days. My conversion had begun an extended time of sorting, appreciating, and regretting much in my earlier life. I had recently taken a course in the spiritual life which had advocated the rediscovery of older traditions. I arrived in the late morning, and the old priest-confessor was waiting for me. The retreat house was in the country, and the idea of laying down burdens I had carried for a while and leaving them in the woods like that poor scapegoat in Leviticus occurred to me. I had a lot to say, including one memory from earlier life. It was something I had done in elementary school, an act of gratuitous cruelty, followed by glib dissembling. I had not thought of it for many years. It was in one way trivial but in another way not at all. My confession included that story, and the shame accompanying it. In subsequent years, when on the rare occasions I think of it, I am comforted by the fact that although the cruelty was real—it happened—but the confession and the forgiveness that followed happened too. I am no more able to erase the latter than the former. This consolation is a capsule of the gospel, and the floor under my feet.

Confession and absolution seem strange or even foreign in many of our churches today, including liturgical churches like the Anglican Church where it is not uncommon to see the confession regularly omitted from the order of worship. It isn't simply that the repetition of a liturgical formula or practice may lack authenticity for some people, but that the confession (and the concomitant call for repentance) is difficult to align with our notion of a faith that is understood to help us become all that we can be.[1] When our conception of God has been largely conscripted by a moralistic and therapeutic understanding of faith, it is not surprising that the regular practice of confession may appear contradictory and offensive to Christians.

In an Anglican Church where I (George) was the priest, a parishioner heard the traditional Prayer of Humble Access: "We are not worthy so much as to gather up the crumbs under thy table."[2] After the service she complained, "All week the world tells me what's wrong with me, and then I am supposed to come here so you can tell me to grovel under the table!" (Never mind that the sentence is alluding to a word from Jesus!) Hers was a valid point which the pastor needed to hear! Similar examples of confusion or complaining about spending Sunday morning hearing how loathsome one is may be found across denominations, whether or not they recite that particular prayer of Thomas Cranmer's.

1. See the study by Princeton sociologists Christian Smith and Melinda Lundquist Denton: *Soul Searching*. See also Dean, *Almost Christian*.

2. *Book of Common Prayer* (1979), 337.

But of course the point of Cranmer's prayer is not to make that parishioner feel worse. It is to announce to him or her the shocking and counterintuitive news of the gracious forgiveness and welcome from God of his child while yet a prodigal. The justification of sinners is good news indeed, especially when we look harder at ourselves and see self-justification, pride, anger, etc. hiding.[3] After a deeper and more honest account of ourselves, grace is yet more amazing. One of the greatest challenges for pastoral leaders is to allow others to hear the good news in confession and forgiveness and to experience the tension produced by the reversal of their expectations with regard to the faith, rather than offering an empty affirmation that God will take care of all their needs and wants.

In Ps 51, as David turns to God in confession he prays, "Against you, you only, have I sinned." In the context of the rape of Bathsheba, his abuse of power, the betrayal of his commander Joab, and the murder of Uriah, David's prayer might seem a failure to take responsibility for what he has done in inflicting harm on so many people. In fact, David's prayer serves to define what sin is (and as a result, what confession and repentance are as well). As abhorrent as his actions have been, the starting point in addressing his sin is to acknowledge his basic rebellion against God and God's desires for his life. He has not only violated God's commands, but he has acted (lived) in a manner that denies the call of God on his life. The root of sin is not our misbehavior or disregard for a set of rules, but our alienation from God, in which we live in a manner that denies God and God's lordship in our lives and our world.[4] Just as confession and repentance involve a willingness to take responsibility for our actions and the ways in which we have hurt others or ourselves, they also involve a regular intentional realignment of our lives in the light of God's desires for us; they are a recognition that God's narrative is different than and often diametrically opposed to the narrative of the world and the narratives by which so much of our daily lives are ordered. Repentance involves the regular acknowledgment that the operative social imaginary

3. Sumner, "You Have Not Yet Considered," 261–73.

4. "The heart of the confession is found in 6a: 'Against you, you only, I have sinned.' Some commentators (see the summaries in Perowne, 415; Gunkel, 222) have noted the absence of any confession of sin against other human beings and have assumed that such awareness is missing from the confession. But other OT passages make it clear that from an early time in Israel sins against persons were believed to be sins against God (Kraus, 543); see 2 Sam 12:9, 10, 13; Gen 39:9; Prov 14:31; 17:5. Violation of the commandments of God is construed as sin against God himself (Kraus, 544; Weiser, 403)." Tate, *Psalms 51–100*, 17.

of our culture (and our lives) is false: It is a mirage insofar as it is an endeavor to create and sustain an understanding of the world and a way of living in the world that does not allow for God or God's intentions for us. And this brings us back to the tendency to root pastoral theology in the social sciences and to narrow pastoral theology to a therapeutic understanding of pastoral care in line with the work of Anton Boisen and the development of Clinical Pastoral Education.

Counseling is such an important a part of pastoral theology that some would simply equate the latter term with the former. Yet this results in a corresponding narrowing and diminishment of the significance of both pastoral care and pastoral theology within the church. This dynamic plays out in several ways: First, pastoral theology has become synonymous with pastoral care to the neglect of the breadth of the many disciplines that are part of pastoral theology. Second, a focus on counseling has tended almost inevitably toward the professionalization of pastoral care, retaining little room or understanding for the way in which the gathered community can and should play a significant role in caring for the needs of those within and beyond the community. So, for example, we see the development of streams of counseling and psychotherapy within seminaries as alternate paths for training for ministry, where the graduates envision a career that is independent of the church proper. In this way, the potential benefits resulting from developments in secular schools of psychological healing are lost in the church, and church leaders are often reticent or ill-equipped to direct people to appropriate professionals.

Third, the shift toward professional practices of psychotherapy and counseling and the requirements of accreditation has in turn resulted in the displacement of the theological from pastoral theology. An assumption has arisen that practitioners should keep their own faith or theological persuasion distinct from the practice of pastoral care. As we noted in the opening chapter, there are multiple reasons why pastoral theology has been informed by the social sciences rather than theology, but here it is of particular note that the subsequent professionalization of pastoral care carries with it a displacement of Christian theology. All efforts at self-improvement or endeavors to deal with difficult issues in our lives, including addiction or other elements of healing, are at best partial if they do not take into account the root problem, which is human alienation from God. However, once this foundational truth is in place, we have things to learn from the counseling arts, and thus pastoral theology is called to a robust dialogue with these forms of secular therapy.

Speaking about our struggles and regrets and hearing a word of comfort in reply are elements common to both the counseling arts and Christian ministry (and that is one reason why we are dealing with the therapeutic at this point in our book). But it is equally clear that in Christian worship, actions of confession and absolution are placed in a wider, older, and more decisive context than that of the therapeutic. Here the order of the eucharistic service is instructive. Our struggles and regrets are offered to God. We do this collectively, as a people. Then a definitive word of divine forgiveness is spoken to us. Absolution makes a decisive difference: Properly understood, it cannot be absorbed into a purely psychological framework. As a result we can greet one another in peace, and proceed to bring our offering (Matt 5).

Let us consider in more depth what this implies about how we understand the human being—that is, about theological anthropology. That we are wounded, wandering, at a loss, out of sync (put it as you will), and need an intervention is a shared assumption across all the healing arts. But secular accounts of the human bracket out the very assumption of the divine which is the starting point for liturgical and theological speech. And once God is bracketed, then other meanings are excluded as well. "Sin" refers to our being guilty before God, not just in our self-apprehension. "Forgiveness" is more than making peace with an acquaintance or dealing with turbulent feelings; it implies having one's relationship to God changed. Here the divergence between social imaginaries in our culture is most stark. And as for the therapeutic, we are speaking not only of the practice of counseling itself, but of one of the dominant themes in our secular imaginary as a whole, and a rival way of understanding the human being per se.

ABSOLUTION AND JUSTIFICATION

At the heart of the interchange that is confession and absolution is the pronouncing of the latter by the presbyter. The church does not understand him or her to say these words as if they came from their own powers. They are charged to say them by the risen Christ, as his ambassadors given to speak his word (John 20:23). It is spoken to the penitent, and as such is not merely an aspiration, but an event, a declaration of fact. (In this way it is the same as the pronouncing of absolution in private confession, which closes the matter and cannot and should not be brought up again—it has been "put away.") To be sure, the description of the life of the converted is always dialectical insofar as we are "already" hidden in Christ with God,[5] although we continue to struggle here and are "not yet" free totally of the old Adam.[6] These perspectives do not compromise the decisiveness of God's act on our behalf in Christ. The absolution requires the act of addressing the penitent, for otherwise it would remain another thought in his or her mind, liable to the changeability and manipulability of all our internal life. It comes from without, and as such is heard.[7] Again, this does not depend on the inherent powers of the priest to utter it, but rather on the word which he or she has been authorized to speak.

It must also be noted that confession and absolution are acts of the community of faith which affect the whole. They are to be celebrated even though confession's inner content is somber. This was clear in the early church, where penitents were isolated from the community so that, after sufficient time (longer than we would imagine), they could be restored to the community. In the Middle Ages, penitence came to be offered to individuals, and the rite carved out of the liturgy as a separate sacramental act (and the accompanying arts of spiritual diagnosis developed, for example, in the Celtic Church), but the larger body was still implicitly in view. During the Reformation a stress on bringing one's sins before one's fellow Christians came to the fore.[8] While reconciliation is available as a rite for individuals, this element of the collective, as well as its celebration, remains as its tacit premise.

Here the philosophical category of the performative can inform our understanding.[9] There are words whose utterance does things. The world is different thereafter. Hence the function they perform is, according to analytic philosophers, different from that of statements which describe, order, or imagine, for example. Our point here is simply to note by way of analogy how different kinds of words can do radically different tasks. This offers a good segue to the manner in which theology understands the pronouncing of the word of absolution (and as a result, how it can aid in understanding other words aimed at healing). The word of absolution is God's. The word is spoken and what it says comes into being, not just

5. Col 3:3.

6. This dialectical quality is the point of the *simul justus et peccator* motto.

7. Hence the Lutheran emphasis on *fides ex auditu*: faith from hearing (citing Rom 10:17).

8. Dietrich Bonhoeffer retains this Lutheran emphasis in his *Life Together*.

9. Austin, *How to Do Things with Words*.

by social understanding, but ultimately because it is spoken by Christ, whose Word itself creates and redeems. It is spoken to us "while we were yet sinners," and as God's word it does what it says. These beliefs are constitutive of the Christian social imaginary. In this event and this from-beyond-oneself quality, absolution is a fitting sacramental sign for the wider category of justification. The verb behind the Greek word for justification includes the active meaning of "putting in the right," so that the noun in turn means "the state of being put in the right," which has a different connotation than the English word *righteousness*.[10]

This performative understanding of the pronouncing of absolution is consistent with a Reformation understanding of justification, but it is also open to misunderstanding. The contrast it assumes is that between divine and human agency. This is not to say that there is not human agency galore in the life of the church, thoroughly laced with sin. The church as a whole is also *simul justa et peccator*. The speaker of the absolution is a sinner, as is the body of the faithful to which he or she speaks. So its practice can indeed corrupt their purpose, consciously or unconsciously.[11] But just the same, God is capable of making himself heard, and doing his work, in spite of us![12] Secondly, we do well to note that this word is spoken to the faithful gathered (though also available to the individual penitent). The body needs forgiving, and disciplines like sociology and history help us to see the how.[13] Third and finally, we need to remember that the doctrine of justification does not obviate the need for a doctrine of sanctification, but on the contrary assumes it. As the forgiven we strive imperfectly, gradually, to address wrongs, to bind up wounds, etc.[14] The spoken word is free, but at work in the body of Christ it must take on embodied form, for it is spoken, after all, of men and women of flesh and blood.[15] We are indeed to be "ambassadors of reconciliation" (2 Cor 5:20),[16] though the word we bring has its own power and mandate (John 20:22–23).

10. *Dikaioun* and *dikaiosune* in Greek.

11. Winner, *Dangers of Christian Practice.*

12. This assumes the eschatological perspective found throughout this work, which Jones actually contrasts with what he calls "therapeutic forgiveness" (of the "I'm okay, you're okay" type). See Jones, *Embodying Forgiveness*, 35–69.

13. Coutts, *Shared Mercy.*

14. Katongole and Rice, *Reconciling All Things.*

15. Jones, *Embodying Forgiveness.*

16. Myers and Enns, *Ambassadors of Reconciliation.*

A note on ecumenical availability: But what about traditions which do not practice a formal confession and absolution? The central point at issue is still relevant. The unilateral nature of the practice and the claim that it makes a crucial difference are not rooted in the practice itself as a human act. Behind it is an understanding of the gospel and the word which proclaims it. The gospel is the proclamation of a prior reality: namely, what God has lovingly and effectively done on our behalf. While the hearing of it is of utmost importance (Rom 9), what is heard, the news of the finished work of Christ (which is prior, complete, sufficient, and from beyond us) is what sets it apart uniquely. In short, the agent heard is the Word himself who speaks, and what he says (creation, redemption, consummation) comes into being. In the same way, one may notice in an "ecumenically available" document like *Baptism, Eucharist and Ministry* that what Jesus had already done in his death and resurrection preceded discussion of the sacrament and its different understandings.

This explication is indeed ecumenically shared (by Roman Catholics too, as the joint statement on justification made clear).[17] In other words, what we have said about the logic of absolution is, in the worship of many evangelical churches, lodged in how the proclamatory nature of preaching, praying, and blessing is understood. Because of the gospel, these, too, have a performative aspect. And of course the saving work on which the pronouncement depends is our common inheritance! From an ecumenical point of view, the practice of absolution serves to make this wider reality especially clear. One might say, as Ramsey did notably, that a catholic practice is best understood as it conveys evangelical (in the sense of gospel-bearing) content.[18]

Although the debate over justification and sanctification led to mutual condemnations (*Anathemas*) in the Reformation, modern ecumenical perspectives have converged with startling agreements. These have built on several ideas, one being the idea of the fruits that grow from being set right, though not fully mature until the eschaton.[19] Another key reason for this convergence is the insight that different images can provide complementary and non-contradictory insights. Justification is infused into our hearts, as love looks at the event and its consequence

17. For example, the Lutheran World Federation and the Roman Catholic Church, "Joint Declaration on the Doctrine of Justification," October 31, 1999.

18. Ramsey, *Gospel and the Catholic Church.*

19. Luther is happy to talk about works as fruits. We might compare the Catholic distinction around concupiscence.

from our side, while imputed has to do with the divine act itself. The action of God is, from beginning to end, in the forefront.[20] While the word *grace* has a considerable and nuanced semantic range,[21] this element of God's action which precedes[22] and prevails is implied in it. Paul emphasizes that "while we were yet sinners" God intervened for us in Christ so that he might bring about our restoration (Rom 5:8–10). Hence it is an act distinguishable from ours. His saying it makes it so, as with the creation itself. In the technical language of the Reformation it is imputed—put in us—so that we have now been given the status we will have on the last day.

Our reason for retracing this somewhat technical history is that this decisive "spoken from outside" quality of justification finds its sacramental correspondence in the word of absolution uttered to us by the ordained. And yet the ways of describing this unilateral event in terms of growth and the virtues open a space for talking about how God's grace does its work over time within us, as "sanctification." While spiritual growth and the virtues are not synonymous with secular descriptions of healing, they do help us to imagine how these latter descriptions could have a role distinct from, subordinate to, and illuminative of the prior and sovereign act of God. So much of Christian discourse, including but not limited to worship, has to do with this work of sanctification in and through us, but all such talk presumes the prior justifying Word of Christ. God can work in and through us because he takes the initiative first to work upon, and even in spite of, us.

In short, justification (and by implication the act of absolution) is shorthand for a wider principle in Christian theology. It bolsters the claim that God's grace both precedes and prevails in the midst of all our own efforts in the world. Thus it confirms what healing, understood in more immanent terms, cannot: reconciliation beyond and in spite of ourselves. God's grace also has the power to show its effects on this still fallen realm and upon us, its inhabitants. To describe such effects, Christians have borrowed secular terminology ("despoiling the Egyptians" as a prime example in St. Augustine[23]) to account for the nature and the

20. This remains no less true even when its original application is the relation of Jews and gentiles, as N. T. Wright has rightly shown; see, e.g., *Justification; Jesus and the Victory of God.*

21. Barclay, *Paul and the Gift.*

22. Hence the technical word *prevenience.*

23. Augustine, *De doctrina Christiana*, 2.40.

transformation of the human soul. Justification takes pride of place, and yet it opens a subsequent space for borrowed illustrative accounts of the means through which God continues to work through time in us—that is, forms of sanctification. These accounts presume a fruitful conversation with secular schools of therapy. Theological distinctiveness need not and should not mean being closed to conversation with our intellectual neighbors.

SIN, GUILT, AND WOUNDEDNESS

The justifying work of God addresses our condition of being guilty before God; by contrast, the arts of psychological healing address our condition as wounded. As we have already made clear, these key terms come from different disciplines, although they are not unrelated to one another. To suppose that they are somehow equivalent would, as we have indicated, evacuate theology of its unique message and make pastoral care a form of secular therapy fitted out with some ancient metaphors. So we need to articulate in more detail the proper relationship between these contrasting but interrelated terms: between being guilty before God and being wounded.

We do well to examine the question twice: once from each direction, as it were. We might begin first from the theological side. Consider someone from a home of neglect or abuse who mistreats his children: His family history shows the same perpetuation we see in the biblical theme of the sins of the fathers visited on the third or fourth generation (or in the plots of Greek tragedies). In other words, there is contained within the idea of sin the victimhood of the sinner, but he or she is at the same time a perpetrator. In our sin we are both at once. Ours is a single, complex agency, so that attributing guilt separately and solely to one agent or generation is difficult. Father and son can live within one another, as do their respective guilts.

This is more than a matter of spreading the blame among all those involved in the tragedy of human relations. It also perceives that the human heart misuses its victimhood, making of it an excuse. We actively participate in the turning of our victimhood into perpetration. Adam thought himself a victim, what with that arbitrary rule God placed on him (Gen 3:12). Cain, too, had a grievance, and ever since the idolater makes of his own yearning and need the occasion for grasping control and self-elevation. In other words, theology at once sees that guilt ultimately lies with Adam—with humanity as a whole—and yet refuses to obscure the real part which each human being has in this tragic drama, which no simple blame-shifting toward our all-too-real woundedness will do away with.

And what about considering the matter from the other side, from the healing arts? There, we assume the bracketing of explanations that are beyond the immanent terms of psychological explanation itself. Yet sometimes these arts inch close to the divine chasm, perhaps in the question of radical evil, or of one's ultimate destination. The healing arts cannot pronounce absolution, which is to say they cannot fundamentally resolve the problem of the human urge for rebellion or harm.[24] A therapist friend has told me (George) that many clients ultimately long for the effective word of forgiveness.

In spite of this limit, secular healing arts do have articulate things to say about family systems and about taking responsibility. They, too, know something of the two-sidedness of the human heart, but only within the terms of their own delineated domains of description. The interplay between collective and individual may be found here, too, but the "mystery of iniquity" remains. Even while acknowledging their own limits, these arts tacitly attest to the qualitative difference of grace.

The area where the gap between guilt before God and human woundedness[25] is most nearly closed may be in those more extreme conditions in which human capacity and agency themselves are compromised. These include, for example, addiction and extreme sociopathy, where agency and empathy are called into question; the functioning of these qualities is assumed if one is to be able to recognize wounds but also take responsibility for the concomitant wrong. An excellent study of the question of the nature of sin at the boundary with psychology and in relation to agency is Alistair McFadyen's *Bound to Sin*.[26] In the case of addiction, therapy can acknowledge the effectiveness of a group like AA, although its language places powerlessness and responsibility cheek to jowl with one another. McFadyen argues that there at the boundary, therapy can see its limits, and ought at least to note the explanatory

24. See Dostoevsky, *Notes from Underground*.

25. The popular contemporary psychologist Brené Brown has been articulate in describing a similar dialectic around shame.

26. McFadyen, *Bound to Sin*.

power of the vocabulary of sin in coming to terms with an event like the Holocaust or child abuse.

McFadyen also uses the term "concrete idolatry" to explain what is going on with an addict who will sacrifice everything he holds dear for the sake of his addiction. This is a negative image of worship: Again, a religious word brings explanatory aid to a boundary reality. Such conditions shed light on the relation and the distinction between "guilty before God" and "wounded." (This is one reason why ministry to addicts is so important in the life of the church. One might say that many churches have, in their basements on Thursday nights, amid AA banners with self-help slogans, a reminder of the vocabulary of sin and redemption as well as the grass-roots empowerment of the laity.)[27]

PASTORAL THEOLOGY AND THE HEALING ARTS

Once these central theological distinctives are in place, we are in a position to have our fruitful conversation with the secular healing arts. We do well to assume that humans must be understood holistically, as ensouled bodies, and as individuals who are irremovably social, whose memories, wills, and relationships are knit together in such a way that each affects the others. Put most simply, the various types or schools of healing prioritize one aspect or another as central, or as most patent of improvement. What they all share is the goal of helping move the client from their own despondency to claim their own agency, in spite of their woundedness (which, again, is not inconsistent with the action of the divine agency, operating as it does on a different plane). While an individual may need to choose one particular kind of help, we cannot but step back and observe that they are best seen together and complementary, consistent with an embodied and social anthropology.

At the outset we need to distinguish types of therapy which do or do not have some relation to religious belief. The former include therapies that make direct appeal to Christian resources, such as pastoral counseling as a para-church reality (Clinical Pastoral Education, chaplaincy, etc.) and the help offered by pastors and trained lay ministers in congregations which may borrow from such sources and guide members toward sources of help. Given the prominence of psychological terms and categories in

27. See *Alcoholics Anonymous*, first published in 1939.

our culture at large, we can readily see the importance of such ministries gaining clarity about the kind of help they are offering.

As we described earlier in the treatment of Hunsinger's *Theology and Pastoral Counseling*,[28] the psychological understanding must be taken up and transposed into the theological, and not vice versa. The two kinds of insights are not on the same plane. At the end of the day, pastoral theology must have an asymmetrical relationship with secular counseling (or with appeal to secular insights in one and the same ministry). This is the witness of the Letter to the Ephesians, which makes clear in chapter 2 that our reconciliation to one another is the anticipated result of God having first reconciled us to himself in Christ.

We can enumerate the types of secular therapy with special reference to the aspect or part of the admittedly holistic human person each prioritizes. The first kind of therapy looks within, to our inner experience. It is especially interested in past events, for example in our early lives, and the way that these continue to exert an influence on our present emotional life. Freudian analysis is the famous pioneer, and while classic psychoanalysis may now have become rare, its continued influence on the field as a whole cannot be denied. The very idea of an unconscious self which drives our conscious decisions and feelings and has its own laws was groundbreaking, as was the idea of the libido as driving force.[29] The internal power of these early attachments can be seen in the categories of transference and counter-transference with which the therapist works.

From this starting point a number of developments and emendations may be identified. The school of object relations emphasized that the crucial feature of early psychological development was the relationship between infant and mother. Erik Erikson's stages of development included the Freudian ones, but delineated more stages that must be traversed throughout a maturing life. Jungian analysis found in the unconscious universal archetypes by which personal emotional styles could be generalized. In each case, the mode of therapy extends or upends the

28. Hunsinger, *Theology and Pastoral Counseling*. See our treatment of her book in chapter 1.

29. We can note how this view converges with an Augustinian view of the determinative force of our loves, and the basic human distortion of the same. Late in his life, and in a manner evocative for theology, Freud speculated about a third drive oriented toward *thanatos*, death. (His own impending death and the imminent devolution of European culture and Holocaust must have influenced him). See Freud, *Beyond the Pleasure Principle*.

inherited Freudian categories, but its introspective experiential element may still be traced.

A second general school of therapy has turned deliberately toward the cognitive. This does not deny the reality of depth insights and inner dynamics, but asks different questions such as: What can I readily change? How can I improve my situation here and now? This school is action- and evidence-based and was influenced by the behaviorism of such figures as Pavlov and Skinner. It is rooted in the belief that who people are and what they really think can best be revealed by observing what they do. Habits can then be reinforced with positive and negative inputs. One version of this school a generation ago was called Reality Therapy, and such is its underlying philosophical claim.[30] The general category of the cognitive can take another turn when the decision called for has to do with one's general life orientation, akin to a philosophy. One could cite Frankl's Logotherapy, in which a person decides about the larger framework of meaning by which they will live.[31]

A third type of therapy looks not within the patient, nor at his or her behavior, but rather between the patient and the others with whom he or she has important relationships. We have already mentioned how object relations allowed insight into not just the inner experience, but early life attachment itself. One thinks readily of the usefulness of these insights for couples or family therapy. Focusing on significant relationships and communications within them can lead to strategies for improved insight or behavior on the part of those involved.[32]

Our interior, our behaviors, or our relationships: in addition to these, a fourth general category of therapy looks at the somatic dimension, or expression of human wounds. We are psychosomatic unities, and advances have been made on a number of medical research fronts (psychopharmaceutics, neuroscience, etc.). One may think here of frontiers like sensory motor dimensions of trauma,[33] the role of the vagal nerve in fight

30. Glasser, *Reality Therapy*.

31. Frankl, *Man's Search for Meaning*. A similar trajectory may be found in existential or Gestalt therapy. Another might be narrative therapy in which the person retells their tale in a coherent and meaningful way. This trajectory of a search for meaning has some of its roots in ancient philosophy, but also interacted with the 1960s counterculture.

32. A fifth type of therapy, akin to the relational, might be called the liberative. It is neo-Marxist in orientation and thus akin to liberation theology. It has value as a source of analysis and critique, but as an account of the human person per se is reductionist.

33. Ogden and Fisher, *Sensorimotor Psychotherapy*.

or flight, etc.[34] Despite the dangers of reductionism or financially driven therapy shortcuts,[35] such therapies remind us how our experiences are encrypted in our bodies themselves.[36] In so doing, they help overcome inherited but overlooked dualisms in our approach to therapy. In some ways, therapy here comes full circle, since Freud himself was originally a neurologist with a physicalist view of the working of the human brain.

Let us return to our starting point. Pastoral theology allows us to view the panoply of therapies together and so to see their complementarity, or at least their non-contradictory aspects. Taken together, we can see the distress of the human being and the longing for help from angles which give a better, holistic picture of human beings as they are before God. Humans possess memories, wills, relations, and bodies, each and all of which may be wounded and patent of healing. Pastoral theology reflects on how these therapies, placed in the wider worldview and fellowship of the church, could cooperate in the healing work of the Holy Spirit. In other words, these arts can be helpful for a Christian in the worshiping context of the church. But these therapies on their own assume a movement toward human wholeness, maturity, and flourishing in their own right, and in a value-free manner. A Christian vision will find this wanting. Theology can take such schools up into its vision, but cannot understand the schools in themselves as providing sufficient accounts of healing. As Christians, "nothing human is alien to" us,[37] yet these human systems as such are limited, and hence deficient. We should in this regard note the larger framework of our survey: the eucharistic way of the Christian life. This has a vision of ultimate flourishing at its very center. Christ takes up the few loaves and fishes of our own efforts and multiplies them. He is himself the telos toward which these arts now can sub-serve.

The therapies mentioned here not only have a general relationship to the Christian life, but some are also close cognates to self-consciously Christian ministries of spiritual healing.[38] These make use of psychological categories more directly, but for the purposes of distinctly Christian

34. Porges, *Polyvagal Theory*.

35. The limits of long-term medication use is an open question in the discipline.

36. We can compare studies of the effects of meditation on brainwaves to the popularity of mindfulness in contemporary therapy.

37. From the Latin comic author Terence (Publius Terentius Afer), *Heauton Timorumenos* 1.1.77.

38. Kelsey, *Healing and Christianity*. The Order of St. Luke is also a good resource.

practices and thus as reminders of the more comprehensive meaning of healing.[39] It becomes crucial to help parishioners to distinguish these from therapy per se, and to bring them into relation with the central affirmations of our faith, one of which is that we are headed for our ultimate healing on the last day (Rev 21:4, 22:2). Again, in worship we bring "ourselves, our souls and bodies"—that is, our need for healing and our partial remedies—as we are oriented toward that last day to which they witness. The ministry of healing is real because the Healer whose word we bring is real. But whenever the subject is spiritual power we must immediately differentiate our agency from God's. This leads us back to the place where we started: the doctrine of justification.

Let us close this chapter with a coda in a different key.

Justification indeed reminds us of that which only the church has to offer, in contrast to any other healing or helping endeavor: namely, the Word of Christ which makes us forgiven. But we must be careful to note what this "having" is and isn't. A kind of triumphalism might result. The justifying word does not belong to the church to use as it wills. Rather, God, by his gracious will, has placed it there for his purposes. It is only by means of the forgiveness of the church's sins that the church has the word of forgiveness to pronounce. Thus justification, although found in the church, stands over against the church's presumption and failure.

Most who have taken the church's ministry seriously are deeply disappointed sooner or later. The priest midway through his or her decades of ministry, or the young convert after a year of throwing himself or herself into service, or the Cursillista on fire for Christ now back in his or her sleepy or conflicted parish, or the immigrant who finds in the pew similar prejudices as in the world at large—what do they, and we, do with our disappointment? The first answer, easy and hard, is humility, for in the moment of being bereft of the Spirit's power we, too, have met the enemy and they are us. Upon further reflection the question comes to this: Why would the Lord commit his gospel to a disorderly lot like this, including me? The question goes back to Jesus's seemingly faulty disciple selection process. The Lord, the One who has *exousia*, "authority," deigns to be present among us in powerlessness. This is clearly so in persecuted churches, and now more evidently so in our post-Constantinian

39. For styles of prayer see Thornton, *English Spirituality*. A contemporary typology is derived from the thought of Richard Rohr. Insofar as he is a Jungian, his work has a gnostic tinge which makes its pastoral appropriation problematic.

situation.[40] We are reminded not to think of power, not least in worship, in worldly terms.

The point is this: We need to think theologically about how the Lord submits himself to powerlessness in his body the church in the world today, and bring this question into contact with our own sense of disappointment. It is not only a surprise that Christ would use such a church, but even more so that he would identify himself with it and die for it. As disciples, we echo the refrain "Where shall we go? You have the words of life" (John 6:68). This cannot be an excuse for corruption, sloth, or lukewarmness. Instead, it must be an occasion to measure the tower (Luke 14:28–30) and ask ourselves what a postmodern congregation following the path of the crucified looks like. We, as ministers of the divinely powerful word of absolution, need to find solidarity in this powerlessness with the struggle of those who come to us in pain and confusion, together with the gracious confidence that here may be found the doorway to a "peace the world cannot give" (John 14:27). On such an occasion we recall where power comes from and whose it is. This following of the crucified one will be particularly important in an era in which the church's prospects are in many places and ways humbled. In the liturgy, the Confession precedes the Peace, and so must include in our hearts a will to be reconciled, for Jesus says this must take place before we would approach the altar. To this latter movement we now turn our attention.[41]

40. See the poetry and later reflections of Bonhoeffer in *Letters and Papers from Prison*.

41. Here we see the inherent relationship between our spirituality and ministries of reconciliation for wrongs past by repentance and truth-telling, for example between races in South Africa and North America between black and white, and in repairing the wounds inflicted among Indigenous peoples in residential schools.

8

Responding to God's Gracious Word

The Offering

THE OFFERING OF BREAD, WINE, and the collection of gifts are a physical (practical) way of offering "ourselves, our souls and bodies"[1] in grateful response to God's grace. This lies at the heart of a theology of the stewardship of creation, wealth, and bodily life together. Our lives, our work, and our families are transformed as they are offered and directed toward God. Ministries of the life-cycle may be understood in this way too. These offerings, underpinning a reordering of our lives, are essential to congregational life and are basic elements in any study of pastoral theology.

The flight to Kingfisher Lake, in the far northwest of the province of Ontario, Canada, took several hours out of Thunder Bay, and involved several stops in small villages along the way. At one point the wheels froze and had to be de-iced before we could take off again. Once I (George) arrived, I stayed in a room in the back of the country store. The next day at breakfast I heard stories from an old man about the complex art of trapping, which involved reading the subtle signs nature offered him. But I also heard about how it had become harder to interest the young in these skills, which require slow attention. Perhaps particularly when the young all carry smart phones.

I was visiting Kingfisher to teach and celebrate Holy Week, 2009. While there I heard about the services which had been previously available to those in need of help at the community center but were now

1. *Book of Common Prayer* (1979), 136.

discontinued. The mischief on Wall Street two thousand miles away had reverberated all the way to this small village in the True North. The globe was unified for ill in its greed and deception as well as, we hope, for good in the gospel. Indigenous people that I got to know were suffering at the further edges of a continent that gave them no mind, although the eldest there remembered what might have been of aid. The bishop in Kingfisher was Lydia Mamakwa; her vast diocese Mishamikoweesh was sparsely populated with small, isolated communities. The Anglican Church continues to have a significant impact in the North in spite of a checkered history. Several years later she gave one of the shortest and best commencement addresses I have ever heard: a description of braiding her grandmother's hair while the old woman sat on her bed in the twilight and quietly chanted Evening Prayer from the *Book of Common Prayer* in Oji-Cree. About unity and diversity there is little more to say.

We must once more at the outset bear in mind how we are to consider our offering. On the one hand the witness of the Reformation, elaborating on the articulation of St. Paul, is that we do not simply or directly make any such thing. Rather we recall that the Eucharist as a whole is a celebration of the "one oblation of himself once offered" of Christ, and the grammar of oblation permits us to speak of our own activities only as a "sacrifice of praise and thanksgiving."[2] In short, the emphasis is not on us and what we might bring, but on the One who always goes before us and to whom our efforts are at best a partial response. Each of the subdisciplines considered in this chapter is different from and consequent upon the prior divine offering upon which the Eucharist is based. This grammar of grace and response underlies everything we will subsequently say.

Let us linger over this premise a moment longer. Most denominations have some form of offering; I (George) have heard it said that the collection is the most widespread of all practices in the universe of religions. To be sure, not all bring elements of the Eucharist (the bread and the wine) forward as a part of the offertory—indeed, not all Anglican Churches do so. But the central point of this chapter stands, namely that in the grammar of Christian faith our offering of "ourselves, our souls and bodies" is always a response in gratitude to what God has already, and sufficiently, done. All Christian traditions, likewise, understand human activities and concerns such as ecology, labor, marriage, etc., as

2. *Book of Common Prayer* (1979), 82–83.

responses to who God is and what God has done in us and for us. As a result, insofar as everything that follows is understood under the rubric of "Christian life as gratitude," all of what follows has immediate relevance across Christian traditions.

BORROWING FROM SECULAR DISCIPLINES

Here in the middle of things at the offertory, let us think about the question basic to all pastoral theology: How may we borrow from and offer back for the benefit of our non-Christian neighbor? By the Christian imaginary we understand that we are in the midst of the nations as exiles, heralds, and friends, in this time of the mission of the church to the nations in the wake of the resurrection of Jesus. Led by people like Lesslie Newbigin in the late twentieth century and continuing into the twenty-first century is a renewed understanding that mission is fundamental to the identity of the church, rather than just one element of its life. Thus, we can learn from the paradigmatic experience of the cross-cultural missionary. First, the missionary must have a deep and sincere empathy and affection for that culture (while remembering that he or she is not a native). Second, the missionary must proclaim the whole counsel of God: the parts that seem readily consonant and assimilable (whether they are to be offered first is a strategic question) as well as the parts that represent a potential "stone of stumbling" to their hosts and neighbors. Doing both simultaneously and convincingly is the challenge of the pastoral vocation. Only when appreciated and transformed can the gifts of that place and time be offered to Christ so as to be a "sacrifice of praise and thanksgiving" (so Rom 12:1–2) and a response of gratitude. This appreciation and transformation, and how we are to live into it, has everything to do with the concept of the Christian social imaginary presented in detail earlier in this book.

To this may be added a third point: The nations are by their nature widely diverse and distinct, as are their gifts, challenges, and circumstances. This array is not contrary to God's will, for we recall that there existed many cities and nations prior to the Tower of Babel and the resulting confusion of tongues described in Genesis chapter 11. This original diversity begins to be healed at Pentecost, yet without erasing the distinctiveness of differences, so as to be finally put right as exhibited in the polyphonic hymn of the nations (diversity in unity) before the throne in Rev 5.

As we also indicated at the outset, pastoral theology has consisted largely of a profusion of subdisciplines addressing the needs and concerns of a profusion of specific subgroups and a great variety of types of congregations. We have in mind here not just worship practices and principles, but all the vocations and ministries which are offered in a response of praise and thanksgiving to Christ on behalf of fellow Christians and for the life of the world. In each case, expertise from the secular realm has been borrowed so as to shed light on the ministry of the church. Diversity may also be found both in how these studies are conducted and among whom, as well as the way in which they might then be offered back to God. For this reason, it is hard to consider them all together or to do justice to the breadth of issues to be considered; this chapter therefore runs the risk of seeming a hodge-podge. The analogy of the missionary aids us in the task of synthesis, for in each case elements of empathy and of challenge, welcome, and transformation can be identified.

What difference does this perspective of empathetic transformation make as we turn to these specific subdisciplines? There is not one single answer to this question. In the case of addiction ministry, a name is added at the altar of the "unknown God" (Acts 17). In the case of stewardship, the arts of listening remain vital, but the human desire for a monument is called into question. In the case of conflict, the identification of complex dynamics is helpful, but distinctly Christian virtues and God's place in the midst of our struggles also have their say. More generally, we can say that each wisdom-based practical account comes into dialogue with the ultimate end of the gospel, and some dissonance results from the "transvaluation of values." Exposing secular wisdom to the light of the Christian telos deepens, complements, revises, or transposes its insights, so that each case becomes a theology of culture in miniature.

THE SACRAMENTAL ACTION OF OFFERING

The place to start our conversation is with what actually happens at the offertory of the Eucharist in a typical congregation (we will use the term *Eucharist* rather than *communion* or *Lord's Supper* in this chapter to emphasize the thanksgiving that is at the heart of this celebration). The elements, bread and wine, are placed on the table, sometimes after having been brought forward by lay people. Meanwhile, a collection is taken up and also brought forward. The first action involves the fruits of the earth and underscores the close connection between creation and redemption in the celebration of the sacrament. The second more closely denotes the human sphere and evokes a secular economy in relation to the *oikonomia* of salvation, of which the sacrament is an efficacious sign. We are aware that the world is not under our control and even we ourselves as creatures also come before the Lord. In other words, these spheres, although distinct in our minds, are both under his lordship as our Creator and Redeemer.

At the same time, this section notably evokes three sensitive and urgent areas of ministry in our time. One might say that they all display our outsized sense of our own powers and autonomy—our Promethean side—and as such, require from us a moment of contrition. We have not been stewards of creation, and now have come to realize that our very existence is threatened. Similarly, we have in the modern era seen world economies lurch from corrupt and oppressive collectivisms to a manipulative market economy which has exacerbated iniquities. Catholic social teaching has succeeded in offering a balanced and prophetic word to both.[3] That these twin distortions to our stewardship appear together is no accident. The church can claim expertise neither in climate science nor in economics, but it can, in hearing the word of God, offer a counter-witness in both arenas. In other words, what makes the church's witness different from social activism (which has its valid place in the secular realm) is its ability to place these issues in relation to the doctrines of creation, sin, and redemption. And as to the third area of essential ministry, marriage, in our hyper-sexualized and contested culture there is special need for counter-witness that reveals the divine generosity "from the beginning" (Mark 9:4) and the deeper mystery of "Christ and his church" (Eph 5:32).

Let us then turn first to a Christian theology of ecology. Sustainability is related to humility and to a sense of our place in the created order and our vocation of care (here especially we may refer to Gen 2:15). Biodiversity is related to our handing off of the environment to succeeding generations; to our vocation as "parents" in an extended sense.[4] For example, a witness against pollution resulting from extraction industries is a vocation where creation and economics coincide—often workers

3. Schlag, *Handbook of Catholic Social Teaching.*

4. Maclaurin and Sterelny, *What Is Biodiversity?*

are exposed to risks, and countries suffer damage to their lands. In the Global South, battling erosion through the planting of trees is a vocation equally at the intersection of creation and economics.[5] Finally, we can catalogue the ways in which disregard of the created order has distorted our sense of ourselves: our theological anthropology.[6] We have lost a sense of our bodily life, especially in relation to procreation, birth, and death, as well as of time. A vocation of attention to our place in the created order reminds us what people are for.[7] We cannot imagine a return to some mythological bucolic time but must make use of the wisdom of contemporary ecological science for the sake of self-restraint and a greater sense of our own welfare over the long haul.[8]

STEWARDSHIP

If we turn to the question of stewardship, in the economic sense it is clear that money has come to mean something else to us, culturally. Even as Christians we sometimes have more infrastructure to maintain than we would wish. If money is our idol, generosity conversely assumes a major role in the practice of discipleship. We monetize everything, but in contrast, we need to transvalue money itself. (Obviously prosperity gospels are a corruption of this trajectory, often, understandably, in settings which lack the benefits of Western economies.) The deeper theological issue is that of flourishing itself. Sometimes success denotes blessing, but it needn't. We ought not to be surprised that where Aslan is now on the move, evidence of new life should be found. But it is a different matter to claim the converse: that blessing automatically shows God's favor. From there we are well on our way to works-righteousness. Yes, success may mean blessing, so long as we realize that there are different, harder kinds of flourishing as well.

5. This was an emphasis at Lambeth Conferences 2008 and 2022.

6. See Radner, *Time to Keep*.

7. Berry, *What Are People For?*

8. More could be said, here and in many places in this work, about the effect of romanticism on both the distortions and the renewal of theology. The excessive sense of ourselves and our own experience is a child of romanticism, but so is a sense of the importance of nature, however contrived it may have been at times. The sense of ecological wholeness cannot be mistaken for salvation, but it offers a salutary contrast to our present situation.

The collection for the saints in Jerusalem, the *locus classicus* for considerations of stewardship, was at once highly practical and utterly theological. It witnessed to the churches' oneness as well as their connection to the origin of the gospel. Jerusalem was the "mother church." This shared stewardship was associated with sharing both suffering as well as the global reach of the gospel from Jerusalem to the ends of the earth. Significantly, it does not come from abundance but resembles more the widow's mite. In short, its offering of money partakes of their understanding of both word and sacrament. It is a liturgical act in the fullest sense.

Most literature on stewardship seeks to glean what it can from the insights of secular philanthropy while restoring Christian giving to its theological roots. Sometimes it appeals to the individual's sense of vocation or an optimistic view of beatitude as a mentality of plenteousness. Clergy are inclined to list the parish's needs, and this honesty has the virtue of sharing the load but risks a downturn in support when one crisis or another passes. Throughout, the wider, corporate vocation of the body of Christ as seen first in the Jerusalem collection should never be far away, especially since this also raises questions about the contemporary meaning of money. How we understand and seek prosperity or flourishing is a question never far from all treatments of stewardship.

"THE WORK OF THE PEOPLE" (LITURGY) AND WORK

A primary kind of "sacrifice of praise and thanksgiving" the faithful might be most likely to bring with them as they gather is one most closely related to economics: their work. Worship itself was, in a Greek inheritance from their pagan neighbors, "the work of the people": liturgy the *ergon*, work, of the *laos*, the people.[9] This understanding would surely shed light on our own work individually. This is so large and important a topic that it is surprising how often it is overlooked or subsumed within a secular/sacred divide. We tend to think in terms of responsibilities lay people are willing to shoulder within the church itself, but what of their own labor? Understanding work in a Christian manner is a vital issue to many believers that is too often unexamined.

9. In ancient Athens the wealthy donated for the sake of the glory of the whole polis.

Our reflection begins as we consider the second chapter of Genesis. God placed Adam and then Eve in a fruitful garden to tend it, to enjoy one another, and to delight in naming the profusion of fellow creatures. Stewardship on behalf of God was delightful. But as a result of the fall, it became toil, with exhaustion and anxieties about survival, domination, and death in its train. The terms are thus set out: Work was stewardship but has become toil and awaits what it shall yet become as the story stretches forward. In other words, work is enmeshed at every stage in salvation history. The postmodern who feels as if he or she were on a treadmill experiences the ripple effects of our primal exile. The intention to render our work fulfilling or meaningful on our own is doomed, but it also is a portent and shadow of the hope for the restoration of stewardship and, as such, could be a *praeparatio evangelica.*

We need at this point to distinguish two obstacles for a theology and a spirituality of work, which although distinct, may reinforce one another. The first comes from the theological tradition: namely, the contrast between faith and works. We may seek to earn our own worth, or to make ourselves too busy to consider death. To be sure, the works Luther rebelled against were religious observances (most vividly in medieval Catholicism in Masses as *opus Dei*, the work of God). However, one might pursue works-righteousness in any domain of one's own will. To be sure, human work, now understood as vocation, was part of the solution for Luther. Work was viewed not in order to justify ourselves, but rather to place this significant part of our lives in relation to faith's imaginary, so as to see what is put "in our hand" anew as an aspect of discipleship. A great deal of writing on labor should be informed by the rubric of a Protestant theology of vocation: for example, advice for Christians in the marketplace.[10]

The second horizon for a Christian theology of work is a pervasive sense of alienation. This category goes back to Marx, although it would be hard to find anyone today who would really believe that it could be removed simply by a revolution in the means of production. This kind of critique is telling, even if Marx's naïve and atheistic remedy is not. A contemporary way to describe this alienation is commodification, whereby workers are reduced to things, assets, or resources. There is a considerable literature about how society might preserve its generation of vast wealth without the objectification, and so dehumanization, of

10. For example Stevens, *Work Matters.*

workers.[11] Alienation has been intensified and sometimes hidden by the dominance of technology, which is in no way neutral. We have internalized our own compulsive overworking, our addictions to distraction and illusion in social media and our moral torpor.[12] We must navigate today around both of these challenges in developing a practical theology of Christian work.

We need to begin where the Reformers did: namely, in placing our work more compellingly within a distinctly Christian social imaginary. To do so, it is helpful to borrow from Alasdair MacIntyre's definition of a "practice." This now popular term signifies the tacit dimension of a normative activity within a tradition.[13] Practice implies a narrative—it occurs someplace: namely in midstream of the life of a community with a past rendering who they are. It assumes certain virtues which the practice is performed to further (as opposed to producing extrinsic goods, even though they could be by-products). And finally it assumes that in all this, the community is going somewhere: that is, there is a telos.

When it comes to work in the post-modern predicament, practices of the church should be paradigmatically instructive for our labors in the world. By grace they would help us to see our efforts not primarily as toil, but as stewardship. Let us begin at the end, with the telos: the kingdom of God in Christ. We cannot bring it in, so it stands as a challenge to our works-righteousness. As such, it is also a comfort and a relief, since as much as we must work toward it, it is not ours to accomplish. Significant voices in a contemporary theology of work appeal to the retrieval of eschatology as both a spur and a challenge to our assumptions and efforts.[14] One task of preaching is setting the lives and work of the listening community against this horizon.

The anthropological category in dialogue with which a theology of work must operate would be play.[15] Play spawns culture. It can be serious or whimsical, but in both cases it has a cathartic effect: think of *Oedipus*

11. See, for example, Novak, *Spirit of Democratic Capitalism*; and for a critique, Sennett and Cobb, *Hidden Injuries of Class*.

12. The elegist for this condition is Byung-Chul Han; see, for example, *Burnout Society*.

13. We spoke earlier of Alasdair MacIntyre and his important place in the shaping of current understandings of pastoral theology. The fullest account is in MacIntyre, *Whose Justice? Which Rationality?*

14. The works of both Volf and his teacher Moltmann are interpreted and critiqued by Darrell Cosden in *A Theology of Work*.

15. The classic study is Huizinga, *Homo Ludens*.

Rex offered at the original Olympic games.[16] Play encompasses children's playgrounds and great sporting events (even though we have managed to commodify it almost completely!). It is the context of imagination, and holds the key to the door of dreams. It can be brought into the service of the gospel, as the seventeenth-century Anglicans understood when they permitted soccer on the village green after worship on the Lord's Day. It is viewed in contrast to work, for it does not render material benefit, although it requires concerted effort in a manner that absorbs us together into its world. Liturgy is also play insofar as it, too, is to be differentiated from work, and as that against which the week's workdays borrow their meaning. Here we should recall the Sabbath (from Gen 2:3), the original practice in contrast to work. Even the funeral, while hardly playful, has a place. It sings and processes, in anticipation of resurrection day, even as it pulls us up short in requiring us to remember our mortal selves and count our days. These practices offer, in our imaginary, a backdrop for work, reminding us of work's limits and pretensions. When our expectations of work are delimited and we understand it to be from God's hand, we can scatter our seed and build our house (Ps 127). We eat our resulting bread with the pleasure that the Preacher would have us enjoy.[17]

No subject is more freighted and contested in our culture than the third gift of creation in the foreground of our discussion: marriage. Its consideration requires here more extended treatment. Around this topic intersect choice, the givenness of our bodies, desire, the history of the relation of the sexes, and the most intimate claims we have on one another. Here is the most intense of cultural flashpoints. It is thus both especially surprising and important that marriage be set in its full theological meaning.

The *locus classicus* is Eph 5:22–33. Paul is speaking of the uniquely Christian calling of the husband and the wife, as he describes it in terms of mutual self-giving and self-surrender (itself a countercultural claim in the Hellenistic world). But he grounds this ecclesial meaning in the doctrine of creation. Then he goes on to say that it is a "*mysterion* (*sacramentum*) . . . of Christ and his church" (Eph 5:32). Marriage is an embodied symbol of Christ and his intimate relation to the church. It

16. We write this book amid justifiable anxiety about AI and the possible end of work. Others wonder if the machines might emerge into consciousness. But they will never play! Or pray for that matter, and that points toward an answer to the theological anthropology question.

17. Eccl 9:7.

informs and reminds us in regard to Christology and soteriology. The vocation of the married couple, in their difference and in their union, is to show this forth—to mirror this to the body of Christ. Husband and wife are important, first of all, for what their union says to the church: not about themselves, their needs, failings, and gifts, but rather about the church itself.[18] In this sense they resemble priests, of whom the tradition could speak in nuptial terms.[19] Grounding the theology of marriage in vocation in the service of Christology serves to frame and give order to all subsequent issues that must be dealt with. Far from avoiding urgent issues of the day, this theological perspective allows the latter to be addressed scripturally, charitably, and patiently.

Beginning with Eph 5:32, we realize how the image of Christ the bridegroom Messiah runs throughout the New Testament.[20] Because we are by grace called in the church into an intimate relationship with Christ,[21] marriage is a key metaphor for our destiny in the kingdom, where we will sit down to the "marriage feast of the Lamb" (Rev 21). This is one of the paradigmatic metaphors[22] for defining the goal toward which the church moves; another being the priest, and yet another the steward/prince. (Levering points out how these symbols overlap and complement one another, dramatized in the coronation of the bride and groom in Eastern Christian weddings.)[23]

It is no accident that all three of these symbols may be found in the Genesis creation account, where caring for the garden is stewardly, naming the creatures priestly, and being presented to one another conjugal. We are "in the image of God" with respect to all three, and we are so not

18. In Sumner, *Being Salt*, I explore this semiotic ecclesiology, in which various stations of life such as marriage, disability, and singleness speak to one's fellow Christians about who the church is. As to the last, Henri Nouwen likes to emphasize that singleness bespoke ultimate devotion to God alone. Hence this is the first meaning of monastic callings, which put in order other callings of intercession, asceticism, stability, etc.

19. This is found in Orthodox theologies of both.

20. This is shown with considerable detail by Matthew Levering in *Engaging the Doctrine of Marriage*. In chapter 3 he draws on the church fathers to show how Adam and Eve as a couple commit the original sin.

21. It is in this context that mystical literature, which is sometimes erotic, is best to be understood. The poetry of St. John of the Cross is the finest example.

22. We may cite here Barbour (see *Myths, Models, and Paradigms*) and through him the whole field of science and religion, which according to him, speak to one another as they both come to see the centrality of such metaphors or models to their enterprise.

23. Levering, *Engaging the Doctrine of Marriage*, ch. 6.

just as individuals, but yoked together.[24] (The point is not that only the married are "in the image," but rather that this relation helps to reveal who we are in relation to our Creator.) And these three symbols are conjoined at the end, where human beings are to celebrate the intimacy with God that they, his creatures, are graciously given and are henceforth to enjoy. But Genesis also makes it clear that we are yoked together, and yet fallen: Adam and Eve descended into recrimination and subjugation (Gen 3:16–19). Marriage first says something about who Christ is in relation to us (and who we shall be finally in relation to him), but it also must be redeemed by his grace. As with the church as a whole, so with marriage; it is a flawed vessel where the treasure is found (2 Cor 4:7).

At this point let us first offer a liturgical note and then a word of moral theological advice. We have so far considered marriage in relation to its intrinsic meaning, but we can only see this in contrast against our culture, and in particular, the ways in which it resists or is in contrast to the witness of Christian marriage. This countercultural dimension becomes clear as we consider the liturgy of marriage. First of all, the witness of marriage should be an anti-gnostic bulwark in the life of the church. It guarantees that God's gracious work in creation and redemption are held inseparably together. The twin goals of "mutual joy" and "procreation" are not to be severed, whether or not the granting of children should be God's will.[25] All impulses to turn the church into a human resource for psychological wellness, family values, or political action are impeded—the church is irreducibly bodily, inter-personal, and spiritual at one and the same time. And that bodiliness has a distinct form in the male and the female, which it retains in the wake of the bodily resurrection of Christ.[26] Secondly, the marriage rite is thoroughly covenantal. God has made a covenant with us by grace in Christ, and we are to witness to this by covenantal fidelity. This is a direct challenge to our propensity to turn everything into a contract characterized as a cost-benefit based transaction. "For better, for worse, for richer, for poorer, in sickness and in health" is an affront to all utilitarianism. The vow is a deliberate archaism, and as such speaks directly into modern culture. Thirdly, we may consider the aesthetic side of self-giving for the sake of mutual joy. The vows of marriage are folly to the world, which would think them reckless

24. This is where Barth's definition of the *imago* as the relation of man and woman comes into focus. He in turn was influenced by Buber's philosophy of "I–Thou."

25. See *Book of Common Prayer* (1979), 423.

26. O'Donovan, *Resurrection and Moral Order.*

in relation to the changes and chances of the future. In this contrarian sense, every marriage is something beautiful for God.[27]

This chapter seeks to expose an empathetic and serious correlation or dialogue between theology in service of the word of God and the congregation with its forms, gifts, and challenges. This means that while we need the clarity of beginning with marriage in the light of Christology, we cannot ignore the perplexities of the culture in which the flesh-and-blood members of the congregation live. Congregations and all their members (the pastor, too) are messy and complicated, and their lives are in flux. The pastor must navigate from the center (who is Christ) and yet welcome all, keeping the periphery open and taking seriously the struggles of those who come to him or her. In emotion as well as thought, the pastor must cleave to a "generous orthodoxy." In this book we are challenging a bifurcation of the pastoral and the theological, but this does not in itself remove the day-to-day tension between center and periphery.[28] In a time of great confusion this is a real and constant challenge for pastors. The closest to an answer one can offer is the virtue of prudence. One must discern the time in the narrative of the parishioner for patience and for advice when it seems it can be heard. One must be attentive to the factor of trauma beneath what people say and do in the present.[29] One must lead with patience and charity.

The theological depth and high calling of marriage stand in contrast to the daunting state of marriage in North America in our time (which is not so different from the rest of the Global North). (It should be noted as a preface that COVID actually made it slightly less likely that couples would get divorced, in spite of the stress involved, as they needed to lean on one another.) Statistics here can be helpful, if only as shock treatment. Half of all first marriages end in divorce, and the outcome for subsequent marriages is worse; two-thirds of all marriages end within forty years. While committed Christians are a quarter less likely to be divorced, the number remains high. These numbers are twice what they were fifty years ago. Outcomes are worse for those with less education and fewer

27. This motive opens onto a theology of the arts and aesthetics in general, all of which assume the countercultural possibility of a gracious intimacy with God.

28. This application of the image from set theory originated with the missiologist Paul Hiebert.

29. In trauma, too, mind and body cannot be severed. Its study is a new frontier in pastoral work. See, for example, Hunsinger, *Bearing the Unbearable*.

resources. Couples are also likely to wait longer to marry, which means that they are likely to have fewer children.[30]

The children of divorce suffer both economically and emotionally; the latter holds true even if they are in early adulthood. As a result, it is harder for them to form lasting attachments.[31] This does not mean they hold marriage in less esteem. On the contrary, they long for its stability and trust, but these seem to be harder or more unlikely to achieve. The demographic challenges to marriage in our culture present us with the risk that marriage itself will become a counter-sign, something signifying the opposite of what is intended. Yet Christian marriage is thus all the more important as a counter-cultural sign.

The church does too little to emphasize marriage's theological importance, even though occasionally the long-married may be recognized or deployed as mentors.[32] Premarital instruction usually includes something about making expectations explicit, facilitating communication, and dealing with conflict. Roman Catholic Pre-Cana programs are often more extensive than other denominations, and hence worth borrowing from. As throughout this book, secular counseling can be a wise source of help, though it needs to be "taken captive" (Eph 4:8, citing Ps 68:18). The habits of fair fighting, listening, "turning toward one another," avoiding contempt,[33] etc., are valuable, but a common practice of prayer, a shared sense of marriage as a vocation, and a commitment to mutual forgiveness, all born of a spiritual imaginary toward the "marriage feast of the Lamb," can place those habits in a different, more coherent frame. Episodic opportunities such as the renewal program called Marriage Encounter can reinforce this difference. These sessions can help the couple to think of their own relationship in explicitly faithful terms. But a deeper nuptial theology of the church per se places the couple in a covenantal matrix of fidelity that is wider than themselves. It is not so much that the church is a resource for their individual relationship (though one hopes it is) as that their relationship has a vocation within the larger family of faith.[34]

30. Barna Group, "Marriage and Divorce in 2025."

31. Wallerstein et al., *Unexpected Legacy of Divorce.*

32. One may point to examples such as the Episcopal Diocese of Connecticut's annual celebration of fiftieth wedding anniversaries, or of parishes that bring the long-married into pre-marital instruction.

33. Gottman and Silver, *Seven Principles of Making Marriage Work.*

34. David Brooks's March 2020 *Atlantic* essay is feeling its way toward this deeper and wider social (and spiritual) bond. Brooks, "Nuclear Family Was a Mistake," 55–69.

As we noted at the beginning of this chapter, most denominations have some form of offering—the feature of bringing something before God in thanksgiving is virtually universal among Christian groups. For this reason, the central point of this chapter stands: namely, that in the grammar of Christian faith our offering of "ourselves, our souls and bodies" is always response in gratitude to what God has already, and sufficiently, done. All traditions, likewise, would understand human activities and concerns such as ecology, labor, marriage, etc., as response. As a result, most everything we have to say has immediate relevance to other Christian traditions.

LIFE TOGETHER

We have considered the telos and some of the fitting practices by which we can understand our work. What then are the virtues implied herein? Since this book is organized around the Eucharist, it will be no surprise that the first is gratitude. As we are given these practices, so we are given things we are called to do, although our salvation and the world's do not depend on us. We are called to them together, yet we tend to depend on ourselves. We are summoned to rejoice, even playfully, although in our acedia we often suppose the world to be as tired and degraded as we feel.[35] We are grateful when we are given to feel his pleasure in us.[36]

The "tacit dimension" (Polanyi) of what we have been saying is the Christian congregation in its particularity, which together offers its gifts amid its flaws and failings. We will mention a number of pastoral approaches, often in ministry to suffering church members or neighbors, that all have as their tacit assumption the whole—the congregation. It is the congregation that gathers and then scatters to the offering of praise and thanksgiving. While some in the contemporary church may think we are in a post-congregational moment or may prefer to focus on the larger society, the congregation cannot but be the focus in our eucharistic approach. It is, as we noted earlier (chapter 3), at the center of God's work and activity in the world. In a more sociological vein, we note that most approaches one might cite assume collective dynamics and interactions or processes. Furthermore, the particular congregation itself is an organ

35. As seen in Gerard Manley Hopkins's poem "God's Grandeur."

36. The classic line by Eric Liddell from the movie *Chariots of Fire*.

in a greater body and across a longer stretch of time (universal and apostolic).

Each congregation has its own story to tell, or a number of stories, depending on which parishioner does the telling! It is important to hear these stories as a unique web of local symbols with wider significance (for example, Hopewell), and to do a careful collection and analysis of their own self-understandings (for example, Browning). Likewise, one can chart the relations within and between its families in a systemic way (Friedman), chart how the dynamics of different sized congregations compare with one another (Alban Institute), or ask how well they can adapt to their changing neighborhoods (Ammerman).[37] One could also offer a critique based on wealth, race, age, class, neighborhood, etc. (to be sure, this would also show how many congregations are often more mixed and complicated than other associations in their neighborhood).

These local narratives are a necessary background for gleaning wisdom about how best the pastor can proceed. But they also must be resolved into the larger narrative from which their identity is ultimately derived and against which their identity is formed and corrected. The liturgy itself is taking up, "breaking," and blessing that congregational story into the great narrative. Particular areas of focused pastoral ministry serve their purpose in significant measure as they are subordinated to the Bible's story, retold in word and sacrament every Sunday morning. Still, the particularities matter—it is that congregation of those people in that place, with its own history—indeed with its own pathologies as well as gifts—that the Spirit draws together and forward.

Some of the practices considered here seem outward facing, and others inward. In the ancient church, the offertory was the moment when only the baptized faithful could remain and receive, and yet the church as a whole is always a sign to and for the world. Pastoral theology also has a purpose in finding the outward-facing, gospel-oriented aspects in the seemingly most "in house" activities. This includes the building itself, which is not infrequently the object of near idolatrous care or fatalistic neglect, or both at the same time. (While visiting a church in southern New Brunswick I [Peter] was told that the ancient and decrepit carpet could not be replaced since it had been donated by the matriarch's grandmother.) As we proceed we will consider each subdomain, whether

37. See especially Hopewell, *Congregation*; Browning, *Fundamental Practical Theology*; Friedman, *Generation to Generation*; Ammerman, *Studying Congregations*. Alban Institute resources are now available through Duke Divinity School.

initially inward or outward facing, and the dialogue that ensues therein, using a verse from the Bible as our headings.

PLACE

Congregations have almost universally to do with place. In the Anglican Church the idea of a parish entails this emphasis on the locale and community in which the congregation lives and for which their ministry is intended.[38] To be sure, our sense of place has changed, not least with the advent of the automobile—it is said that most contemporary mainline believers drive by several churches to get to the one where they pray. Still, congregation implies place and is not unrelated to a burgeoning ecological, even anti-technological, sense that has a connection to the doctrine of creation.[39] Here we can find theological significance and a pastoral vision in the very idea of a network of congregations scattered through places. It is in relation to the people in particular places that the idea of the parish as representative remnant is best understood.[40]

Finally, we realize how all accounts of a congregation as a body inevitably swim against the current in mainstream North America (although less so in some more socially traditional ethnic congregations). A generation ago, *Habits of the Heart* laid out the challenge of affiliational communities as lifestyle enclaves[41] in which the individual choices and evaluation of need-fulfillment are the dominant factors. It is against this reality that the congregation coheres and is given to participate in Christ's narrative. All Christian communities are gathered by grace against some gravitational force (secular, pagan, nationalistic, etc.) of its own. In each subsection we will identify the pervasive underlying issue against which all Christian treatments offer a countervailing view.

38. Rumsey, *Parish*.

39. One might here consider the contributions of the Canadian poet Tim Lilburn, especially the idea of "living in the world as if it were home" (in the book by that name). This sense of place is a good reminder in light of the financial straits in which many rural congregations find themselves.

40. Thornton, *Pastoral Theology*.

41. Bellah et al., *Habits of the Heart*.

EIGHT SECULAR DISCIPLINES ECCLESIALLY TRANSFORMED

1. "Before You Bring Your Offering"—Addressing Conflict

Conflict in human communities is to be expected (see discussion in chapter 3). But as the people of God it comes into focus specifically as evidence of original sin and as opportunity for reconciliation. We are ministers of reconciliation only insofar as we are servants of the One who effected reconciliation (2 Cor 5:20). Thus, reconciliation must be sought in relation to the parish's history and its complex demographic and generational make-up, but only after it has been considered in light of the whole of the historical salvation narrative. It is precisely as a conflicted community that the offering is brought to the One who commands obedience and promises peace of a kind the world cannot give. Conflict's resolution requires "speaking the truth in love" (Eph 4), surrendering wrath (Eph 5), and recognizing that the forces of conflict are both in us and beyond us (Eph 6). These all have as their background our life as disciples of the Crucified and Risen One. Against this stormy background the true nature of the vocation of the already and graciously reconciled becomes clear.

What can we say about Christian conflict resolution more practically? The literature is largely concentrated on enabling people to look honestly at conflict and recognize its inevitability, structuring processes to move through it, and accessing all available resources from mediators to resolution practices.[42] Church conflict is not less intense for being religious, since it involves close relations and often is in stark contrast with what congregants profess. All these kinds of advice amid conflict open onto a gospel perspective: We the conflicted share a mediator, a theologically informed account of conflict's source and possibility, and a telos to which the Spirit leads.

Put another way, at the end of the laying bare of conflict, the church has the absolution of Christ to offer, unlike secular helpers or groups. This does not magically remove the fault-lines, but it does place those divides against a brighter horizon and on a more hopeful map. Another way to put the matter is this: The core issue in church conflict is anger and how it is to be expressed but also laid to rest "before sundown." Christ was

42. A case in point is Speed Leas's "Levels of Conflict." See Leas, *Moving Your Church Through Conflict*.

crucified because of and in victory over anger. In light of the Christian social imaginary, the church has something unique and decisive to offer, often in spite of itself, to human beings in their anger.

2. "Gathered from North, South, East, West"—Diversity

Sometimes secular emphases are vestiges or shadows of themes in the Scriptures in a kind of cultural parallel to natural theology. As we noted at the outset of this chapter, although we hear much in contemporary Western culture about diversity, the biblical correlate is the gathering of the nations back to Zion (Isa 2) in anticipation of their being reunited at Pentecost (Acts 2) and on the last day (Rev 7). In short, the redeemed assembly of the peoples is a feature of the church as it offers its sacrifice of praise and thanksgiving. Diversity points to the redeemed community, though it has become the occasion for political debate in recent conversations. The core issue is identity in Christ as the redeemed, the baptismal, the church catholic, to which secular accounts of diversity point and against which they seem thin. As with all the issues in this chapter, the background of the Christian social imaginary theologically grounds diversity in who we are as a church gathered by the Spirit, as opposed to seeing it functionally, politically, or from a marketing viewpoint.

Given the interest in diversity, the emphasis on segmentation in seminal studies of church growth uncovers an element of theological tension.[43] Gatherings of like-minded individuals might offer a source of connection and enhance church growth (new Christians want to pray with people who look like them) but are antithetical to our calling as Christ's body. Meanwhile, theologies of enculturation and contextualization raise the same issues in different ways. How are church communities in particular locales to be formed in response to both the gospel and culture? A missional practice requires flexibility and attention to the local, although the philosophical roots of indigenization in romanticist notions of the genius of a race of people rightly come in for critique.[44]

43. The key author here is McGavran, e.g., in *Bridges of God*.

44. One finds a good diagnosis of this in Sykes's *Integrity of Anglicanism*.

3. "The Young Will Have Visions, and the Old Dream Dreams"—Youth Ministry

Much of the literature on types of Sunday school assumes modern theories of the stages of child development (for example, James Fowler's application of the groundbreaking work of Piaget and Erikson). The recognition that children learn and think differently has been a welcome insight, especially as they bring an element of wonder and awe before God.[45] At the same time, the traditional elements of memorization as well as liturgical incorporation provide a balance. A movement like Godly Play, which integrates learning theory, worship, and habit is an edifying example. As with all approaches to formation, it is hoped that the mind, feelings, and will are addressed together in keeping with the nature of the Christian imaginary itself. In short, Sunday school education must acknowledge that children may have their own charism to bring to the body's worship. Thus, their integration into the wider church is vital both for them and for the adults. For this reason, the older practice of sequestering, or half-sequestering, children from the liturgy is being debated and rethought. (The stress and trauma experienced by young people in the pandemic, especially with respect to mental health issues, has exacerbated disturbing trends already in evidence. This has made the embodied and personal dimensions of worship, as well as the empathetic mentoring role of youth ministers, all the more important.)

4. "Living or Dying We Are the Lord's"—Life Cycle

As with Christian education for youth, most writing on gerontological ministry is based on theories of the stages of human development. In particular, ministry to the aged involves helping people come to terms with death, which is inseparable with coming to terms finally with ourselves and the whole course of our lives. "Ego integration"[46] assumes a spiritual solitude which would seem to lead naturally to coming to terms with ourselves before God, although without him it might well lead to despair. The stages of dying have been decisively articulated by Kübler-Ross in a kind of quasi-secular work in the "art of dying."[47] (Death and dying

45. Isaac Bashevis Singer speaks of this wonderment, as does Albert Einstein in another context.

46. See Erikson, *Childhood and Society.*

47. Kübler-Ross, *On Death and Dying.*

in cross-cultural perspective is an important additional literature which has grown out of her research.) This background of mortality, of "being toward death,"[48] or what we might call the Ecclesiastes theme, brings into relief for the community what it means to walk in the light of the resurrection of Jesus, both in regard to its place in the human struggle at the end of life and its unique and decisive gift that makes the Christian imaginary truthful and gracious. In Christian ministry to the dying there is a forthright acknowledgment of death as the final enemy (1 Cor 15), as opposed to the culturally facile adoption of a circle of life gloss. But in the case of each age group, Eriksonian developmental identity, generativity, and ego integrity are healed and raised into baptismal identity, nurture in discipleship, grasping the hope of the resurrection, etc.

The ministry to the old can also be understood against the ethical debate about euthanasia, beneath which lies a utilitarianism which is, in the end, vitalistic and nihilistic (see Hauerwas's argument for being "useless and a burden").[49] We can by contrast consider theological and spiritual treatments of incapacity in general, which find in it a witness to human dignity which is not found in our own capacities.[50] Particularly articulate on this front is Swinton's deeply theological reflection on disability. His works also shine a light on the sheer gratuity of grace, as did the theology of implicit faith in the Middle Ages. Here the witness of L'Arche displays the distinctly Christian idea of human dignity against the spirit of the age.[51] The radically different evaluation of the disabled by the people of God as aligned to a distinctly Christian social imaginary is its own critique of the prevailing culture.

This chapter assumes a distinctively Christian understanding of offering. We ought to understand the self-offering of the dying and the witness of the Burial of the Dead in just this way as well. We offer our frailty, fear, and incapacity in a way inseparable from hope, and thus in a way that secular culture cannot.

48. In Heidegger, *Being and Time*.

49. See Hauerwas and Bondi, "Memory, Community, and the Reasons for Living," 439–52; see also Meilaender, "I Want to Burden My Loved Ones."

50. Keck, *Forgetting Whose We Are*.

51. L'Arche was an influence on Henri Nouwen's later work at the intersection of disability and spirituality.

5. "Tell Them How Much the Lord Has Done for You"—Addiction

One way to look at ministry is as the thanksgiving we offer, as gentiles freed from the worship of idols to lives submitted to the living God. Ministry is always as opposed to the worship of false gods, as we see in the second, third, and fifth commandments. One prominent form of ministry in recent years addresses addiction, which may be understood as a type of idolatry. This helps to explain the perverse devotion, forsaking all others, which the addict has. In other words, addiction ministry may be understood as insight into the old life, as well as insight into the dynamics of coming to the new life. It has concealed in it the traditional language of sin, redemption, and contrition. Part of the life of recovery is telling what God has done for the restored person before "the assembly," which might constitute an AA meeting before it is the church congregation itself.

The other great challenge and encouragement to the church presented by the recovery movement is the fact that AA is entirely led by its members—there is no staff that ministers on behalf of the others. It is a secular, or better yet, a quasi-religious group which embodies the ministry of the whole people of God. Its decentralized face-to-face form is a working out of the original insight of the Methodists (see our discussion of small groups below).

6. "Do Not Quench the Spirit"—Renewal

It has been said that any adequate ecclesiology must take into account both what have been called the Petrine (structures of traditional and formal authority) and the Ignatian (informal, voluntary societies and sodalities for prayer and mission)—the warp and woof of the church. We might in many cases call the latter para-church. Often a freer and more collaborative kind of ministry can take place there. We see dramatic evidence of this in the historic monastic and missionary movements. In other words, the people offering their gifts by grace stand together not only as formal members of the church, but also as brothers and sisters in a number of complementary and overlapping ministries within, at the edge of, and on behalf of the church.

Renewal ministries have sometimes been criticized as leading to cliques in the church: After the mountain-top experience the quotidian seems boring. The key is to see the Petrine and Ignatian as together subserving the same goal of edification of the whole body of the faithful. The

Pentecostal is seen as a part of a larger whole, in light of all that builds up charity (1 Cor 13).

There are also groups which take part in renewal (even if they at times mistakenly suppose themselves to be an alternate understanding of the church itself). They are creative ports of entry into the church, though they often lack the capacity for endurance and fail to reproduce themselves over time. We have in mind here the informal gatherings of parents and children called "Messy Church," as well as gatherings in diverse non-religious settings called "Fresh Expressions." Tellingly, the origins of both are in evangelical outreach within the more traditional church.

7. "Where Two or Three"—Small Group Ministry

The congregation is in fact made up not only of individuals, but of a multiplicity of small groups and ministries. There are gatherings at many levels. The choice of collectivity or individuality is a false one, and contrasts with the variously unified sense it has in the New Testament. *Ecclesia* is verb as well as noun—it entails and comprises the *ecclesiolae*. So the gathering of two or three in Matt 18 is the gathering of the body, which includes the Spirit, not some fraction thereof. This is true throughout the history of the church, in the lay movements of the late Middle Ages, the *devotio moderna*, devotional societies in Catholicism, classes in Methodism, mission societies, underground churches, Bible study groups, etc. The small group movement in secular as well as religious culture in our time is an outgrowth of this. The church comprises an interaction of intimacy and assembly, and the inclusion of the former is surely a key factor in much growth (consider for example the role of fellowship groups in the East African Revival).[52] Obviously the skilled small group leader must make sure the group conduces to the welfare of the whole koinonia rather than a clique and must recognize when it should undergo mitosis.

As an addendum, there is in all small group ministry a sense of the part existing for the whole, or on behalf of the whole. Another form of this is in the biblical idea of the remnant, when the whole seems somnolent or confused in some way. We have already mentioned how in the Anglican tradition there is something of this in the very idea of the parish, which assumes that its membership consists of all who live in an

52. Warren, *Revival*.

area, even though they may in fact have no interest in participation. So the congregation itself comes to be a kind of remnant.[53] Even outside of this idea of the parish, one may also find in the congregation a minority who are spiritually energetic and have bought into the goals of the ministry. They may emphasize their formation not as a preference but so as to broaden the ministry and influence among their fellow lay people (as in Moses's selection of the seventy elders). It is not in the experience of the small group alone, but in its contribution to and participation in the whole, that the gathering of two or three matters most.

8. "Do Not Pass Your Servant By"—Hospitality and Friendship

We have already noted that the offertory was the point at which catechumens would be exorcised, blessed, and dismissed in the early church. The meal that followed was for the faithful. But this brings into relief the need for the church to take care to nurture a ministry of welcome, of making space for the visitor, the seeker, the skittish, or the curious. There is a place for the *ger*, the fellow traveler, who may along the way become a member. One may also cite the tradition of a gentile visitor at the Passover meal—likewise we need to give the outsider in our midst an honored place. Helpful in this regard are recent studies which treat friendship, its nature, and its cultivation.[54] Likewise, local cultures which have retained a fuller practice of hospitality, of washing the hands and slaying the last chicken to feed the guest, have much to teach us.[55] The grounding of a theology of friendship is in the One who called us friends (John 15:15), and a theology of hospitality is grounded in the One who as God pitched his tent in our midst (John 1).[56]

We are focusing on hospitality when the body is gathered, but this implies practices of inviting in and visiting afterward. Congregations should discern how inviting they are in the eyes of visitors. Is it easy to navigate the books involved in reciting the order of service? What about finding a place to sit? How sensitive is the congregation to both people who want to be welcomed in and those who want to be allowed more

53. Thornton, *Pastoral Theology.*

54. Austin, *Friendship.*

55. These examples are from personal experience of East African culture (George).

56. The offering of communion to the unbaptized might seem to forward this goal, but actually it breaks down the very distinction which gives meaning to the category of visitor.

space and time? Likewise, the wise congregation keeps an eye out for newcomers at coffee-hour, so that the most socially astute members can come alongside them and help them feel at ease.

Studies have shown that newcomers who have been visited in their homes soon after the service are most likely to return. This ought to be part of an ongoing discipline of parish calling by the pastor, for during these calls he or she learns most about the lives of church members. To be sure, comfort with calling, or even familiarity with it, has declined. Many people would be surprised by or even opposed to a pastoral visit, so clergy may need to find alternative locations such as a nearby coffee shop. This is related to a justifiably heightened awareness of safety and boundaries which needs to be considered when fostering an atmosphere of welcome.

In contrast to calling on newcomers, there is a regular rota of bringing communion to shut-ins. This is an area where lay people can take their rightful place in the administration of the sacrament. (It is also the best example of the valid place of streaming and technology for the sake of including all in the common prayer of the body.) It may be hoped that the shut-in members can see themselves as having an active ministry of intercession, for their lives are by necessity characterized by an unusual stability which could allow them to see themselves as the equivalent of anchorites.

A vivid example of the art of invitation and making space comes from the recent period of pandemic. In the Cathedral of the Episcopal Diocese of Dallas an outdoor service was initiated for pandemic safety; this proved fruitful in drawing newcomers. The space of the service was literally more open, and everyone was new in the sense of adjusting to a new environment. Seekers felt most comfortable attending this service, the reasons for which are informative for other settings as well. It was particularly attractive to young families. This ministry continued to grow after COVID restrictions were relaxed.

The general category of hospitality and welcome extends beyond the service itself in another way. Congregations often make their space available in a myriad of ways for the sake of neighborhood events. This might take the form of a blood drive, a public lecture, an AA meeting, or on a more permanent basis, a daycare or a quinceañera. These are enactments of hospitality in themselves, and possible invitations to "come and see." One important question arises as to when an invitation may be extended to those of other faiths or traditions. The congregation must show friendship, but it also must avoid confusing the faithful. We respect other believers by recognizing and acknowledging their differences. Still, space can be found which threads this needle. For example, congregations in the Anglican Diocese of Egypt have for many years welcomed Muslim neighbors into the parish halls for the breaking of the fast during the evenings of Ramadan. Worship by another religious tradition in the church proper is more problematic, although one can also cite carefully prepared community Thanksgiving services which manage friendship and devotion in a way that takes seriously the differences of belief and the consciences of the communities and individuals involved.

9

The Communion Proper

THE SYMBOL HERE IS THE BLESSING and consuming of the body and blood of Christ. The ancient adage *lex orandi lex credendi* encapsulates the unity of praying and believing found in the Christian social imaginary. With the help of anthropologists as dialogue partners, it is evident that sacramental realism, understood broadly, may now been seen as ecumenically available and a mainstay against the postmodern social imaginary.

He was accustomed to a more pallid sort of religion: unobjectionable and socially conscious. Yet at seminary he experienced something strange, ancient, and profound when introduced to Latin chanting, billows of incense, and the ornate ceremonial around the sacrament. He had read in class of Rudolf Otto's description of the "mystery earth-shaking and fascinating," and soon after he would read of the young secular Jew Franz Rosenzweig, who emerged shaken from his experience of the traditional Yom Kippur liturgy. A decade later Robert Webber of Wheaton gave voice to this kind of discovery in *Evangelicals on the Canterbury Trail*. Forty years later, having moved to the Episcopal Church, a succession of would-be ordinands would continue to find their way to his more traditional diocese. In time he would also see the moral failings, the mere aestheticism, and formational shortcomings of the Anglo-Catholic world. But the lessons remained powerful, and Webber went on to write more than forty books on worship. He wrote of how the divine presence was really in the liturgy, about dimensions of the Christian faith that needed to be recalled, and that the critique usually pointed at faith would need to be redirected upon modernity itself.

Although the organizing principle of this entire book is eucharistic, we need a chapter that deals specifically with liturgics as a discipline, including special attention to the specific practice of celebrating the Eucharist (in more evangelical parlance this would be a chapter on worship). The study of this topic is aided by a recent perspective which goes by the Latin adage of Prosper of Aquitaine: *lex orandi lex credendi*, or "the law of praying is the law of believing." Just as we have considered in this book how best to relate the practices of the church to its doctrines in the context of our corporate experience, so the church ancient and modern used this idea of *lex* or "rule" to accomplish the very same task. It restates in a liturgical vein an answer to the question of method: Practice and theology can never be very far from each other. Yet the relationship between the two continues to be understood in many different ways, with some seeking to avoid any emphasis on practice altogether, while others seek to retrieve worship practices as a way of enriching our worship. Alan Jacobs has written a scathing critique of evangelical retrievals of practices, mainly for their lack of seriousness and weak understanding of historical context.[1] But the desire for such retrieval itself is both admirable and indicative of a wider movement. Still, one would do better to see the practice, in the full sense in which MacIntyre used the word (telos, narrative, virtues, accounts of rival narratives), as the Eucharist itself, as this has the advantages of universal use, flexibility and familiarity, a clear grounding in both Scripture and tradition, and an avoidance of exoticism. So we will consider the strengths and weaknesses of this sentence, *lex orandi lex credendi*, as an informative way to continue our reflection on the theology of liturgy and worship.

In the ancient church, and especially in debates related to pneumatology, appeal could be made to inherited liturgical usage to settle theological debates already by the fourth century. The worshiping life of the community was not simply determined by doctrine but was itself a witness to the theological interpretation of Scripture. When the question of the status of the ancient heterodox churches of the East came up in the nineteenth century, this earlier kind of appeal again proved useful. Since Eastern Christians prayed to the triune God in a similar way, their seeming divergences could be seen in a more lenient light.

Fast forward yet again, and the ancient formula became popular in the twentieth century for traditions such as Anglicanism, with a primary

1. Jacobs, "Do-It-Yourself Tradition," 27–32.

emphasis on liturgies over against doctrinal theology proper. In some cases, the sentence was the springboard to a theologically robust account, while in others the *lex orandi* side of things was equated simply with contemporary experiences of worship—evolving worship practices were deemed to affirm or even redirect doctrine, and so progressivist change carried the day.[2] In other words, the formula can become not so much a solution as a restatement of controverted questions, or a "wax nose." To be sure, the formula depended for its usefulness on a stable liturgical tradition. As a result, in an era of frequent liturgical innovation (closely linked as it is with our secular social imaginary valorizing constant change) it ceased to be possible to find an implied teaching lodged in the liturgy.[3] Of what use then could the adage be?

We return to Alexander Schmemann, whom we briefly mentioned in chapter 5 as one of the central advocates for the relationship between *lex orandi* and *lex credendi*. Within his own tradition he was at times accused of advocating for the evolving nature of liturgy and failing to affirm tradition. Schmemann explains that the "essence" of the liturgy is the *lex orandi*, which "is ultimately nothing else but the Church's faith itself or, better to say, the manifestation, communication and fulfillment of that faith."[4] That would suggest that liturgy which has become disassociated from the Nicene Faith no longer has the capacity to transform people into relationship with God. The liturgy alone cannot function in shaping a social imaginary. It requires both the liturgy and the faith. Or to put that more directly, the liturgy and the faith must cohere to maintain their integrity. And as we discussed in chapter 5, this is not individual faith as much as it is *the Faith* of the community, which is ultimately the person of Jesus Christ and by implication his body the church.

The faith, Schmemann argues, gives birth to and shapes the liturgy. The liturgy fulfills and expresses the faith, and therefore the liturgy "'bears testimony' to faith and becomes thus its true and adequate expression and

2. The classic text is Wainwright's *Doxology*.

3. Schmemann, whom we shall discuss later in this chapter, is concerned with giving full weight to the "law of believing"—the last thing the adage should be taken to mean is as weighted toward innovation and experience.

Throughout he assumes the stability we speak of here. In liturgy we witness to and inhabit the divine truths themselves. See, for example, his article on liturgical theology. We hope this work shares his desire to overcome an unhelpful dichotomy between theory and practice, although we live in the midst of the modernist social imaginary. See his "Debate on the Liturgy," 217.

4. Schmemann, "Debate on the Liturgy," 217.

norm: *lex orandi et credendi*."[5] This is neither to collapse faith into liturgy nor confuse the two, nor to negate the place and importance of doctrine. "Here liturgy is viewed as the 'locus theologicus' *par excellence* because it is its very function, its 'leitourgia' in the original meaning of that word, to manifest and to fulfill the Church's faith and to manifest it not partially, not 'discursively,' but as living totality and catholic experience."[6]

The question underlying all these debates about *lex orandi lex credendi* is that of stability and change in worship, a question recapitulated in every congregation, of whatever tradition, not least at the introduction of a new hymn tune or the moving of chancel furniture. In some more progressive Anglican churches it has become the norm for the congregation to write their own worship liturgy. While this serves to encourage more active participation and acknowledges the need for ongoing revision of both practice and liturgy, it fails to allow for the integrated relationship reflected in *lex orandi lex credendi*. This is not a new problem, although recent expressions of it reflect cultural assumptions of atomistic individualism. Thomas Cranmer was insistent on the need for liturgy to be readily comprehensible in the vernacular while preserving as much of past practice as possible. His openness to revision was in part a recognition of the need to undo rather than compound theological error.[7] Creativity and a reminder that liturgies are not Scripture itself are necessary. Still, repetition has a relation to formation, and a stable text can allow one to attend to adoration (instead of finding the page). For many, that stability serves as a reminder of the stability of God's grace, although this can sometimes lapse into obsessiveness or even idolatry. This takes us back to patience, prudence, and the golden mean.

THE SIGNIFICANCE OF INHERITED LITURGIES

A consistent theme in this book has been the importance of the social sciences as conversation partners and clarity about their proper relationship with theology. In this spirit we will consider three of this era's most influential anthropologists, who have often been cited in considerations of the dynamics of Christian worship. We can listen first and profitably to Mary Douglas, a devout Roman Catholic as well as a famous social

5. Schmemann, "Debate on the Liturgy," 218.
6. Schmemann, "Debate on the Liturgy," 219.
7. See preface to first *Book of Common Prayer* (1549).

scientist of the Durkheimian school. She reflected on the relationship between the social imaginary of a group and its own social structure and dynamics which influence how members appropriate and express that imaginary. In the church an important part of this is the liturgy.

Douglas analyzed this interaction with the help of two interpretive tools. Together they amount to an account of the abiding social dimensions of an imaginary. First she posits a parallelism (she calls it an homology) between the way a people understand their own bodies, the body politic, and the universe or body cosmic. The porousness or permeability of the boundary of one will mirror that of the others. Secondly, societies are distinguished by the strength of the bonds between members over against strangers (what she calls group) and the stringency of their rules (grid). For example, modern societies that are prone to looser bonds and more verbal self-expression are less able to understand formal and inherited rituals.

Douglas offers a telling example from liturgy. In Vatican II the abandonment of the requirement to eat fish on Friday was seen as a historically and socially enlightened view, distancing itself from prior legalism. But in fact, it simply displayed the preferences of leaders and teachers who were moderns in the upper middle class (mobile, with weak links to relatives, given to wordy explanations, etc.). They were not more evolved believers, but rather more limited in their appreciation of how traditional liturgies functioned. (Douglas went on to note that such mobile and individualist twentieth-century types were not so different from the nomadic, entrepreneurial XuiXui of the Kalahari.)[8]

In her analysis of this attempt at modernization, Douglas kicks one of the legs out from under an unreflective and facile project of contextualizing liturgics. How a liturgy is understood inevitably has a strong social dimension. How worshipers understand the world in a pervasive way, how they imagine their relation to society and the world, and what sense of agency they assume reside behind concrete liturgical proposals. In our desire to revise practice we may be naïve to the set of practices that are informing our own revisions, and indeed informing how we think of revision in the first place. So one might with the best intention propose what seems to be a locally sensitive way to pray which may imply a notion of change, a vision of the world, and a propensity to manipulation

8. Douglas, *Natural Symbols*, ch. 3.

which are foreign to the local worshipers.[9] Issues of class, race, or wealth may also come into play; they will inevitably come into play particularly when we do not allow for their influence. We are not suggesting that such projects should be abandoned: indeed both Cranmer and Schmemann have already established the need for revision and renewal. But those offering revisions should show more self-awareness and humility. Douglas's analysis offers a kind of social scientific apologetic for the profundity of inherited liturgies enduring over time.[10]

This example of a liturgical change at Vatican II is a telling one, since it is a prime example of one of the most prominent liturgical factors of our time: namely, the liturgical movement spurred on by the rediscovery of worship's patristic roots. It can be praised for increased theological seriousness when we pray ancient texts anew, the seamless garment which *lex* seeks at its best. But it could also comprise modernizing goals about which it was not always candid or which brought unforeseen consequences (of which Douglas's Vatican II citation is a vivid example). Still, the ostensive desire to reclaim is not unrelated to the present project. Douglas would reinforce humility about change and respect for what we have inherited.

To our consideration of tradition (via the *lex orandi* adage) we should add a new factor which has emerged first from New Testament studies and as a result, from systematic theology in the modern era: namely, the influence of eschatology on liturgy. Albert Schweitzer's rediscovery of Jesus as an eschatological figure marks in many ways the end of earlier modern liberal New Testament interpretation. The ripples of this rediscovery permeated theology in the twentieth century, although in ways as various as the interpretations of the last things themselves. For example, for the theologians of hope, it meant imagining the intrusion of the God of the future into the present, while for the liberationists it was an appropriation of a vision of the coming kingdom into their praxis. For

9. Douglas, *Natural Symbols.*

10. One could readily add other anthropological voices which, while not as prominent as those discussed above, do make observations immediately relevant to our task at hand. James Clifford, for example, would note the fissures and conflicts in culture, so as to overcome an inherent bias toward the holistic (and romanticist) in traditional societies. See Clifford, *Predicament of Culture.* As we shall see, reflection on the Eucharist, the "sacrament of unity," has ironically been a battlefield during some stretches of Christian history. Or one may think of James K. A. Smith, who lays our rite alongside implicit secular rites. See Smith, *Imagining the Kingdom.* Both are, in a more granular way, related to Mary Douglas's matrix of conditions for local reception.

a theologian like Barth the central recollection was that "my ways are not your ways, nor my thoughts your thoughts" (Isa 55:8). This rediscovery found fruitful ground in the eucharistic origins in Scripture: "until he comes again" (1 Cor 11:26), "until I drink it anew in the kingdom" (Matt 26:29), and "from north and south and east and west to sit at table in the kingdom of God" (Luke 13:29). Since the Eucharist grows out of the meals of the Risen One with his disciples, the resurrection as an eschatological event puts this dimension of our faith at the boundary of already and not yet at the center of eucharistic life.[11] The impingement of the kingdom on the quotidian life of the church because of the resurrection of Jesus, and thinking in light of this reality, lie at the heart of the imaginary within which the pastoral theologian does his or her work.

This emphasis on eschatology in relation to liturgy, albeit in a patristic and largely platonic idiom, has been found historically especially in Eastern Orthodoxy, whose celebrations take place under a heaven-like ceiling in imitation of the heavenly court. More recently, Alexander Schmemann was able to work out an eschatological, eucharistically centered Christian imaginary consistent with the whole biblical narrative.[12] In the garden, we human creatures had a sacramental relationship to the whole created order, which we shall be given by grace once more in the kingdom. The sacrament is given "for the life of the world" by Christ, who gives himself, until such time that the world as a whole is revealed as the sacrament of the divine indwelling. Now, in the time of redemption and mission, we can "taste and see that the Lord is good" already in the sacramental life of the church, which is literally a foretaste from the One who is both beginning and end. In short, Schmemann shows how life together, understood eschatologically, is best experienced as a dense symbol for all of life before God.[13] In the same spirit, and by its light, liturgy comes to inform the rest of ministry, such as, for example, the social ethic of early Anglo-Catholic thinking.[14]

11. Because Christian life, in light of the gospel, is seen to be at the boundary, the *limen*, the collision of the times, and because Christian believing and living share this imaginary, we can also understand theology eschatologically, as *doxology*. This insight can be explicated on the one hand epistemologically (for example, Pannenberg, "Analogy and Doxology") or with reference to the history of liturgy (see, for example, Wainwright, *Doxology*).

12. Schmemann, *For the Life of the World*.

13. See Wainwright, *Eucharist and Eschatology*.

14. The classic example was the outreach to the London docks.

Understood eschatologically, the Eucharist represents the journey—the pilgrimage—on the way to the eternal holy of holies described in Hebrews—to communion with the Father, and to the heavenly banquet. This pilgrimage has typically comprised at once the *via dolorosa et gloriosa* of Jesus himself, the progress of the Christian soul as he or she does these last things, and the church in and toward the end of the world. All three dimensions of eschatology, of Jesus himself, of the individual believer, and of the church moving through history, are included in the eucharistic vision of the Christian life.[15] We remember how Jesus ate with his friends, suffered, and was raised to the Father's right hand. At the same time, each of us says Jesus's prayer of intimacy with the Father as our own, and we are each fed by the heavenly food—the viaticum—at the climax of the service. And we, Christ's body, anticipate this same road for the world at large. Holding these three readings together is entailed in a genuinely Christian spirituality. All of the Christian writings can be understood as midrash on the paschal passage of Jesus himself. All three are to be found in the Eucharist symbol.

THE LIMINAL

This emphasis on eschatology also has a conversation partner in anthropology. We have in mind Victor Turner and his oft-cited concept of the *liminal.*[16] His theory depended on the contrast between structure and what he called "anti-structure." Societies depend on moments of what he called "communitas" to release the pressures that build up as a result of conformity.[17] Liturgies give shape (structure) to these moments of the anti-structural, and as such, allow passage into and out of these periods of dis-articulation (hence the term *liminal* from the Latin for doorway). The theory is quite supple and can be applied to a village, a society, a feud between clans, or to adolescence, etc. It also provides at a high level of generality an account of what liturgies do. But we want to emphasize how it gives expression to the edge between the ordinary and the extraordinary and to this awareness of standing in the doorway: the Christian sense that the kingdom and the end already confront us in worship.

15. They correspond in the fourfold sense to the typological, the tropological, and the analogical.

16. Behind his thinking is Van Gennep's *Rites of Passage.*

17. Turner, *Ritual Process*, ch. 3.

Sometimes a new era makes an old debate simpler, as it brings the question into starker outline against a darker horizon. An example of this would be the older debates about ecclesiology which were cast in a new light for the younger churches of India by the shared and looming challenge of Hinduism, all of which contributed to the eventual formation of the Church of South India. Liminal moments like this are, as Turner suggests, a normal part of human life, and this includes the life of the church.

In the church the liminal is not simply episodic, but is at the center of who we are. At the Lord's Supper, the congregation is invited into that state of "communitas" which presages the kingdom even as it narrates the moment in which, by Christ's death, the old aeon died and the new was born. In other words, for Christians, Eucharist both describes and represents experientially that ultimate liminality which lies at the center of our life in Christ. In Christian liturgy "the kingdoms of this world are always becoming the kingdoms of our Lord and of his Christ . . ." (Rev 11:5). The term *liminality*, in its anthropological idiom, offers an analogy to the ordering and the intrusion of the times which lie at the heart of the Christian social imaginary, and so the church's gathering.

We cannot avoid the question of how the contentious historical theological debate related to the Eucharist might be heard, and how it might inform contemporary pastoral practice.[18] Most attention has been given to the question of how Jesus was present in the sacrament. Some of the options, for example, present by conformity to the promissory word (Lutheran) or by the Holy Spirit (Calvinist), would a half millennium later seem now to be better understood in a both/and manner. We have already noted how a thoroughgoing eschatological view transposes these earlier debates into a new key. We may also note how each position, in ruling out a defective understanding rather than prescribing the correct

18. What may seem a side issue is to what extent conscious assent and understanding of the meaning of the sacrament is required. We may here compare the sacrament of baptism administered to babies who have none such, even though in some traditions the lack is made up later in confirmation (likewise a conscious confession of faith). What of those who cannot in any way "discern the body," if by this we mean making out what the reception entails? This question may be applied to the reception by infants, as in the Orthodox tradition, and equally to reception by the cognitively impaired. Note, in spite of its rejection by the Reformers, the tradition of "implicit faith" and its primary usefulness here. By believing in church per se and by participation, they believe what the church believes. One might add that for them, the eating and the believing imply one another: "taste and see that the Lord is good."

one, can contribute to agreement.[19] For example, Martin Bucer's mediating position among the Reformed (not least in England) was essentially a negative rule: A eucharistic theology should not understand the elements and their consumption as immaterial to the presence of the Lord.[20] These perspectives allow a more stereoscopic comprehension of the older debates without devaluing the questions at stake.

One suspects that, whatever their denomination and liturgical stylistic preference, many contemporary believers really have what might be called a symbolist view in the modern sense.[21] For many Christians the sacrament is a vivid illustration of a general truth in a movingly ancient form (there is some appeal both to anthropology and romanticism here too, though unacknowledged). This may be contrasted with what we might call a general realism, whether Lutheran, Roman Catholic, Orthodox, Calvinist, or Anglican. The division between modernist experiential and traditional retrievalist approaches in theological method recapitulate themselves in understandings of the sacrament. In other words, for us post-moderns the main question has become simpler: Is Jesus understood to be present in some real sense other than in the imagination of the believer? Otherwise, in the modern era, we are all Zwinglians. The telling question is whether this predicament is grasped and whether we can overcome this prejudice. In the Eucharist, taking a Christian social imaginary seriously comes down to being first of all a sacramental realist, whether Reformed or Catholic; one way or another, this is one dimension of a realist dimension to one's eschatology.

THICK DESCRIPTION

At this turn let us listen to our third major anthropological voice, Clifford Geertz. While Turner gave us liminality, Geertz has given us thick description. It is another way to name what Taylor called a social imaginary. Geertz thinks that the more abstract, universal, and general that anthropological judgments are, the less interesting and fruitful they prove to be. Better to begin at the ground level, with the local, and try to appreciate how people there actually see themselves, however imperfect

19. See Morse, *Not Every Spirit.*

20. He is referred to in Gerrish's *Grace and Gratitude.*

21. The anecdote is in O'Connor, *Habit of Being*, 125, where she famously replied on the Eucharist to the writer Mary McCarthy, "Well if it is only a symbol, I say 'to hell with it.'"

this imaginative effort may be. Geertz prefers a more narrative approach, since stories are particular to the one by and about whom they are told. He advocates the building up of a particular understanding, layer by layer (as one might with old-fashioned technology add one image atop another with an overhead projector). Local history, a sociological study, a fable, an anthropological study of a rite—lay one after the other on top of each other until one has a sense of what a particular practice means to local people as one takes into account the assumed as well as the explicit (as for example, famously for Geertz, a Balinese cock fight).[22] In the same way one might do an anthropological study of Eucharist in the New Testament to understand what it meant to the early church, or for a church of the Middle Ages, or in the Reformation era.[23] One can readily see the implications for our task at hand. The meaning of the Eucharist is unique to the Christian narrative and tradition, although other local overlays will affect how it is received and expressed. Thick description helps to free us from the modernist prejudices we too easily fail to notice even as it leaves plenty of room for particular ways of expressing and living out the grammar of faith.

What does such an anthropological perspective contribute to an ecumenically tradition-attentive retrieval of a realist understanding of Christ's presence in the Eucharist? A thick description of our own celebration of the Eucharist would include layered understandings from the New Testament, from the ongoing tradition, and from modern efforts to reclaim the faith, as well as narratives and social factors particular to our own situation. The list could be elaborated: the words of institution in the New Testament as well as denominational articulations, the musical evocation of God's presence, the local culture of feasting and promising, the weight of memory of generations in a congregation. There is in such a thick description a kind of working history of effects of the tradition as well as the accompanying virtues and practices which endure in the church. Elucidating the distinctness of a Christian worshiping imaginary with such thick descriptions helps us to grasp the strange and strong claims that are being made about the risen Christ's presence. They help us to see a different or distant culture on its own terms, and so to resist the blinkers of our own modern assumptions.

22. See Geertz, "Deep Play," 412–54.

23. Meeks, *First Urban Christians*.

FOUR THEMES IN LITURGICAL PRACTICE

With respect to the discipline of liturgiology proper, what themes or questions have had the greatest effect on pastoral practice? We can identify four. They are anything but arcane, for they are given expression every Sunday in every congregation, of whatever size and circumstance. The first, going back to Gregory Dix's magisterial *The Shape of the Liturgy*,[24] finds in the Eucharist an essential order derived from the New Testament accounts of the Last Supper itself. While Dix did not have this intent, one could see in his highlighting of "take, bless, break, and eat" a framework with ecumenical import. It is patent of various views of ceremonial and denominational tradition. The shape is at once a remembrance and also a starting point for such contentious theological questions as the place of sacrificial language and the nature of real presence. In an earlier era, both Protestants and Catholics could have agreed on the centrality of the words of institution, but the shape focuses on the liturgical action.

This leads naturally to the second general emphasis in liturgics of the past two generations, namely the rediscovery of the action of the whole assembly—the body or *laos*. This is accompanied by a sense of the consecration as including the whole liturgy of the word. One can find a parallel emphasis on the people of God as the dominant image for the church in Vatican II.[25] A number of influences here conspire: the Reformation theme of the priesthood of the whole body of the faithful, a democratizing movement in church culture, as well as an anthropological sense that with the celebrant, the whole people are represented and act.[26] In forgetting themselves, in actions in remembrance of him, they act out who they in fact all are.

The third seismic shift in liturgical study in the past two generations has been ecumenical declarations about the Eucharist which have assumed a weight of authority. In particular, the *Baptism, Eucharist and Ministry* document of the World Council of Churches offers its own kind of "shape" argument (invocation of the Father, remembrance of the Son, communion of the faithful, and meal of the kingdom). It sets the action in the wider context of meals in the Old and New Testaments. It seeks to square the circle of older debates by appealing to the deeper meaning than our word *remember*, expressed by "anamnesis," by agreeing on

24. Dix, *Shape of the Liturgy*.

25. For example in Second Vatican Council, *Lumen Gentium*.

26. See for example Borgeson et al., *Reshaping Ministry*.

real presence but prescinding from the "how" question, and by seeing, for example, the use of bread and wine as normative but not universal. This strategy of a wider framework of consensus has been used in other ecumenical achievements, especially the Final Report of the Anglican–Roman Catholic International Commission, which managed to square every inherited doctrinal circle among Anglicans themselves and with Roman Catholics. This same notion of the consensus view derived from New Testament retrieval and a wider angle of consideration has a bearing on the approach of this book as a whole. By means of such a strategy, reflection on the Eucharist proper can inform a eucharistically shaped and ecumenically available vision of Christian common life, and so pastoral practice within it. This development is consistent with the emphasis on realism just articulated.

The fourth area of liturgical study may seem to be a departure from the interests of the first three. We easily forget that traditionally, distinct devotions preceded reception. Furthermore, this was not only for the catholically inclined. Preparing one's heart was especially important for those of a receptionist bent (the ancestors of present-day evangelicals). (Many of Isaac Watts's hymns were written in order to prepare the believer for communion.) Nor does infrequent communion imply that the sacrament is devalued. (In East Africa communicants would bring a card called "my journey [safari] with the Lord" to have signed by the celebrant, so as to recall this special event of the celebration.) Piety around the sacrament, or the lack thereof in recent times, can have a dramatic effect on how it is valued and understood. Here practice takes the lead in making doctrinal understanding possible, and assumptions about sacramental seriousness are challenged.

THE EUCHARIST AS THE PRACTICE OF THE BODY

Based on what we have learned from liturgical study, the cognate science of anthropology, and the theological tradition we can now summarize our conclusions about the Eucharist itself as practice. We can do so in reference to three pastoral theological guideposts, with a fourth, relevant to the present moment, appended. First of all, *culture matters, but does not matter finally*. Whether you are an innumerable assembly meeting at a cathedral or a tiny country parish, the church catholic is there gathered. Both a simple Lord's Supper and an ornate high Mass involves taking, blessing, breaking, and eating. And yet the density of social bonds and rules will affect how the action is understood. Communion is not redesigned for the individual congregation, but the catechesis by which it can be appreciated may be. An anti-modernist apologetic making the case that our thin sense of ritual is our deficit, not the tradition's, can be made with the aid of modern and yet anti-modernist thought.[27] The universality of the action and its ultimacy are encouragements to the pastor, for whom questions of achievement or even survival seem to prevail for much of the week.[28] In other words, insight into the effect of culture on worship is keen in our time, but as an author like Mary Douglas shows, sometimes it reveals more about our own cultural constraints than it frees the sacrament from the distant or hidebound.[29]

Secondly, we can find a correlation between the anthropological insight into *liminality and the rediscovery of eschatology*. The meal is of the kingdom to which the gentiles come from east and west and north and south (Luke 13:29), the banquet of fat things after death is defeated (Isa 25:6), and the glimpse of the beatific vision. The voice of the anthropologist helps us to see how liturgy can be a hinge between the two worlds. All our practice of ministry requires both perspectives: we are seated at once at the heavenly banquet, and yet also at a meal where the rich eat well and push aside the poor (1 Cor 11), and where the betrayer and doubter have places in this *corpus mixtum*. As with the bread, at once bread and body, so too the event as a whole. The wise pastor sees in stereo.

Thirdly, eucharistic realism is an ingredient in a Christian social imaginary. Whatever position one may take and however one thus actually celebrates the Supper, realism is a consequence in practice of

27. We have in mind Geertz and Douglas here, but also the likes of Wittgenstein, Gadamer, etc.—that is, the friends of a cultural-linguistic post-liberalism.

28. See for example Ineson, *Ambition*. Another contrast is revealed in the literature on wellness and on leadership.

29. At this point we do well to recall a kind of footnote to the Eucharist as emblematic of ecclesiology: the at once mysterious but evocative claim in Orthodox theology that the whole of the church is found in each congregation and its celebration. The church is not the arithmetic aggregate, but at once everywhere and in its entirety in each place. However mystical it may seem, this belief is cogent in the life of the local congregation. It is true because the congregation participates in a single eucharistic reality across time and space, which is complete because the ascended Christ is present, no matter how small and otherwise distressed the congregation may be. The doctrine of the real presence in this encompassing vision challenges tacit tendencies to consider the church a kind of non-profit, or a society for religious individuals (however useful such analogies to other kinds of groups may at times be).

a full doctrine of the presence of the risen and ascended Lord in the church. Take for example the historic division between Calvinists, who understood the ascended body of Christ as absent in heaven so as to send the Spirit, and Lutherans, who understood the ascended body as present everywhere in creation and hence in the sacrament especially. Both views moved from a realist understanding of the ascension to one of the Eucharist, and so shared the underlying realism of which we speak here.

To this may be added a postscript relevant to our technological era in general and the COVID time in which this chapter was written in particular. Thick description implies an event in history taking place among actual persons. People, place, history, and ecology are what make it thick. Expressed theologically, the elements of the Eucharist are creaturely by design, and the action is at the intersection of the domains of creation and redemption.[30] It is a moment where at least "two or three are gathered" (Matt 18:20), and Christ is among the faithful. For these reasons, the Eucharist sets a limit on the intrusion of the technologically distanced into the life of the church.[31] Someday the embodied nature of pastoral practice may itself seem counter-cultural, but a purely cyber communion or a consecration by machine at a distance would be Zwinglian memorialism in the extreme. It is to humans—ensouled bodies—by grace bound to that place where they shall be spiritual bodies in the presence of the Lamb who was bodily wounded that the Eucharist is administered. The Eucharist as anachronism will become yet more pertinent.

30. Wingren, *Creation and Gospel*.

31. Bishop Andy Doyle of Texas has written on this in his dissertation. See Doyle, *Embodied Liturgy*.

10

"Go in Peace to Love and Serve the Lord"

The symbol here is the Dismissal not as an ending, but as a sending—the sending out of the congregation into the world. Having been gathered together as God's people to be built up together in Christ they are now sent out into the world for the sake of the world. This movement of gathering and sending is the regular heartbeat of the church's life and orients us toward the centrality of the *missio Dei* in how the church is to understand itself.

I (George) met Philip Turner in graduate school, at Berkeley-Yale Divinity School, where he was the dean; he had served in East Africa a decade before me and under the rigors of the Amin era. He had studied anthropology with the likes of Mary Douglas and Victor Turner as well as theology, and these different facets of learning shaped his practical understanding of ministry. In him I could see how important the returned missionary continued to be. He served as a dean around whom gathered younger scholars who were keen to reclaim the traditional faith in an era of church decline. Years before, he had written an article about the early missionaries as eponymous ancestors to the first generation of African Christians. A light bulb went off in my head, for I had met old Tanzanian priests who resisted the critiques of their grandchildren with the reply that the pioneer missionaries had brought the inheritance (the urithi) of the gospel. It is too easy to dismiss the whole history of mission under the label of colonialism. Inculturation for an East African was not only what you said but also how you thought about things being handed on. This was crucial in a traditional society. Philip helped me to look at the how as well as the what, and thus to see another vector in missiological thinking. The lesson reverberated back home in the years of ministry to come.

On its face, the Dismissal serves the obvious function of telling the congregation that the service has ended. The language, however, is freighted biblically and theologically. The border it calls the worshipers to cross is not simply that between the service and the rest of their day (or week) but symbolically, the one between sacred and secular time—between the mount of transfiguration or the upper room and the disciples' road and their assignment to go to the ends of the earth.

At one church I (Peter) served in there was a brass-colored sign that hung above the main entrance to the church that said "Servant's Entrance." It was on the interior rather than the exterior wall of the church, so the congregation would see it as they left the church. The meaning was plain: As the congregation left following the service they were going into the world as servants—to serve the needs of the world. The gathering together was never simply for the sake of the congregation and their catechesis or edification; it was as much for the sake of the world. At the end, the kingdoms of the world shall be "the kingdom of our God and his Christ" (Rev 12), but for now they are still distinct, and the congregation must still fulfill their particular callings in the kingdom of this world. (Our earlier discussion in chapter 9 of Turner and his concept of liminality comes to our aid here in imagining this crossing of a threshold.)

But first we do well to go behind both these usages and elucidate an even more basic meaning, understood in relation to the imaginary which is the bass note of our whole treatment. With the resurrection, the time of the gentiles has come. The church lives in, or lives into, this gospel time and subserves it as herald and witness so that the nations might be gathered into the people of God. We see this connection in the Great Commission in Matt 28, in the references to the "eternal gospel" and the "rider on the white horse" in Rev 14:6 and 19:11, in the Johannine glorification on the cross which will "draw all nations" to himself (John 12:32), in the apostle of the gentiles' completed passage to the "ends of the earth" (Romans chapter 15), and so forth. For the post-resurrection church, neither time nor space is neutral. They are defined as the theater for the mission to the nations.[1] This lies as the background of all that follows.[2]

The area of the pastoral life which pertains most closely to the Dismissal is mission, but what do we mean by this word? Stephen Neill, one of the great historians of mission, famously commented that "where everything is mission, nothing is mission."[3] As much as mission—God's mission—is at the center of the church's life and calling, to put everything under the category of mission is to confuse and distort this area of the church's life. We begin, then, with the more traditional meaning of mission as a distinct, organized activity of sending those who are called across some geographic boundary in the service of the gospel, or in the extended sense of the word, as the ministry of the church more generally. The two senses are connected. The power of the latter, broader use is both supporting and shaped by the historic meanings of the former. In this chapter, the cognate disciplines serving as the middle terms are all those which have informed the somewhat amorphous discipline of missiology over the years: church history, biography, semantics, and finally cross-cultural and, in our time, post-colonial studies.

To be sure, including all pastoral ministry under the rubric of mission as in the widespread use of the term *missional* is an evocative act of imagination, yet it blurs the understanding of the church's call to build itself up alongside of its call to serve the world. This is seen especially in the church's tendency to negate the one for the sake of the other. Some churches focus only on their life together at the expense of their service to the world, while others put their primary emphasis on social action and neglect their own gathering together to be built up.

The traditional sense of mission as sending and our own missional situation[4] are actually connected by a series of concrete historical cases where practices from the mission field have been borrowed (and invariably tailored) for pastoral ministry in congregations in the Global North. These examples of borrowing are informative. Donald McGavran's theory of church growth began among the people movements of India before it

1. The wider scope of God's mission as elucidated by people like Chris Wright takes on particular nuances in light of the resurrection and the institution of the church. See Wright, *Mission of God*.

2. See especially Cullmann, "Eschatology and Missions in the New Testament"; and Jeremias, *Jesus' Promise to the Nations*.

3. Neill, *Creative Tension*, 81.

4. An example of this usage is Guder and Barrett, *Missional Church*.

transformed church planting in North America.[5] "Total ministry," with the emphasis on lay vocations whose promotion is the main task of the pastor (aptly called Teach Each a Ministry in Alaska) spoke to congregations and ordination processes in the 1980s, but began with the eccentric Anglo-Catholic missionary to China, Roland Allen.[6] And the moniker for this wider sense of mission, the *missio Dei*, began with post–World War II missiologists giving voice to a new understanding of the relation between younger and sending churches.[7]

In each case the transition from the missionary to the missional poses challenges, but in each case there was an enduring insight that proved useful in our context as well. In the case of church growth, the insight was that people tend to join congregations where there are others who look like them. In the case of "total ministry" the insight was a reclamation for the laity of the Reformation concept of vocation. In the case of the *missio Dei* it was the insistence that mission, however conceived, is not optional to the life of the church, but is rather an ingredient of or entailed in the very notion of being church, or those gathered by Christ (mission the diastole, as it were, of which the gathering is the systole).

For the purposes of this chapter, we will find value in both the stricter sense of mission as found in mission history and missiology proper and its extended sense in pastoral theology more generally, as well as the link between the two: the similarity and difference that the analogy includes. The exemplar of this connection in modern church history is Lesslie Newbigin, whose life well illustrates in a concrete way our central argument about mission.[8] He began his ministry in old-fashioned evangelical-style beach evangelism in England using pamphlets. There followed four decades of missionary labor in South India, where he became a noted scholar of Tamil, a friend of Bishop Azariah, the first Indian prelate, and a pioneer in ecumenical creativity with the inception of the Church of South India. Each of these activities embodies something vital to missionary practice. Upon his return to the United Kingdom he was in

5. See, for example, McGavran and Wagner, *Understanding Church Growth*. The insight lent by segmentation cannot be denied, but the question of how the church remains catholic is the challenge for this approach.

6. Allen, *Missionary Methods*. Again, churches are not isolated, and factors like the inheritance of the sending societies should not be occluded. Something similar can be said of Donovan's *Christianity Rediscovered*.

7. Rosin, "Missio Dei."

8. Newbigin, *Unfinished Agenda*.

the forefront of all the major movements in missiological thinking that came in turn to strongly influence theology in general: the breaking down of the distinction between ecumenism and mission (with both under a single World Council of Churches), advocacy of the idea of the *missio Dei*, and exploration of mission's relation to Trinitarian theology (with its own missions).[9] Eventually, Newbigin worried about these movements as they came under the sway of the dominant cultural currents of the secular West. In this spirit of re-thinking he sought to hear again the neo-orthodox voice of Hendrik Kraemer from the 1930s and thus to challenge the rising tide of inter-religious pluralism. Finally, and also as a result of his reading of Karl Barth, he sought to "turn the lens" and to see the individualist, overly Cartesian, supposedly scientific West as a mission field whose cultural assumptions also needed to be challenged. In short, in a life that summed up modern missiological thought, Newbigin arrived at an emphasis on the imaginary of credal, scriptural Christianity compatible with our approach.

The most interesting part of his now classic *The Gospel in a Pluralist Society* is its closing chapter, which claims that the real hermeneutic today is found in the concrete, local congregation itself. This evocative claim underlies a good deal of this book. It assumes, for example, that such a congregation indwells God's word, although it be "folly to the Greeks," and that the congregation is sharing a "truth to tell" in public, namely the "open secret" of all history in the gospel.[10]

Newbigin's work was not only the most significant bridge between missionary and pastoral practice, not to mention between missiology and theology proper, but also the source of an ongoing intellectual project that seeks to look at all church life from this vantage point. We are referring to the Christ in Culture movement.[11] It should come as no surprise that the import of this movement has itself become a point of contention in response to questions around the relationship of the church and culture. In this context, an emphasis on contextual theology often serves as shorthand for giving all voices equal say. Newbigin was not opposed to contextualization, but rather an excessive kind that gives too much away to secular (that is, neo-pagan) culture. But how much is too much, and what are the criteria by which we will know?

9. Newbigin, *Open Secret.*

10. Newbigin, *Gospel in a Pluralist Society.* I am alluding to other titles by Newbigin: *Foolishness to the Greeks* (1988), *Truth to Tell* (1991), and *Open Secret* (1995).

11. See Hunsberger, *Bearing the Witness of the Spirit.*

Although missiology, like pastoral theology more widely, has been something of an orphan discipline, first in practical handbooks for missionaries, then variously part of biblical studies or church history, it finally came to be lodged in systematic theology because of the kind of thinking we find in Newbigin. The best answer to such a question about academic lodging may be the simplest: that missiology is a subdiscipline of ecclesiology, where its neighbors are ecumenics, evangelism, apologetics, catechetics, and diaconal studies, while its locus is in an understanding of how God makes himself present to us.

"Go in peace to love and serve . . ." Let us return to the central claim of the scriptural imaginary, namely the realist presence and initiative of the risen Christ. This is not just any voice that is commanding and sending, nor any peace such as the world can give. The sentence overflows with allusion to the Scriptures. The sending voice is that of the risen Jesus. The destination is the nations of the earth (and behind that, the prophetic hope that they would be gathered to Zion in the "latter days" [Isa 2:2–4]). For this day the cosmos itself has been groaning (Rom 8:22). In this drama, the gentiles are a character in the historical plot of salvation. As a sign of the end-times that have been ushered in by the resurrection, they must be summoned (Matt 28, Rev 3). Salvation may be of the Jews (John 4:22), but now it must go out to all humanity.[12] Only when Paul's circle is complete—when they reach "the coastlands" (Jer 31) and the God of Israel is glorified by them (Malachi, Rom 15)—can the end come.

"Go in peace . . ." Indeed, the imperative provokes a pervasive question. Each nation or tribe to which the gospel goes has its own culture. How far am I to go? That is, what is the relation of the culture I reenter to the life of the church and its expression in worship? Culture is at present the rubric under which virtually all the subsequent missiological questions may be found. This question has always been with us: Think, for example, of Gregory's advice to Augustine about borrowing temple sites and pagan festival dates. But it has become the organizing category in modern times under the influence of intellectual romanticism and the new-born discipline of anthropology. We can find here an epistemological question: namely, how can there be a plethora of cultural settings in which the same gospel is faithfully expressed? This is a concern relevant to our appeal to a single Christian social imaginary. But there continues to be in our time a moral question as well, one which we see in the very

12. The centrifugal is found in Blauw, *Missionary Nature of the Church*.

skittishness about the word *missionary* itself.[13] Doesn't conversion invariably involve cultural imposition, and hence colonialism, whether explicit or implicit? We need to address both these questions and the best way to do so is to pay attention to the actual history of mission, especially in the Global South.

But a useful preparatory question asks, What is the governing metaphor according to which we understand the relation of church practice to the wide varieties of culture? We can identify three metaphors which can be placed in relationship to one another. First, one might appeal to the incarnation, and by analogy we inhabit the culture in which we minister (even though as an analogy this includes dissimilarity as much as similarity; here we note our discomfort with the recent tendency to speak of incarnational mission). There is no neutral, pure, or disembodied gospel: it always comes embodied in a particular cultural setting. The Word made flesh is what must be communicated, and so a second analogy is to translation. There is an original text prior to translation, and a complicated process of finding an approximation of semantic equivalence.[14] Thirdly, this linguistic analogy leads to the related idea of becoming bilingual. We have a mother tongue, but we can also speak another language. There is such a thing as being truly bilingual, although a true one-to-one correspondence in denotation cannot be found. Indeed, it is not enough to simply know the words of another language. We must also know its cultural settings and nuances; we must indwell it in order to truly communicate. This interlocking set of analogies is evocative for pastoral ministry, for local congregations too must find appropriate ways to express the gospel they have heard and continue to hear from the one voice of Jesus Christ. Here, the idea of a language's grammar can help us imagine how a single structure of speech can allow us to say a range of different things.[15]

Inculturation, indigenization, contextualization—call it what you will, the challenge in communicating in this particular place is central to each, as is the challenge to make sure it is the same gospel that is being communicated. To this end, here are a dozen missional rules of thumb which can be applied relevant to our situations. The important thing to

13. For a contemporary example of this, see Spellers, *Church Cracked Open*.

14. Nida, *Toward a Science of Translating*. On the implications of translation for mission, see Sanneh, *Translating the Message*.

15. See Lindbeck, *Nature of Doctrine*; and Davidson, "On the Very Idea of a Conceptual Scheme," 5–20.

note is that they have been gleaned from the history of mission itself. We might call this bottom-up thinking in a manner that is coherent with our whole approach to pastoral theology; we look and see what actually happened on the ground and draw possible lessons from it.[16]

First, and most simply, listen to local Christians who in their lives act out their new commitments (this is not to overlook the ways in which local Christians themselves may err in their understanding).[17] Newbigin highlights this issue in speaking of missions when he notes that it was in learning to listen to those they hoped to reach with the gospel that the missionaries themselves came to understand the gospel more clearly. This listening is part of a process of mutual, global discernment whereby the church catholic, with sufficient patience, can be helped to discern and recognize particular expressions as true to the gospel or not.[18] Ground-level decisions over many years in real life situations convey a wisdom greater than any imported theories. While the examples here are primarily from the history of the Global South, the lessons are the same in the contemporary North. I (George) recall a national church convention near to the mission to native people where I was working which invited medicine men to chant without first consulting local indigenous Christians.

Secondly, much energy and ink has been expended noting the rise of the church in sub-Saharan Africa and wondering what it portends for world Christianity.[19] Bengt Sundkler notes in his magisterial *A History of the Church in Africa*[20] how evangelism originally depended on converts who were somehow or other "in between."[21] They knew the cultural settings but were not safely ensconced at its center. A youngest son, a woman fleeing an arranged marriage, a man back from war or a job away on the railroad, young men at court who learn to read—their second foot was

16. Here we borrow from the theologian-physicist Polkinghorne; see, for example, *Faith of a Physicist.*

17. In addition to scholars like Akiri and Okorocha, see Karanja, *Founding an African Faith.*

18. A particularly painful example of this process is the ongoing debate over human sexuality. It can be understood as just this kind of process of global struggle whether to recognize (or not) a development. Here the analogy to the debate over polygamy in the African Church is instructive, as it points to charity and patience on the one hand, and yet a continued distinction between pastoral generosity and a change in doctrine on the other.

19. See Jenkins, *Next Christendom.*

20. Sundkler and Steed, *History of the Church in Africa.*

21. On liminality, see classically Turner, *Ritual Process.*

already in another culture and they were open to new thoughts, although still natives of the context in question. Who would represent analogous "amphibious" in-between figures for us?

Connected to his claim about the outside-insider is Sundkler's observation about *mfecane*, the churning (in Zulu).[22] The word refers to a time in the later nineteenth and early twentieth centuries when war, drought, migration, and cultural cross-pollination created a moment of promise for the gospel. So, thirdly, there seem to be times of disruption, of more dramatic change, when the order of things is broken open and people are themselves more open to change. While this is not an historical law, it seems to have prima facie plausibility. It is not hard to see the signs of *mfecane* in our own situation.

The fourth lesson has to do with where we look for evidence of adaptation. We might suppose we need to use, say, the music, clothing, or idiom, of Gen Z . . . but adaptation is more socially complicated than simple emulation. For example, often the first generation of converts are traditional in their Christian beliefs and strongest in their rejection of the old life (which, ironically, they understand most intimately). Furthermore, we need also to consider unconscious adaptations. It could be that the way the convert thinks about the new beliefs conforms to a view of tradition native to their inherited customs. They think new things in a way consistent with the old.[23] The example concerning Philip Turner in Uganda is apposite here.

Likewise it may be that the adaptation is found in first order activities where there may be an implicit theologizing, such as social groupings or in styles of music.[24] Another example might be how inhabitants of a culture think of religious power, so that behavior that might seem harsh is interpreted in terms familiar to power evangelism. This emphasis helped me (George) to understand, as a pastor to native people, why episodic Pentecostal revivals had success, which was surprising given their stringent view of traditional folkways.

This last point opens up another front of debate in what we might call latent domains of New Testament witness. Any culturally and historically steered account of the life of the church (which means all accounts) will emphasize some elements derived from Scripture and shortchange

22. Sundkler and Steed, *History of the Church in Africa*, 789ff.

23. Turner, "Wisdom of the Fathers and the Gospel of Christ," 45–68; and Steltenkamp, *Black Elk*.

24. Taylor, *Growth of the Church in Buganda*.

others. The second generation of African Independent Churches offered ministries its members could not find in the missionary churches: exorcism, healing, prophecy, angelology, etc. (we might here compare the charismatic movement in Western churches).[25] While the missionaries offered some justified warnings about relapse into paganism, the argument about "the whole counsel of God" when it comes to the New Testament is fair enough. Here is yet another place where a more global sense of the church reminds us of areas which have been occluded from our view. Thus, fifth, what parts of Scripture can my context hear especially, and to which do we tend to be deaf?

Another general (and sixth) question relates to what Roman Catholic theology called the doctrine of accommodation. This refers to offering those truths of the faith which outsiders are able to understand and appropriate, and waiting to teach others which can only be grasped later, after baptism and further formation. We can see a dramatic example of this in the famous approach of the Jesuits in the seventeenth century, especially in figures like Alexander de Rhodes in Vietnam, Roberto de Nobili in India, and Matteo Ricci in China.[26] By contrast, the Dominicans protested that the truths of the faith are intertwined, and that witness shorn of the cross forgets that the gospel is always offensive (*vide* 1 Cor 1). They walked through the streets of Beijing with crucifixes crying "repent" to surprised crowds. One can see a version of this very debate in the literature about missional approaches today. Put another way, one might say that all are agreed that there needs to be catechism so that new Christians come to ask new kinds of questions and find answers built on new assumptions, but in what order should one present the faith, and over what time frame?

Seventh, at the same time such debates have sometimes obscured how other factors are really at work. While the Jesuits emphasized intellectual adaptation to Brahmin Hindu belief, the mass movements amounted to a challenge to the oppression that the whole social system represented. This amounted to an insight into what contextualization and liberation looked like as opposed to what might have seemed to be inculturation. A very different example could be cited in Tanzania, where a creative expression of confirmation as circumcision by Anglo-Catholic missionaries was resisted because questions of control and autonomy

25. See, for example, Barrett, *Schism and Renewal in Africa.*

26. See Phan, *Mission and Catechesis*; Spence, *Memory Palace of Mateo Ricci*; Cronin, *Pearl to India.* See also Dunne, *Generation of Giants.*

over the rites of passage lay beneath the surface. We, too, need a sharper sociological and anthropological eye in such matters, and must be sure to include in our analyses questions such as "by whose lights?" and "controlled by whom?"

Earlier we mentioned the widespread sense that we are post-Constantinian Christians. But usually this implies an alignment with the situation and strategies of the pre-Constantinian early church.[27] So eighth, we once again live among other faiths and curious but uncomprehending pagans, although whether post-modern seculars fit this description or are sui generis is an outstanding question. Of course, the high bar the early church required for someone to qualify for baptism surprises us, as well as their lively sense both of the hints and seeds of the gospel in pagan thought and of its being riddled with demons. It has been argued that the key factor in their evangelism was a mix of virtues, among them humility and patience, which their neighbors found surprising.[28] Often in our own circumstances we find some, but not all, of these features. At any rate, the implied alignment[29] has led in our time to the retrieval of a vision of evangelism borrowing from the extended process of moral preparation and teaching found in the early era.[30] A more stringent version of this underlying claim of alignment would be the school of thought around the "Benedict Option."[31]

The ninth point follows on this retrieval or analogy to the situation of the early church. Contemporary rediscovery of catechumenal formation grows out of a sense that we live in a post-Constantinian situation. This does not mean that young people need formation more than their parents did (or their great grandparents)—the church did poorly at this in previous generations as well. But it does mean that we cannot hide from the conclusion that marination in contemporary, post-modern culture has virtually no relation to Christian formation. Here Smith and

27. A profound development of this analogy with the early church in catechesis is Abraham's *Logic of Evangelism*.

28. See Kreider's *Patient Ferment of the Early Church*.

29. George Lindbeck once commented that the church of the future needed to find a way to be both catholic in content and a sect in sociology.

30. See Abraham, *Logic of Evangelism*. The liturgical renewal seemed to grasp the observances without the rigors of teaching and moral expectation.

31. Dreher, *Benedict Option*. His more recent interest in authoritarianism would seem to belie his earlier argument.

Denton's telling account of the culture's catechesis in the breach, which amounts to therapeutic deism, has proved decisive.[32]

The liturgical movement included this rediscovery of the extended catechumenate used in the pre-Constantinian church (especially as seen in Hippolytus). This dovetailed with anthropological insights into rites of passage and the sense that the post-modern situation has analogies to the first phase of Christian history.[33] (Once again we are reminded of Victor Turner's work.) Its elements, works of charity, moral instruction and the credal *traditio* (handing over), separation, and *ascesis* (not to mention teaching on the other side of initiation), represent a holistic vision of what conversion ought to look like in their era, and in ours. Contemporary liturgical forms tend to shortchange the elements of *ascesis* and *traditio* and follow a more expressive educational theory; we would do better to reclaim the process in its entirety.[34] (This is the problem with theories like those of Westerhoff or Groome, for whom secular stages of self-discovery militate against the truly countercultural nature of catechesis.)[35]

In the same vein, a popular program like Education for Ministry, the lay education program out of the University of the South School of Theology, which would fall more in the mystagogical basket since it is post-baptismal, retains a Tillichian assumption that Scripture gives pictures for our own experiences.[36] Its usefulness is actually found in its discipline of regular Scripture reading, small group koinonia, and encouragement of lay calling. These are formative in spite of the accompanying theological assumptions, for the entailed exposure to Scripture has a transformative power. (This is aligned to what Calvin meant by the *testimonium* of the Spirit through the Scriptures.)

If we take a wider ecumenical view, we can say that in our denominational scene, prior experiences in another Christian tradition often amounts to part of one's formation. In the Anglican world, those who join from more evangelical backgrounds have already had a fuller education

32. Smith and Denton, *Soul Searching*. It would be a mistake to see this cultural shift as something new—it goes back several hundred years. Some scholars suggest that the seeds of this understanding go back to the Reformation.

33. This is implied in the New Evangelization of the Roman Catholic Church.

34. See, for example, the liturgical version in the Episcopal Church's *Book of Occasional Services*, and writings in support of it.

35. See, for example, Westerhoff, *Living the Faith Community*; or Groome, *Christian Religious Education*.

36. See especially its correlation of personal experience with biblical images.

in the Scripture, so that the "Canterbury Road" amounts to the addition of an historically catholic element to their collective catechumenate.[37]

Another question at the intersection of culture, mission strategy, and theology is how the church orders and organizes its life for mission. So, tenth, in regard to the question of adaptation of ordination itself, confessional traditions obviously have different understandings. But across the board there are questions about which and how much expectations from the missionizing church may be adapted to the newer church. Where should flexibility, native forms of leadership, and evangelistic opportunity be shown? Neill thinks that timidity on this question had a great deal to do with limited success in church growth in India.[38] We can find a parallel debate today about residential seminary and online education in North America.[39] Disentangling theological understandings of orders from modern notions of academic theology and a professional pastorate is difficult since expectations are inherited, and financial stress may motivate excessive jettisoning of standards.

Mission history in Africa teaches us that the typical heralds of the gospel and the typical leaders of village congregations were native evangelist/catechists. Africa is simply too big and missionaries too few to have made any other answer possible.[40] We might compare these leaders to those in minor orders in the medieval period. So, eleventh, reviving such a tradition would require, in some traditions, rethinking the emphasis, born of the liturgical revival, of the goal of the Eucharist celebrated in every congregation every Sunday. In evangelical Anglican Tanzania, occasional celebration conduced to a sense of the importance of the event, and so to a piety of spiritual preparation which more overtly sacramental strains of our tradition had forgotten.

In point twelve, David Martin has claimed that the central adaptation of the Protestant side of Christianity to modernity was Methodism, and in particular, the cell, the class meeting, and the prayer group.[41] These have proven portable and amenable to mitosis and replication. We can see secular confirmation of this in our own setting in the tremendous

37. See Webber and Ruth, *Evangelicals on the Canterbury Trail*. Something similar could be said of the large number of evangelicals who become Orthodox.

38. See his chapter on India in Neill and Chadwick, *History of Christian Missions*.

39. See, for example, Banks, *Reenvisioning Theological Education*.

40. This becomes clear if one reads Sundkler and Steed, *History of the Church in Africa*.

41. Martin, *Tongues of Fire*.

success of self-help in small groups, often in the basements of churches.[42] It is likewise worth noting that the beating heart of a number of megachurches is not the large gathering on Sunday morning (where the service may have more of a seeker quality than one would have guessed), but rather the small groups to which newcomers are steered and where formation takes place.

Let us summarize our answer to the challenge of culture. Epistemologically, the doctrine of the faith has been like a grammar making possible various expressions which can be tested and corrected across generations and continents. Morally, the weight is placed on the agency of local Christians and the fruitfulness of the gospel through them, sometimes with and sometimes in spite of their missionary colleagues.[43] If Newbigin were to rise from the ground, like Saul summoned by the witch of Endor, what might he observe about our cultural situation and its missionary implications? The points he might make are all treated elsewhere in this work, but it may be useful to offer them as a summarizing list, in the wake of our inculturation rules of thumb.

For us, choice and hence the marketplace are king. Pastors must make use of this and the energy it affords without surrendering to it and the commodification it entails. We are forever on our phones, and so the simple fact of gathering bodily will take on a compelling counter-cultural significance. In a generation that has been defined for many by divorce, the traditional, the lasting, and the promissory will have evangelistic power. In an age where joining is on the wane, the power of the small group must also be harnessed, but how?[44] Even contending parties in the church agree we are now post-Constantinian, and more so after COVID. In such a world, a core of lay leaders—the well-catechized remnant—are all the more important. But how are they to be recruited and trained? Likewise, how will the intensity of training which residential seminary provided for previous generations be continued in the crisis to come for such schools?[45] In the "next Christendom" in American cities, who will be able to make room for the nature of "the church catholic" in our midst?[46]

42. See Wuthnow, *"I Come Away Stronger."*

43. However, we do not lose track of the first generation of missionaries, who knew they faced likely death.

44. Putnam, *Bowling Alone*.

45. The shift toward hybrid rather than residential learning, which was already well underway, rapidly accelerated during COVID.

46. See, for example, Hanciles, *Beyond Christendom*; or Cho and Page, *No Longer Strangers*.

And finally, in a time wary of authority in general and doctrinal claims in particular,[47] can the present generation reconceive of its leaders as less powerful and more spiritually authoritative?[48] (And in light of these last questions, can para-church organizations like sodalities, mission societies, and seminaries reimagine themselves so as to be agents of renewal, as they have historically been, in the interstices of the declining institutional church?)

Although culture is the question that has dominated the missiological landscape for the past several generations, several classic older questions continue to accompany it, phrased in new ways. First, what is the relation of mission to evangelism? Secondly, what is its motive? And thirdly, why do the peoples of the earth tend to hear and respond? While these questions have understandably persisted in reflection, we can note a shared quality to the answers we now tend to hear. Each generates answers characterized by holism: the balancing of different answers and a tendency to see each in a both/and way. Complementarity and mutual entailment are the order of the day.

As to the first question, we might say that mission refers to all the activities involved in response to the summons of the risen Christ in going to the nations. After considerable debate between evangelicals and ecumenicals (as they were called in the 1960s) it was understood that witnessing and serving—the Great Commission of Matt 28 and the imperative of Matt 25—were inseparable and belonged together.[49] Missiologists such as Vinay Samuel and Chris Sugden have noted that the idea that evangelism and social action (or service) could be separated is a luxury assumption of the church in the West.[50] It is worth noting that throughout mission history they were inseparable—even the Baptists like Carey who went to India determined not to squander their energies in good works ended up building schools and hospitals. Conversely,[51] the freeing of slaves in West and then East Africa led naturally to their evangelization by the mission societies. We might say that this holism is simply witness to the kingdom in body and soul.[52] One can see this in

47. See the research of the Barna Group, *Engaging the Spiritually Open*.

48. One wonders if a more exilic church will mean an authority more rabbinic.

49. This is laid out well in Verkuyl, *Contemporary Missiology*.

50. Samuel and Sugden, *Mission as Transformation*.

51. See, for example, Oliver, *Missionary Factor in East Africa*.

52. To this may be added recent research from Barna about reticence to make claims lest they seem overly aggressive, even among evangelicals in our culture. Evangelism

gatherings of the Global South Anglican Churches, which are preponderantly evangelical yet are all deeply involved in social outreach due to the great needs of their dioceses.

At this point, however, we should make an important distinction. While Christian service to alleviate poverty may be impelled by Christian reasons in the heart, it may not look significantly different from the service of a compassionate secular person. It is particularly in witness—in the hope of conversion and the call to believe—that the distinctiveness of the Christian mission as a whole comes clearly to the fore. While serving and witnessing go hand in hand, the latter invariably has a distinct role in marking the activity as defined by devotion to Christ, and it reminds us that the human cannot live by bread alone. Otherwise, advocating holism can become a means of avoiding giving one's testimony, which is truly counter-cultural. However, whether this is done in person or via media, in a group or as an individual, to strangers or after a time of getting to know one another, after serving or alongside of it, are matters of strategy and not per se of theological principle. (However, we can say that Christians who actually do witness can pose questions about the salvation of non-believers or about adherents of other religions from a real-life perspective and not just speculatively.)[53]

The second of these classic, inter-related, and holistically inclined questions is that of the motive for mission. The following answers are mainstays: the saving of lost souls, the planting of churches, the alleviation of misery, and obedience to the Great Commission. It is hard to disagree with any, and one can easily see how the answers are more a matter of emphasis in particular moments in history than as a result of different doctrinal stances. They seem complementary insofar as they are answers to the same question from a different angle. Recently, strong arguments have been made for a more doxological response to God in mission—namely, that having a role in the divine summoning of the nations in the end-time is a way to praise him and at the same time an invitation for the nations to join in this symphony of praise.[54] As we are graciously given a share in the invitation we are enabled to "do something

---

that comes alongside, listens, takes time to serve, etc. may prove simply the most effective. See Barna Group, *Engaging the Spiritually Open*.

53. See Sumner, *First and the Last*.

54. For example, Sunquist, *Understanding Christian Mission*. See also Begbie, *Voicing Creation's Praise*.

beautiful for God."[55] It is easy to see how this answer fits perfectly with a eucharistic approach to pastoral practice.

While this gives reasons for the messenger, what have the standard answers been as to why people accept the good news? (The best answer is grace, but it is an answer on a different plane, and working in and through the other possible answers.) Here we face epistemological questions: How can the hearer respond in the affirmative if his or her frame of reference is by definition not yet one from which the invitation is issued? Put simply, people are drawn to the gospel for various factors, understood in various degrees. Once in the fold, they come to see those same factors more deeply and from a wider perspective of the new worldview, although the original reasons will not vanish.

At this point we do well to return to the emphasis on holism. Most often, people make a cumulative judgment of heart, will, mind, relationships, etc.[56] These all conspire to show something new, and the change may happen gradually until it reaches a kind of critical mass.[57] To be sure, the confection will be different for different individuals. Here we may return to our second emphasis on the congregation as the "argument" as a whole, per Newbigin. Ideally, the congregation would somehow seek to make the appeal to be reconciled with God (2 Cor 5) with mind, will, conscience, emotion, relationship, and service. It is from this wider angle that we can see the validity, for example, of apologetics, although arguments may serve as much to reinforce new or wavering believers as to convince the skeptic.[58] In other words, all apologetics is ad hoc, insofar as it takes place within a wider worldview and on behalf of an embodied congregation.[59]

The question as to why people have converted, and do convert, is obviously not open to a single answer. But we do well to expand our imaginations with the help of church history and explore reasons that may not immediately come to mind. In the patristic era, for example in Justin, apologetic reasons were given in part to head off persecution and to deflect prejudice. But willingness to suffer martyrdom and the performance

55. Muggeridge, *Something Beautiful for God.*

56. See Mitchell, *Justification of Religious Belief.*

57. Rambo, *Understanding Religious Conversion*; and Kuhn, *Structure of Scientific Revolutions.*

58. Thus Buckley, *At the Origins of Modern Atheism.*

59. See Placher, *Unapologetic Theology.*

of miracles were also offered as reasons for conversions.[60] A quieter and more surprising reason was the demonstration of patience, which the ancients did not even think of as a virtue, and which resulted in a steady "ferment."[61] In the early Middle Ages we see a kind of power evangelism in challenging paganism as well as preserving learning and social order.[62] Another pervasive but more hidden reason is the resolution of conflict between old and new religious values in the second or third generation after the introduction of the gospel, by which a new cultural synthesis is created around the gospel, accompanied by revival or dramatic renewal of some sort.[63] Renewal becomes a bridge or passage from the older to the newer life in a more comprehensive way (and this raises anew the question of what renewal may mean in changed circumstances).[64]

So much in pastoral practice comes back to preaching and teaching, whereby Christians are formed and encouraged to understand the biblical narrative as their own story: to fuse their horizon with its.[65] When they hear "Go in peace," the world into which they go—their familiar neighborhood—is also the place and time of the gentiles now summoned. They are in continuity with heralds going forth across centuries of mission history. And they go forth as members of the body—the congregation—part of the church whose guilt, gifts, traditions, peculiarities, movements, and sufferings they share. In theory, though all are heralds, doubtless some will take up this calling more earnestly. As with all missionaries, these will seek to understand their context and will not be surprised if their own motives and the reasons for conversions they see are holistic and cumulative. They will also stand ready to be surprised by the forms that the "yes" they will hear from the world, also God's, will take, dependent as those answers are on his grace.

60. A good example is Athanasius, *On the Incarnation.*

61. Kreider, *Patient Ferment of the Early Church.*

62. For example in St. Boniface.

63. One thinks of revival in the Pacific Islands and the East African Revival, at once radically new and traditional.

64. One wonders if a functional equivalent of a movement like Cursillo can be found.

65. A good articulation of this is Hauerwas and Willimon's *Resident Aliens.*

Bibliography

Abraham, William J. *The Logic of Evangelism*. Grand Rapids: Eerdmans, 1989.

Abrahamson, Eric. "Using Creative Recombination to Manage Change." *Employment Relations Today* 30 (2004) 33–41.

Achtemeier, Elizabeth. "The Artful Dialogue: Some Thoughts on the Relation of Biblical Studies and Homiletics." *Interpretation* 35 (1981) 18–31.

Alcoholics Anonymous: The Story of How Many Thousands of Men and Women Have Recovered from Alcoholism. 4th ed. New York: Alcoholics Anonymous World Services, 2001.

Allen, Michael. *Ephesians*. Grand Rapids: Brazos, 2020.

Allen, Roland. *Missionary Methods: St. Paul's or Ours?* Cambridge: Lutterworth, 2006.

Ammerman, Nancy Tatom. *Studying Congregations: A New Handbook*. Nashville: Abingdon, 1998.

Anderson, Ray S. "A Theology for Ministry." In *Theological Foundations for Ministry: Selected Readings for a Theology of the Church in Ministry*, edited by Ray S. Anderson, 6–21. Edinburgh: T&T Clark, 1979.

Anonymous. *The Way of a Pilgrim*. Translated by Olga Savin. Boston: Shambhala, 1996.

Athanasius. *On the Incarnation*. Translated by John Behr. Yonkers, NY: St. Vladimir's Seminary Press, 2011.

Augustine. *De doctrina Christiana*. Edited and Translated by R. P. H. Green. Oxford: Clarendon, 1995.

———. *Homilies on the Gospel of John*. In vol. 7 of *Nicene and Post Nicene Fathers*, Series 1, edited by Philip Schaff. New York: Christian Literature, 1888.

Austin, J. L. *How To Do Things with Words*. Oxford: Clarendon, 1975.

Austin, Victor Lee. *Friendship: The Heart of Being Human*. Grand Rapids: Baker Academic, 2020.

Balthasar, Hans Urs von. "Casta Meretrix." In *Explorations in Theology 2: Spouse of the Word*, 193–288. San Francisco: Ignatius, 1991.

Banks, Robert. *Reenvisioning Theological Education: Exploring a Missional Alternative to Current Models*. Grand Rapids: Eerdmans, 1999.

Baptism, Eucharist and Ministry. Faith and Order Paper 111. Geneva: World Council of Churches, 1982.

Barbour, Ian G. *Myths, Models, and Paradigms: A Comparative Study in Science and Religion*. New York: Harper & Row, 1974.

Barclay, John M. G. *Paul and the Gift*. Grand Rapids: Eerdmans, 2015.

Barna Group. *Engaging the Spiritually Open*. Report, 2023.

———. "Marriage and Divorce in 2025: Five Trends Shaping Today's Families." Nov. 12, 2025. https://www.barna.com/trends/marriage-divorce-trends-2025/.

Barrett, David B. *Schism and Renewal in Africa: An Analysis of Six Thousand Contemporary Religious Movements*. Nairobi: Oxford University Press, 1968.

Bass, Dorothy C., ed. *Practicing Our Faith: A Way of Life for a Searching People*. San Francisco: Jossey-Bass, 1997.

Bass, Dorothy C., et al. *Christian Practical Wisdom: What It Is, Why It Matters*. Grand Rapids: Eerdmans, 2016.

Begbie, Jeremy. *Voicing Creation's Praise: Towards a Theology of the Arts*. Edinburgh: T&T Clark, 1991.

Bell, Rob. *Love Wins*. San Francisco: HarperOne, 2011.

Bellah, Robert N., et al. *Habits of the Heart: Individualism and Commitment in American Life*. Berkeley: University of California Press, 2008.

Bernard of Clairvaux. *Honey and Salt: Selected Spiritual Writings of Saint Bernard of Clairvaux*. Edited by John F. Thornton and Susan B. Varenne. New York: Vintage, 2007.

Berry, Wendell. *What Are People For? Essays*. Berkeley: Counterpoint, 2010.

Blackwell, Ben C. *Christosis: Engaging Paul's Soteriology with His Patristic Interpreters*. Grand Rapids: Eerdmans, 2016.

Blauw, Johannes. *The Missionary Nature of the Church*. New York: McGraw-Hill, 1962.

Bloom, Anthony. *Beginning to Pray*. New York: Paulist, 1970.

Boersma, Hans. *Scripture as Real Presence: Sacramental Exegesis in the Early Church*. Grand Rapids: Baker Academic, 2017.

———. "A Wafer-Thin Practice." *First Things*, May 12, 2020. https://www.firstthings.com/web-exclusives/2020/05/a-wafer-thin-practice.

Bonhoeffer, Dietrich. *The Cost of Discipleship*. New York: Simon & Schuster, 1995 [1937].

———. *Letters and Papers from Prison*. Translated by Isabel Best et al. Dietrich Bonhoeffer Works 8. Minneapolis: Fortress, 2010.

———. *Life Together*. New York: HarperOne, 2009.

———. *The Lord's Prayer*. Minneapolis: Fortress, 1976.

Book of Common Prayer. Canada: General Synod, 1962.

Book of Common Prayer. London: Robert Barker, 1549.

Book of Common Prayer. New York: Church Hymnal Corp., 1979.

Borgeson, Josephine, et al. *Reshaping Ministry: Essays in Memory of Wesley Frensdorff*. Arvada, CO: Jethro, 1990.

Bourdieu, Pierre. *The Logic of Practice*. Translated by Richard Nice. Stanford, CA: Stanford University Press, 1990.

Brooks, David. "The Nuclear Family Was a Mistake." *Atlantic Monthly*, Mar. 2020, 55–69.

Browning, Don S. *A Fundamental Practical Theology: Descriptive and Strategic Proposals*. Minneapolis: Fortress, 1996.

Buckley, Michael J. *At the Origins of Modern Atheism*. Repr., New Haven: Yale University Press, 2010.

Buttrick, David G. "Preaching Today: The Loss of a Public Voice." In *The Folly of Preaching: Models and Methods*, edited by Michael P. Knowles, 3–14. Grand Rapids: Eerdmans, 2007.

Carlson, Kent, and Mike Lueken. *Renovation of the Church: What Happens When a Seeker Church Discovers Spiritual Formation*. Downers Grove, IL: InterVarsity, 2011.

Chan, Simon. *Liturgical Theology: The Church as Worshiping Community*. Downers Grove, IL: InterVarsity, 2006.

Charry, Ellen T. *By the Renewing of Your Minds: The Pastoral Function of Christian Doctrine*. New York: Oxford University Press, 1997.

Chester, Stephen. "Apocalyptic Union: Martin Luther's Account of Faith in Christ." In *"In Christ" in Paul: Explorations in Paul's Theology of Union and Participation*, edited by Michael J. Thate et al., 375–98. Tübingen: Mohr Siebeck, 2014.

Cho, Eugene, and Samira Izadi Page. *No Longer Strangers: Transforming Evangelism with Immigrant Communities*. Grand Rapids: Eerdmans, 2021.

Clifford, James. *The Predicament of Culture: Twentieth-Century Ethnography, Literature, and Art*. Cambridge: Harvard University Press, 1988.

Coakley, Sarah. "Can Pastoral Theology Be Saved? Reflections on the Practice of Theology Inside the University and Out." Australian Broadcasting Corporation, June 20, 2021. https://www.abc.net.au/religion/can-systematic-theology-become-pastoral-again-and-pastoral-theol/10095582.

Cobb, David, and Derek Olsen. *St. Augustine's Prayer Book: A Book of Devotions*. Cincinnati: Forward Movement, 2012.

Coggan, Donald. *Sacrament of the Word*. London: Collins, 1987.

Congar, Yves. *Chrétiens désunis: Principes d'un 'oecuménisme' catholique*. Unam sanctam 1. Paris: Editions du Cerf, 1937.

Copenhaver, Martin B., et al. *Good News in Exile: Three Pastors Offer a Hopeful Vision for the Church*. Grand Rapids: Eerdmans, 1999.

Cosden, Darrell. *A Theology of Work: Work and the New Creation*. Eugene, OR: Wipf & Stock, 2006.

Cosper, Mike, host. *The Rise and Fall of Mars Hill*. *Christianity Today* podcast series, 2021–22. https://www.christianitytoday.com/podcasts/the-rise-and-fall-of-mars-hill/.

Coutts, Jon. *A Shared Mercy: Karl Barth on Forgiveness and the Church*. Downers Grove, IL: IVP Academic, 2016.

Craddock, Fred. *As One Without Authority*. 3rd ed. Nashville: Abingdon, 1979.

Cronin, Vincent. *A Pearl to India: The Life of Roberto de Nobili*. New York: Dutton, 1959.

Cullmann, Oscar. *Christ and Time: The Primitive Christian Conception of Time and History*. Eugene, OR: Wipf & Stock, 2018.

———. "Eschatology and Missions in the New Testament." In *The Background of the New Testament and Its Eschatology*, edited by W. D. Davies and D. Daube, 409–21. Cambridge: Cambridge University Press, 1954.

Davidson, Donald. "On the Very Idea of a Conceptual Scheme." *Proceedings of the American Philosophical Association* 17 (1973–74) 5–20.

Dean, Kenda Creasy. *Almost Christian: What the Faith of Our Teenagers Is Telling the American Church*. Oxford: Oxford University Press, 2010.

Deneen, Patrick J. *Why Liberalism Failed*. New Haven: Yale University Press, 2019.

DePree, Max. *Leadership Is an Art*. New York: Currency, 2004.

Dingemans, Gijsbert D. J. "Practical Theology in the Academy: A Contemporary Overview." *The Journal of Religion* 76 (1996) 82–96.

Dix, Gregory. *The Shape of the Liturgy.* London: Bloomsbury, 2015.

Donovan, Vincent J. *Christianity Rediscovered: An Epistle from the Masai.* London: SCM, 1982.

Dostoevsky, Fyodor. *Notes from Underground.* Translated by Richard Pevear and Larissa Volokhonsky. New York: Vintage, 1994.

Douglas, Mary. *Natural Symbols.* 2nd ed. London: Routledge, 1996.

Doyle, C. Andrew. *Embodied Liturgy: Virtual Reality and Liturgical Theology in Conversation.* New York: Church, 2021.

Dreher, Rod. *The Benedict Option: A Strategy for Christians in a Post-Christian Nation.* New York: Sentinel, 2018.

Dunne, George H. *Generation of Giants: The Story of the Jesuits in China in the Last Decades of the Ming Dynasty.* London: Burns & Oates, 1962.

Durnbaugh, Donald F. *The Believers' Church: The History and Character of Radical Protestantism.* New York: Macmillan, 1970.

Dykstra, Craig, and Dorothy C. Bass. "Theological Understandings of Christian Practices." In *Practicing Theology: Beliefs and Practices in Christian Life*, edited by Miroslav Volf and Dorothy C. Bass, 13–32. Grand Rapids: Eerdmans, 2002.

Erikson, Erik. *Childhood and Society.* New York: Norton, 1950.

Evans, Gillian R., ed. *A History of Pastoral Care.* London: Cassell, 2000.

Evdokimov, Paul. *L'Orthodoxie.* Neuchatel: Delachaux et Niestlé, 1959.

Farrer, Austin. *Lord I Believe: Suggestions for Turning the Creed into Prayer.* Cambridge, MA: Cowley, 1989.

Fowl, Stephen E. *Ephesians: A Commentary.* Louisville: Westminster John Knox, 2012.

Francis. "Letter of His Holiness Pope Francis to the People of God." Letter. Holy See. Aug. 20, 2018. https://www.vatican.va/content/francesco/en/letters/2018/documents/papa-francesco_20180820_lettera-popolo-didio.html.

Frankl, Victor E. *Man's Search for Meaning.* New York: Random House, 2006.

Freeman, Curtis W. *Contesting Catholicity: Theology for Other Baptists.* Waco, TX: Baylor University Press, 2014.

Freud, Sigmund. *Beyond the Pleasure Principle.* London: The International Psycho-Analytical Press, 1922.

Friedman, Edwin H. *Generation to Generation: Family Process in Church and Synagogue.* New York: Guilford, 1985.

Geertz, Clifford. "Deep Play: Notes on the Balinese Cock-Fight." In *The Interpretation of Cultures: Selected Essays*, 412–54. New York: Basic, 1973.

Gerkin, Charles V. *An Introduction to Pastoral Care.* Nashville: Abingdon, 1997.

———. "On the Art of Caring: A Meditative Address." *Journal of Pastoral Care* 45 (1991) 399–408.

———. "Pastoral Ministry Between the Times." *Journal of Pastoral Care* 30 (1976) 178–85.

Gerrish, Brian. *Grace and Gratitude.* Eugene, OR: Wipf & Stock, 2002.

Glasser, William. *Reality Therapy.* New York: Harper & Row, 1965.

Gorman, Michael J. *Cruciformity: Paul's Narrative Spirituality of the Cross.* Grand Rapids: Eerdmans, 2001.

———. "Paul's Corporate Cruciform, Missional *Theosis* in 2 Corinthians." In *"In Christ" in Paul: Explorations in Paul's Theology of Union and Participation*, edited by Michael J. Thate et al., 181–208. Tübingen: Mohr Siebeck, 2014.

Gottman, John M., and Nan Silver. *The Seven Principles of Making Marriage Work*. New York: Harmony, 2015.

Graham, Elaine, et al., eds., *Theological Reflection: Methods*. 2nd ed. London: SCM, 2019.

Greene-McCreight, Kathryn. *Darkness Is My Only Companion*. Grand Rapids: Brazos, 2006.

Gregory, Brad. *The Unintended Reformation: How a Religious Revolution Secularized Society*. Cambridge: Harvard University Press, 2012.

Groome, Thomas H. *Christian Religious Education: Sharing Our Story and Vision*. San Francisco: Jossey-Bass, 1999.

———. Review of *A Fundamental Practical Theology: Descriptive and Strategic Proposals*, by Don S. Browning. *Horizons* 20 (1993) 162–63.

———. "Theology on Our Feet: A Revisionist Pedagogy for Healing the Gap Between Academia and Ecclesia." In *Formation and Reflection*, edited by Lewis Seymour Mudge and James N. Poling, 55–78. Philadelphia: Fortress, 1987.

Guder, Darrell L., and Lois Barrett, eds. *Missional Church: A Vision for the Sending of the Church in North America*. Grand Rapids: Eerdmans, 1998.

Guzie, Tad. "Patristic Hermeneutics and the Meaning of Tradition." *Theological Studies* 32 (1971) 647–58.

Habets, Myk. "'Reformed Theosis?' A Response to Gannon Murphy." *Theology Today* 65 (2009) 489–98.

Han, Byung-Chul. *The Burnout Society*. Stanford, CA: Stanford Briefs, 2015.

Hanciles, Jehu. *Beyond Christendom: Globalization, African Migration, and the Transformation of the West*. Maryknoll, NY: Orbis, 2008.

Hart, Trevor. "Humankind in Christ and Christ in Humankind: Salvation as Participation in Our Substitute in the Theology of John Calvin." *Scottish Journal of Theology* 42 (1989) 67–84.

Hatchett, Marion J. *Sanctifying Life, Time, and Space*. New York: Seabury, 1976.

Hauerwas, Stanley. "Which Church? What Unity? Or, an Attempt to Say What I May Think About the Future of Christian Unity." *Pro Ecclesia* 22 (2013) 263–80.

Hauerwas, Stanley, and Richard Bondi. "Memory, Community and the Reasons for Living: Theological and Ethical Reflections on Suicide and Euthanasia." *Journal of the American Academy of Religion* 44 (1976) 439–52.

Hauerwas, Stanley, and William H. Willimon. *Resident Aliens: Life in the Christian Colony*. Nashville: Abingdon, 1989.

Hays, Richard B. "'What Is 'Real Participation in Christ'? A Dialogue with E. P. Sanders on Pauline Soteriology." In *Redefining First-Century Jewish and Christian Identities: Essays in Honor of Ed Parish Sanders*, edited by Fabian Udoh et al., 336–51. Notre Dame: University of Notre Dame Press, 2008.

Healy, Nicholas M. "Practices and the New Ecclesiology: Misplaced Concreteness?" *International Journal of Systematic Theology* 5 (2003) 287–308.

Heidegger, Martin. *Being and Time*. Translated by John MacQuarrie and Edward Robinson. New York: HarperOne, 2008.

Hess, Edward. *Learn or Die: Using Science to Build a Leading-Edge Learning Organization*. New York: Columbia Business School Publishing, 2014.

Hiltner, Seward. "What We Get and Give in Pastoral Care: What We Get: II—Theological Understanding." *Pastoral Psychology* 5 (1954) 14–25.

Hitchcock, James F. "Liturgy and Ritual." *Adoremus* 12 (2006–7). https://adoremus.org/2006/12/liturgy-and-ritual/.

Hopewell, James F. *Congregation: Stories and Structures*. Philadelphia: Fortress, 1987.

Huizinga, Johan. *Homo Ludens: A Study of the Play-Element in Culture*. London: Routledge, 1949.

Hummel, Charles. *Fire in the Fireplace*. Downers Grove, IL: InterVarsity, 1994.

Hunsberger, George R. *Bearing the Witness of the Spirit: Lesslie Newbigin's Theology of Cultural Plurality*. Grand Rapids: Eerdmans, 1998.

Hunsinger, Deborah van Deusen. *Bearing the Unbearable: Trauma, Gospel, and Pastoral Care*. Grand Rapids: Eerdmans, 2015.

———. "Pastoral Theology in a 'Barthian' Key." *Pro Ecclesia* 28 (2019) 4–21.

———. *Theology and Pastoral Counseling: A New Interdisciplinary Approach*. Grand Rapids: Eerdmans, 1995.

Hunsinger, George. "Salvator Mundi: Three Types of Christology." In *Christology, Ancient and Modern: Explorations in Constructive Dogmatics*, edited by Oliver Crisp and Fred R. Sanders, 42–59. Grand Rapids: Zondervan, 2013.

Hunter, Rodney J. "Five Questions and Polemical Suggestions for the Future of Pastoral Theology." *Journal of Pastoral Theology* 5 (1995) 8–20.

Hütter, Reinhard. *Suffering Divine Things: Theology as Church Practice*. Grand Rapids: Eerdmans, 2000.

Ineson, Emma. *Ambition: What Jesus Said About Power, Success and Counting Stuff*. London: SPCK, 2019.

Jacobs, Alan. "Do-It-Yourself Tradition." *First Things*, Jan. 2009, 27–32.

Jenkins, Philip. *The Next Christendom: The Coming of Global Christianity*. New York: Oxford University Press, 2007.

Jenson, Robert W. *Systematic Theology*. Vol. 2. New York: Oxford University Press, 2001.

Jeremias, Joachim. *Jesus' Promise to the Nations*. London: SCM, 2012.

John of Damascus. "The Orthodox Faith." In *Psalms 1–50*, by C. A. Blaising and C. S. Hardin, 8. Downers Grove, IL: IVP Academic, 2008.

Jones, L. Gregory. "Beliefs, Desires, Practices, and the Ends of Theological Education." In *Practicing Theology: Beliefs and Practices in Christian Life*, edited by Miroslav Volf and Dorothy C. Bass, 185–205. Grand Rapids: Eerdmans, 2002.

———. *Embodying Forgiveness: A Theological Analysis*. Grand Rapids: Eerdmans, 1995.

Karanja, John. *Founding an African Faith: Kikuyu Anglican Christianity, 1900–1945*. Nairobi: Uzima, 1999.

Katongole, Emmanuel, and Chris Rice. *Reconciling All Things: A Christian Vision for Justice, Peace and Healing*. Downers Grove, IL: IVP Books, 2008.

Kavanagh, Aidan. *On Liturgical Theology: The Hale Memorial Lectures of Seabury-Western Theological Seminary, 1981*. Collegeville, MN: Liturgical, 1992.

Keck, David. *Forgetting Whose We Are: Alzheimer's Disease and the Love of God*. Nashville: Abingdon, 1996.

Kelly, J. N. D. "The Nicene Creed: A Turning Point." *Scottish Journal of Theology* 36 (1983) 29–39.

———. "Il punto di visto anglicano sulla Constituzione." In *La Chiesa del Vaticano II: Studi e commenti intorno alla Costituzione dommatica* Lumen gentium, edited by Guilherme Baraúna, 1203–12. Firenze: Vallecchi, 1965.

Kelsey, Morton. *Healing and Christianity: A Classic Study*. Minneapolis: Fortress, 1995.

Kierkegaard, Søren. *For Self-Examination/Judge for Yourself!* Vol. 21 of *Kierkegaard's Writings*. Edited and translated by Howard V. Hong and Edna H. Hong. Princeton: Princeton University Press, 2015.

Knox, John. *The Integrity of Preaching*. New York: Abingdon, 1957.

Kreider, Alan. *The Patient Ferment of the Early Church*. Grand Rapids: Baker Academic, 2016.

Kress, Robert. *The Church: Communion, Sacrament, Communication*. New York: Paulist, 1984.

———. "Simul Justus et Peccator: Ecclesiological and Ecumenical Perspectives." *Horizons* 11 (1984) 255–75.

Kübler-Ross, Elisabeth. *On Death and Dying*. New York: Macmillan, 1969.

Kuhn, Thomas S. *The Structure of Scientific Revolutions*. 4th ed. Chicago: University of Chicago Press, 2012.

Langberg, Diane. *Redeeming Power: Understanding Authority and Abuse in the Church*. Grand Rapids, Brazos, 2020.

Leas, Speed. *Moving Your Church Through Conflict*. Washington, DC: Alban Institute, 2012.

Leech, Kenneth. *Soul Friend*. New York: Morehouse, 2001.

Leithart, Peter. *Traces of the Trinity*. Grand Rapids: Brazos, 2015.

Levering, Matthew. *Engaging the Doctrine of Marriage*. Eugene, OR: Cascade, 2020.

Lewis, C. S. *Mere Christianity*. New York: HarperCollins, 1952.

———. *The Weight of Glory*. 1942. https://www.doxaweb.com/assets/weight_of_glory.pdf.

Lilburn, Tim. *Living in the World as If It Were Home*. Connemara, Ireland: Xylem, 2002.

Lindbeck, George A. *The Nature of Doctrine: Religion and Theology in a Postliberal Age*. Philadelphia: Westminster, 1984.

Long, Thomas G. *The Witness of Preaching*. 2nd ed. Louisville: Westminster John Knox, 2005.

"Longer Report on Church and Community." In *The Churches Survey Their Task: The Report of the Conference at Oxford, July 1937, on Church, Community and State*, 188–240. London: Allen & Unwin, 1937.

Longman, Tremper, III. *Literary Approaches to Biblical Interpretation*. Grand Rapids: Zondervan, 1987.

Lutheran World Federation and Roman Catholic Church. "Joint Declaration on the Doctrine of Justification." Dicastery for Promoting Christian Unity, 1999.

Macaskill, Grant. *Union with Christ in the New Testament*. Oxford: Oxford University Press, 2013.

MacDonald, G. Jeffrey. "Congregations Gone Wild." *New York Times*, Aug. 7, 2010, 9.

MacIntyre, Alasdair C. *After Virtue: A Study in Moral Theory*. 3rd ed. Notre Dame: University of Notre Dame Press, 2007.

———. *Whose Justice? Which Rationality*? Notre Dame: University of Notre Dame Press, 1988.

Maclaurin, James, and Kim Sterelny. *What Is Biodiversity?* Chicago: University of Chicago Press, 2008.

Martin, David. *Tongues of Fire: The Explosion of Protestantism in Latin America*. Cambridge, MA: Blackwell, 1990.

McFadyen, Alistair. *Bound to Sin: Abuse, Holocaust, and the Christian Doctrine of Sin*. Cambridge: Cambridge University Press, 2000.

McGavran, Donald A. *Bridges of God: A Study in the Strategy of Mission.* Eugene, OR: Wipf & Stock, 2005.

McGavran, Donald A., and C. Peter Wagner. *Understanding Church Growth.* Grand Rapids: Eerdmans, 1990.

McKnight, Scot. "Five Streams of the Emerging Church: Key Elements of the Most Controversial and Misunderstood Movement in the Church Today." *Christianity Today*, Feb. 2007, 34–39.

Meeks, Wayne. *The First Urban Christians.* New Haven: Yale University Press, 2003.

Meilaender, Gilbert. "I Want to Burden My Loved Ones." *First Things*, Mar. 1, 2010.

Miller-McLemore, Bonnie J. "The Living Human Web: A Twenty-Five Year Retrospective." *Pastoral Psychology* 67 (2018) 305–21.

Mitchell, Basil. *The Justification of Religious Belief.* London: Macmillan, 1973.

Mitchell, Leonel L. *Praying Shapes Believing: A Theological Commentary on the Book of Common Prayer.* New York: Morehouse, 1985.

Morse, Christopher. *Not Every Spirit: A Dogmatics of Christian Disbelief.* London: T&T Clark, 2009.

Moschella, Mary Clark, and Lee H. Butler Jr. *The Edward Wimberly Reader: A Black Pastoral Theology.* Waco, TX: Baylor, 2020.

Muggeridge, Malcolm. *Something Beautiful for God: Mother Teresa of Calcutta.* New York: Harper & Row, 1971.

Myers, Ched, and Elaine Enns. *Ambassadors of Reconciliation.* Maryknoll, NY: Orbis, 2009.

Neder, Adam. *Participation in Christ: An Entry into Karl Barth's Church Dogmatics.* Louisville: Westminster John Knox, 2009.

Neill, Stephen. *Creative Tension.* London: Edinburgh House, 1959.

Neill, Stephen, and Owen Chadwick. *A History of Christian Missions.* London: Penguin, 1991.

Neumann, James N. "Thy Will Be Done: Jesus's Passion in the Lord's Prayer." *Journal of Biblical Literature* 138 (2019) 161–82.

Newbigin, Lesslie. *Foolishness to the Greeks.* Grand Rapids: Eerdmans, 1988.

———. *The Gospel in a Pluralist Society.* Grand Rapids: Eerdmans, 1989.

———. *The Open Secret: An Introduction to the Theology of Mission.* Rev. ed. Grand Rapids: Eerdmans, 1995.

———. *Truth to Tell.* Grand Rapids: Eerdmans, 1991.

———. *Unfinished Agenda.* Eugene, OR: Wipf & Stock, 2009.

Nida, Eugene A. *Toward a Science of Translating.* Leiden: Brill, 1964.

Novak, Michael. *The Spirit of Democratic Capitalism.* New York: Simon & Schuster, 1982.

O'Connor, Flannery. *The Habit of Being: The Letters of Flannery O'Connor.* New York: Farrar, Straus and Giroux, 1988.

Oden, Thomas. *Care of Souls in the Classical Tradition.* Philadelphia: Fortress, 1984.

O'Donovan, Oliver. *On the Thirty-Nine Articles.* London: SCM, 2011.

———. *Resurrection and Moral Order: An Outline for Evangelical Ethics.* Grand Rapids: Eerdmans, 1994.

Ogden, Pat, and Janina Fisher. *Sensorimotor Psychotherapy.* New York: Norton, 2015.

Old, Hughes. *The Reading and Preaching of the Scriptures in the Worship of the Christian Church.* Grand Rapids: Eerdmans, 1998.

Oliver, Roland Anthony. *The Missionary Factor in East Africa*. London: Longmans, 1952.

Orthodox Church in America. "Saint Basil the Great, Archbishop of Caesarea in Cappadocia." Jan. 1, 2025. https://www.oca.org/saints/lives/2023/01/01/100003-saint-basil-the-great-archbishop-of-caesarea-in-cappadocia.

Pannenberg, Wolfhart. "Analogy and Doxology." In *Collected Essays*, translated by George H. Kehm, 211–38. Vol. 1 of *Basic Questions in Theology*. Philadelphia: Fortress, 1970.

Park, Samuel. "History and Method of Charles V. Gerkin's Pastoral Theology: Toward an Identity-Embodied and Community-Embedded Pastoral Theology, Part I, History." *Pastoral Psychology* 54 (2005) 47–60.

Pawley, Bernard C. "An Anglican Views the Council." In *Steps to Christian Unity*, edited by John A. O'Brien, 109–26. London: Collins, 1965.

Phan, Peter C. *Mission and Catechesis: Alexandre de Rhodes and Inculturation in Seventeenth-Century Vietnam*. Maryknoll, NY: Orbis, 2007.

Placher, William C. *Unapologetic Theology: A Christian Voice in a Pluralistic Conversation*. Louisville: Westminster John Knox, 1989.

Polkinghorne, John. *The Faith of a Physicist: Reflections from a Bottom-Up Thinker*. Princeton: Princeton University Press, 1994.

Porges, Stephen W. *The Polyvagal Theory*. New York: Norton, 2011.

Purves, Andrew. *Reconstructing Pastoral Theology: A Christological Foundation*. Louisville: Westminster John Knox, 2004.

Putnam, Robert D. *Bowling Alone: The Collapse and Revival of American Community*. New York: Simon & Schuster, 2000.

Radner, Ephraim. *A Brutal Unity: The Spiritual Politics of the Christian Church*. Waco, TX: Baylor University Press, 2012.

———. *A Time to Keep*. Waco, TX: Baylor University Press, 2016.

Rambo, Lewis R. *Understanding Religious Conversion*. New Haven: Yale University Press, 1993.

Ramsey, Michael. *The Gospel and the Catholic Church*. London: Longmans, 1956.

Reno, Russell R. *In the Ruins of the Church: Sustaining Faith in an Age of Diminished Christianity*. Grand Rapids: Brazos, 2002.

Rice, Charles. *What's the Shape of Narrative Preaching? Essays in Honor of Eugene L. Lowry*. Edited by Mike Graves and David J. Schlafer. St. Louis: Chalice, 2008.

Robertson, Donald. "Stoic Fatalism, Determinism, and Acceptance." Ch. 12 of *The Philosophy of Cognitive-Behavioural Therapy (CBT): Stoic Philosophy As Rational and Cognitive Psychotherapy*. London: Routledge, 2010. https://donaldrobertson.name/2013/03/09/stoic-fatalism-determinism-and-acceptance/.

Robertson, Edwin H., ed. *Dietrich Bonhoeffer's Christmas Sermons*. Grand Rapids: Zondervan, 2005.

Robinson, Haddon. *The Art and Craft of Biblical Preaching*. Grand Rapids: Zondervan, 2005.

Robinson, Peter. "Theological Interpretation of Scripture: 'Not a Method but a Mode.'" *Vestigia Dei: Wycliffe College Blog*, Sept. 17, 2019. https://www.wycliffecollege.ca/blog/theological-interpretation-scripture-not-method-but-mode.

Root, Andrew. *Christopraxis: A Practical Theology of the Cross*. Minneapolis: Fortress, 2014.

———. *Faith Formation in a Secular Age: Responding to the Church's Obsession with Youthfulness.* Grand Rapids: Baker Academic, 2017.

Root, Michael. "Why Care About the Unity of the Church?" In *Why Are We Here? Everyday Questions and the Christian Life*, edited by Ronald F. Thiemann and William C. Placher, 98–111. Harrisburg, PA: Trinity, 1998.

Rosin, Hellmut H. "Missio Dei": *An Examination of the Origin, Contents and Function of the Term in Protestant Missiological Discussion.* Leiden: Interuniversitair Instituut voor missiologie en oeucumenica, Afdeling Missiologie, 1972.

Rowthorn, Jeffrey. *The Wideness of God's Mercy.* New York: Church, 2007.

Rudy-Froese, Allan. Review of *Hearing the Sermon: Relationship/Content/Feeling*, by Ronald J. Allen. *The Conrad Grebel Review* 26 (Fall 2008) 95–96.

Rumsey, Andrew. *Parish: An Anglican Theology of Place.* London: SCM, 2017.

Rutledge, Fleming. *The Crucifixion: Understanding the Death of Jesus Christ.* Grand Rapids: Eerdmans, 2015.

Samuel, Vinay, and Chris Sugden. *Mission as Transformation: A Theology of the Whole Gospel.* Oxford: Regnum, 1999.

Sanford, Agnes. *The Healing Gifts of the Spirit.* New York: Jove, 1982.

Sanneh, Lamin O. *Translating the Message: The Missionary Impact on Culture.* Maryknoll, NY: Orbis, 1989.

Sayers, Dorothy. *Creed or Chaos? And Other Essays in Popular Theology.* London: Methuen, 1947.

Schlag, Martin, ed. *Handbook of Catholic Social Teaching.* Washington, DC: Catholic University of America Press, 2017.

Schmemann, Alexander. "Debate on the Liturgy: Liturgical Theology, Theology of Liturgy and Liturgical Reform." *St. Vladimir's Theological Quarterly* 13 (1969) 217–24.

———. *For the Life of the World: Sacraments and Orthodoxy.* Crestwood, NY: St. Vladimir's Seminary Press, 1973.

———. "The Orthodox Tradition." In *The Convergence of Traditions: Orthodox, Catholic, Protestant*, edited by Elmer O'Brien, 11–37. New York: Herder & Herder, 1967.

Second Vatican Council. *Lumen Gentium.* Dogmatic Constitution on the Church. Holy See. Nov. 21, 1964. https://www.vatican.va/archive/hist_councils/ii_vatican_council/documents/vat-ii_const_19641121_lumen-gentium_en.html.

Sennett, Richard, and Jonathan Cobb. *The Hidden Injuries of Class.* New York: Norton, 1972.

Simeon, Charles. "Directions How to Hear Sermons." In *Helps to Composition; or, Six Hundred Skeletons of Sermons*, skeleton 35, 1:345–48. 3rd ed. London: Luke Hansard & Sons, 1815.

Smith, Christian, and Melinda Lundquist Denton. *Soul Searching: The Religious and Spiritual Lives of American Teenagers.* New York: Oxford University Press, 2005.

Smith, James K. A. *Imagining the Kingdom: How Worship Works.* Grand Rapids: Baker Academic, 2013.

———. "Redeeming Ritual." *Banner*, Jan. 6, 2012. https://www.thebanner.org/features/2012/01/redeeming-ritual.

———. *You Are What You Love: The Spiritual Power of Habit.* Grand Rapids: Brazos, 2016.

Spellers, Stephanie. *The Church Cracked Open: Disruption, Decline, and New Hope for the Beloved Community*. New York: Church, 2021.

Spence, Jonathan D. *The Memory Palace of Mateo Ricci*. New York: Penguin, 1985.

Steltenkamp, Michael F. *Black Elk: Holy Man of the Oglala*. Norman: University of Oklahoma Press, 1997.

Stevens, R. Paul. *Work Matters: Lessons from Scripture*. Grand Rapids: Eerdmans, 2012.

Stott, John. *Between Two Worlds: The Challenge of Preaching Today*. Grand Rapids: Eerdmans, 1982.

Sumner, George R. *Being Salt: A Theology of an Ordered Church*. Eugene, OR: Cascade, 2007.

———. *The First and the Last: The Claim of Jesus Christ and the Claims of Other Religious Traditions*. Grand Rapids: Eerdmans, 2004.

———. "You Have Not Yet Considered the Gravity of Sin: A Key Retrieval for Our Time." *Pro Ecclesia* 25 (2016) 261–73.

Sundkler, Bengt, and Christopher Steed. *A History of the Church in Africa*. Cambridge: Cambridge University Press, 2000.

Sunquist, Scott W. *Understanding Christian Mission: Participation in Suffering and Glory*. Grand Rapids: Baker Academic, 2017.

Swinton, John. *Becoming Friends with Time: Disability, Timefullness, and Gentle Discipleship*. Waco, TX: Baylor University Press, 2018.

Sykes, Stephen W. *The Integrity of Anglicanism*. New York: Seabury, 1978.

Tate, Marvin E. *Psalms 51–100*. Word Biblical Commentary 20. Grand Rapids: HarperCollins, 2015.

Taylor, Charles. *A Secular Age*. Cambridge, MA: Harvard University Press, 2009.

Taylor, John V. *The Growth of the Church in Buganda: An Attempt at Understanding*. London: SCM, 1958.

Teresa of Avila. *The Interior Castle*. Translated by E. Allison Peers. New York: Martino Fine Books, 1961.

Thornton, Martin. *English Spirituality*. Eugene, OR: Wipf & Stock, 2012.

———. *Pastoral Theology: A Reorientation*. Eugene, OR: Wipf & Stock, 2010.

Torrance, James. *Worship, Community and the Triune God of Grace*. Downers Grove, IL: InterVarsity, 1996.

Torrance, Thomas F. *The Mediation of Christ*. Edinburgh: T&T Clark, 1992.

———. *The School of Faith: The Catechisms of the Reformed Church*. Eugene, OR: Wipf & Stock, 1996.

———. *Space, Time, and Incarnation*. Edinburgh: T&T Clark, 1997.

Turner, Philip. "The Wisdom of the Fathers and the Gospel of Christ: Some Notes on Christian Adaptation in Africa." *Journal of Religion in Africa* 4 (Jan. 1971) 45–68.

Turner, Victor W. *The Ritual Process*. London: Routledge, 1969.

Van Gennep, Arnold. *The Rites of Passage*. Chicago: University of Chicago Press, 1960.

Vanhoozer, Kevin J. *The Drama of Doctrine: A Canonical-Linguistic Approach to Christian Theology*. Louisville: Westminster John Knox, 2005.

———. "Interpreting Scripture Between the Rock of Biblical Studies and the Hard Place of Systematic Theology: The State of the Evangelical (Dis)union." In *Renewing the Evangelical Mission*, edited by Richard Lints, 201–225. Grand Rapids: Eerdmans, 2013.

Verkuyl, Johannes. *Contemporary Missiology: An Introduction*. Grand Rapids: Eerdmans, 1978.

Vodopivec, G. "Ecclesiologia Anglicana." *Humanitas* 20 (1965) 131–36.

Wainwright, Geoffrey. *Doxology: The Praise of God in Worship, Doctrine and Life.* New York: Oxford University Press, 1984.

———. *Eucharist and Eschatology*. New York: Oxford University Press, 1981.

Wallerstein, Judith, et al. *The Unexpected Legacy of Divorce: A 25 Year Landmark Study.* New York: Hachette, 2001.

Warren, Max. *Revival: An Inquiry.* London: SCM, 1954.

Webber, Robert, and Lester Ruth. *Evangelicals on the Canterbury Trail.* Harrisburg, PA: Morehouse, 2012.

Weber, Max. *The Theory of Social and Economic Organization*. Edited by Talcott Parsons. Glencoe, IL: Free Press, 1947.

Webster, John B. *Holy Scripture: A Dogmatic Sketch.* Cambridge: Cambridge University Press, 2003.

Welch, Robert H. *Church Administration: Creating Efficiency for Effective Ministry.* Nashville: B&H, 2011.

Westerhoff, John H. *Living the Faith Community: The Church That Makes a Difference.* Minneapolis: Winston, 1985.

Westerhoff, John H., and O. C. Edwards. *A Faithful Church: Issues in the History of Catechesis.* Wilton, CT: Morehouse-Barlow, 1981.

Wilken, Robert Louis. *The Spirit of Early Christian Thought: Seeking the Face of God.* New Haven: Yale University Press, 2008.

Williams, Charles. *Descent of the Dove*. London: Green & Co., 1939.

Williams, D. H. "Monarchianism and Photinus of Sirmium as the Persistent Heretical Face of the Fourth Century." *Harvard Theological Review* 99 (2006) 187–206.

Williams, Rowan. "The Archbishop of Canterbury Concluding Presidential Address to the Lambeth Conference 2008." Anglican Communion News Service, Aug. 3, 2008. https://www.anglicannews.org/news/2008/08/the-archbishop-of-canterbury-concluding-presidential-address-to-the-lambeth-conference-2008.aspx

———. "The Nicene Heritage." In *The Christian Understanding of God Today*, edited by James M. Byrne, 45–48. Dublin: Columba, 1993.

Wingren, Gustav. *Creation and Gospel: The New Situation in European Theology.* Eugene, OR: Wipf & Stock, 2004.

Winner, Lauren F. *The Dangers of Christian Practice: On Wayward Gifts, Characteristic Damage, and Sin*. New Haven: Yale University Press, 2018.

Wolfteich, Claire E. "Re-Claiming Sabbath as Transforming Practice: Critical Reflections in Light of Jewish-Christian Dialogue." In *Religion, Diversity, and Conflict: Proceedings of the International Academy of Practical Theology*, edited by Edward Foley, 247–58. Zürich: LIT, 2011.

Wright, Christopher J. H. *The Mission of God: Unlocking the Bible's Grand Narrative.* Downers Grove, IL: IVP Academic, 2006.

Wright, N. T. *After You Believe: Why Christian Character Matters*. New York: HarperOne, 2010.

———. *Creation, Power and Truth: The Gospel in a World of Cultural Confusion.* London: SPCK, 2013.

———. "Freedom and Framework, Spirit and Truth: Recovering Biblical Worship." *Studia Liturgica* 32 (2002) 176–95.

———. *Jesus and the Victory of God*. Minneapolis: Fortress, 1997.

———. *Justification: God's Plan and Paul's Vision*. London: SPCK, 2009.

Wuthnow, Robert. *"I Come Away Stronger": How Small Groups Are Shaping American Religion.* Grand Rapids: Eerdmans, 1994.

www.ingramcontent.com/pod-product-compliance
Lightning Source LLC
LaVergne TN
LVHW090512110826
845146LV00003B/830

* 9 7 9 8 3 8 5 2 4 9 2 9 9 *